A House on Stilts

A HOUSE ON STILTS

Mothering in the Age of Opioid Addiction

a memoir

PAULA BECKER

University of Iowa Press // Iowa City

University of Iowa Press, Iowa City 52242
Copyright © 2019 by Paula Becker
uipress.uiowa.edu
Printed in the United States of America

Text design by Omega Clay

Printed on acid-free paper

Author note: the names of most of Hunter's friends and their
families; schools; and rehab facilities and all of their employees
have been changed. Some identifying characteristics have also
been altered to protect the privacy of these individuals.

Names: Becker, Paula (Paula S.), author.
Title: A house on stilts : mothering in the age of opioid addiction,
a memoir / Paula Becker.
Description: Iowa City : University of Iowa Press, [2019] |
Includes bibliographic references. |
Identifiers: LCCN 2019002000 (print) | LCCN 2019006623 (ebook)
| ISBN 978-1-60938-660-3 (ebook) | ISBN 978-1-60938-659-7 (pbk. :
alk. paper)
Subjects: LCSH: Becker, Paula (Paula S.) | Parents of drug addicts—
United States—Biography. | Heroin abuse—United States. |
Mothers—United States—Biography. | Teenage boys—United
States—Biography. | Drug addicts—Family relationships—United
States. | Mothers and sons—United States.
Classification: LCC HV5822.H4 (ebook) | LCC HV5822.H4 B39 2019
(print) | DDC 362.29/33092 [B]—dc23
LC record available at https://lccn.loc.gov/2019002000

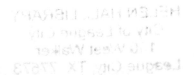

"Let us make a chair with our hands and carry her," said the Scarecrow. So they picked up Toto and put the dog in Dorothy's lap, and then they made a chair with their hands for the seat and their arms for the arms and carried the sleeping girl between them through the flowers. On and on they walked, and it seemed that the great carpet of deadly flowers that surrounded them would never end.

—L. Frank Baum, *The Wizard of Oz*

CONTENTS

Prologue ix

Ultrastrong 1

Didn't Know Anything 17

Chasing It 31

The Squat 44

The Accident 51

Totally Fucked 60

Flying South 76

Waiting 83

Family Week 93

A Hundred Needles 105

Thanksgiving 114

Harm Reduction 120

Lights in the Night 125

The Visit 135

The Climb 141

Jonah 148

The Passport 155

Flying East 161

Market Street 167

Runaway Bunny 177

Drugstore Cowboy 180

Love Is 195

Requiem 198

PROLOGUE

I am in the kitchen baking lemon black sesame seed muffins for my eighteen-year-old son, Hunter. It is a bright mid-July morning, and the sunlight is a soothing coda to the gray Seattle spring we've recently endured. Hunter is newly home from a three-month drug rehab program where—his father and I desperately hope—he has been yanked back from his recent plunge into prescription opioid abuse.

Our lives have veered savagely off the placid road that Hunter and his younger siblings, Sawyer and Lillie, traveled with us in the years before Hunter started using drugs. Our old, safe patterns have become unfamiliar territory, but I am endeavoring to hold on to what is still familiar, baking these small mouthfuls of comfort, a new variation on a recipe I've followed perhaps a hundred times.

These should be lemon poppy seed muffins, since those are Hunter's favorites. This batch is meant to be a welcome home treat for him. But Hunter's sobriety, so fresh, prompts me to substitute black sesame seeds. Poppies are opiates, after all. Consuming them might spur a positive response on the opioid urine tests we are administering randomly. I take conservative precaution, substituting the benign dark specks for their narcotic counterpart.

Hunter, meanwhile, unbeknownst to me, is downstairs in his basement bedroom, shooting heroin.

We realize, finally. We confront. Hunter bangs out the front door, running, clutching his bag of drugs, shouting, "These can't be in *our* house" to me and "Fuck you!" to his father. Bound for the street. Again.

Once he is gone, I knit all day, huddled beneath a quilt in the over-stuffed armchair where Hunter used to fall asleep when he was a toddler, board books and goldfish crackers by his side. I breathe. Light some incense, knit some more. I write a poem, trying to frame the pain, to puncture it, and pin it down like a butterfly fixed to a board, to contain it, but still it seeps and stains. None of my tricks deliver me to solid ground. There is no comfort, and I cannot find a way to save my son.

Memories shimmer before me: Hunter's sweet young face, his easy guileless laughter, his strong small arms slung around my neck as he jumped up to hug me. Where is that little boy, what part of him still lives inside this drug-addicted teenager?

Hunter's drugs mean that he cannot live with us, but we decide that on the nights when he can't find a friend or fellow forlorn one to take him in, he can sleep in what we call the House on Stilts, a treeless tree house in our small backyard. He comes and goes. I leave fresh boxer shorts, jeans, a T-shirt. He leaves his dirty clothes, redolent of cigarette smoke and perspiration. I leave a sandwich, a box of Lillie's home-made cookies, a bottle of water, vitamins, his toothbrush. He leaves a Q-tip, cotton coaxed from its tip for what I guess must be no healthy purpose.

We do not know when he will come and go. Stealthily, he avoids us, coming after dark, leaving before dawn. But I look out the kitchen window, and when my son is present, the stained glass windows of the House on Stilts glow with the light of the small lamp within, like a church on Christmas Eve. This is my only solace and it is fleeting—and I cling to it as I once clung to him, sweet smelling, freshly bathed.

Parenting publications often refer to parenting as a journey, promising to help moms and dads navigate each turn from birth to launch. I contributed for years to a local magazine called *ParentMap*, such a reassuring title because hey, if there's a map, parents can buy one, borrow one, forecast the road to come. Maps mean cartographers have charted the way, road builders have leveled and landscaped it, or at the very least, some traveler has scratched the path with ciphers suggesting left is easy walking, right is the cliff.

But being the parent of a teenager with addiction is like trying to navigate a dark room blindfolded. You bump around, desperate for clarity, feeling the objects in your path to try and figure what they are, tripping, falling. Occasionally, your blindfold shifts enough that you catch a glimpse—in that infinitesimally less dark moment—of what the room contains. Then the blindfold slips back, the darkness rendered even blacker by the fragment of paler dark.

We were a family just like yours perhaps. We loved and protected each other, read Harry Potter books, picked apples and peeled them and added sugar and cinnamon and baked them into pies. We followed the recipe, we followed the rules. Barry and I knew we were not perfect, but we could sometimes feel perfection in the moments we shared. People who looked at us thought, blessed children. Lucky mom and dad.

We did not know it when we lived these years, but we were taking part in opioid addiction's horrific zeitgeist. We numbered among the now legion middle- and upper-middle-class families previously privileged not to have experienced opioid's ruinous effects, among the parents who thought their children impervious to this scourge. America flails now in the teeth of the wolf that is addiction. Opioids—black market and legally prescribed—have become, for millions of families, their personal pathology.

Families have always struggled when a member was abusing, often silently, usually in shame. American society now struggles openly because the growing consumption of illicitly manufactured fentanyl-laced heroin means more people are dying. Use can be disguised or contained within families. Death cannot.

We now acknowledge, and we must, that opioid addiction cuts across all barriers: economic, racial, educational, age, and gender. My family's deeply personal story has become universal.

This is the story of my journey as a mother down years of unmarked road, of grasping blackness, begging for clarity. It is my story, but there were others walking, sometimes crawling, the path with me: my husband, Barry; our middle son, Sawyer; our daughter, Lillie. And Hunter, our beloved eldest child, careening, slashing, plunging, pounding ahead.

Some of us think that we can choose our stories, map our journeys. Being Hunter's mother has shown me we cannot.

A House on Stilts

Ultrastrong

Motherhood offers no guarantees. Opioid addiction, for the addicted and for their families, is a hall of mirrors. I gaze from my looking glass into the darkness, Hunter's memory on the other side. He has grown as tall as me, taller. His hair, silky golden in babyhood, tumbling pecan curls as a teen, is close cropped, receding at temples. His skin is pale, too pale. His beautiful soulful brown eyes meet mine, reflect their yearning. He matches his palms to my palms, turns his sweet head, rests it against the impenetrable hard surface between us. We are the ghostly echo of our old symbiosis.

He was a fearless child. Extremes of every sort delighted him. No dark could ever be too dark, no snow too cold, no story too intense, no bridge or cliff or overlook too high. Hunter began to walk at nine months, to talk when other children were still pointing. He made us know his fearlessness in words and actions. He'd grin and clench his fists and grrr. "Hunter, you're fierce!" Barry and I would say. "Fierce!" he'd reply. "Fierce like a dinosaur! Fierce like a shark!"

We climbed the towering play structure at a park in Maryland. Hunter's small fingers gripped the bars that kept him safe, and he leaned into the winter-cold steel with all his might, as if to push those bars aside. "Long way down!" he chortled. "Long way down!" He turned and launched himself toward the small hole in the structure's floor, the place we'd reached by climbing up a slippery ladder. My fingers gripped the back of his cherry-red snowsuit. "Hunter," I cried, trying to telegraph the need for caution without squelching his spirit, "Hunter, it *is* a long way down. We need to be careful."

There were so many moments just like this in Hunter's childhood. Later, they came to seem like metaphors. As Hunter grew, as he began to rush toward danger ever more deliberately, I wished a thousand times for the ability to grab him, pull him back, make him see how high up he had clambered. How truly far his plunge might be, and what smashing to the ground would mean.

I struggled to know just which well-intentioned choice I'd made might be to blame for my son's drug addiction. To know what flaw I'd let slip into all my plans, to understand what I had missed that led us to this swift unraveling. I was his mother, after all. How could I not have seen this coming?

That little boy, my bright fearless Hunter, flickered inside me as his older incarnation's recklessness, rebellion, and eventual addiction swept us into an inky nightmare. A tiny pocket in the deepest recess of my soul still glowed with that childhood flame as Hunter ripped himself away from me. Glimpsed at a bus stop, homeless, as my car rolled by, he was my boy. Knocking on the front door, terrified of angry drug dealers, hand bruised and swollen from a needle-site infection, he was my Hunter, my child, my darling. Our mutual helplessness changed none of that.

. . . .

When Hunter was born, I was completely clueless as to what being a mother entailed. I had never spent more than an hour with any baby. Because I approach nearly every experience as a research project, I'd read the books, thought I knew What to Expect, but from his first moments on the planet, this tiny creature bucked the trends. How could a baby be so all-consumingly, eternally alert? I could manage an office full of people twice my age, yet I struggled to cope with the demands of this tiny, howling, sleepless person Barry and I had summoned into being.

Most babies nap at least once during daylight hours. Hunter never did. He rarely even dozed. He nursed constantly, and I let him. This was called nursing on demand, or so the books said. Like Margaret Mead, I tried to observe his actions, seeking patterns, a predictable schedule. I kept a list of every time I fed him, start times and end times blurred together, separated sometimes by five or ten minutes. Looking at this relic now, I marvel at my determination to keep my head above the swirling waters of early motherhood, to cling to any rock in the current.

Who was that girl, that twenty-eight-year-old woman whose life thus far had made her think that working hard enough toward absolutely any goal would invariably yield success? So sure that her complete dedication to this motherhood project would control the situation, let her steer her destiny? Hunter was my teacher even then. It took me decades, finally, to learn his lesson.

Barry was slightly better prepared than I had been to float along through early parenthood. We had been married for five years, and he was midway through a three-year family practice medical residency. He'd held newborns, at least, and cared for them and helped shepherd their sometimes weepy mommies through archetypal transitions. I knew how to soothe a cranky theater board member but not a newborn baby; how to exchange opera tickets but not how to change diapers. Barry taught me to cradle Hunter's tiny neck and head, to diaper and swaddle him.

Barry had grown up in Southern California, surfing, riding his skateboard through dusty rural San Diego County, jostling with his three siblings to prove which of them in his ultra-athletic, highly competitive, well-educated family would hold the top spot in their parents' affections. His hair was sun bleached, his skin perpetually tanned. He had a swimmer's build: broad shouldered but otherwise lithe. His hair sprang naturally into curls if allowed to grow. He had the longest, lushest eyelashes I'd ever seen. When we met, he was juggling premed coursework, the requirements of his English major, and a Nike-sponsored career as a professional triathlete.

We started living together the summer before my senior year. Months before graduation, I took an internship with the Kennedy Center in Washington, DC, figuring that arts administration was a safer, more controlled choice than using my drama major to take my chances as an actor. I knew I wanted stability and a family. I was ambitious, capable, and could have stayed at the Kennedy Center when, at the summer's end, American National Theater offered me a permanent position. But I felt compelled toward a life with Barry, who had taken a teaching job in Houston to qualify for in-state medical school tuition. I joined him there.

I spent a year at Houston's Alley Theatre, another four at the Dallas Opera, while Barry went through medical school. We married in the summer after his first year. In spring of his fourth year, Barry was matched with a family practice residency program in Fairfax, Virginia.

Back in DC, I found a job as the subscriptions manager at the Kennedy Center. Working full out through long days, I made my way home by bus or sometimes cab, falling exhausted into bed about the time Barry arrived home from his own taxing days, rising early the next morning to repeat the cycle.

I loved the work, but part of my mind was always counting backward, starting at thirty-five, the age after which women's chances of giving birth to a child with birth defects begins to climb. We wanted three kids. Three years apart seemed like perfect spacing. By that dream calendar, I would need to give birth to our first child midway through Barry's residency program. It sounds crazy now, but somehow we caught that brass ring. Hunter was born when I was twenty-eight; Sawyer, when I was thirty-one; and Lillie, when I was thirty-four.

Hunter was born after I'd been in the subscriptions manager job for a year and a half. I planned to take my three-month paid maternity leave, then come back to my twelve- to fourteen-hour days with the baby in, maybe, a basket I could keep under my desk. I pictured coworkers bouncing this mythic infant on their knees as they took phone orders, freeing me to attend the lengthy meetings that gobbled up my days.

The women who were mothers among my Kennedy Center colleagues rolled their eyes, stifling laughter, when I voiced this plan. "Well," the most generous among them told me, "that works for some people maybe. It depends on the baby really." Yes, indeed. And from the moment he was born, Hunter showed us that he was absolutely positively not that boy.

Ten hours before I pushed him out into the world, I was at the office, growing increasingly sure that what I felt was early labor. Emerging from the stage door into the frigid late January night, I splurged on cab fare rather than risk the crowded Wisconsin Avenue bus. Speeding up Rock Creek Parkway, part of me sighed, nostalgic already for the life I suspected I was about to shed.

I tried to sleep or at least rest lying down, but soon gave in to the urge to stand, sit, squat—I had no idea what I was doing, but my body apparently did. At four a.m., Barry knelt beside me. "Unless you want to have this baby here," he said, "we have to go in right this minute. There is no more time." He shoved my old high-top sneakers onto my bare feet, tied the laces, helped me down the stairs and into the ancient hand-me-down sedan we shared. Only my gritted teeth and stiff-braced legs stopped me from giving birth in the front seat as we careened down Reservoir Road.

When we arrived at Georgetown Hospital, the triage nurse took one look and slammed a wheelchair under me, racing to the labor and delivery floor. I waited an agonizing ten minutes for my nurse-midwife to arrive, trying not to push. "Giving birth is really more an animal thing than a person thing. Let it be animal," she'd said at my last weekly appointment. I was all animal, and when she finally arrived, I pushed twice, she said, "Head's out!"—and in a giant whoosh that transported me completely into the next phase of my life, Hunter was born.

He was perfect, tiny, and a complete stranger. I pined for him when the nurse carried him down the hall for an examination. Friends arrived, said they'd peeked into the nursery and seen him. "Tell them I want my baby back," I said, but Hunter was allowed back only for a brief feeding before the nurse rushed him back to the nursery.

She had seen—or thought she'd seen—discoloration in his hands and wrists during her exam. This might mean problems with his heart, his breathing. An attending physician explained that Hunter was being moved to the neonatal intensive care unit for a brief evaluation. "You can go sit with him there," she added.

It was Friday, February 1, 1992. The staff was reduced on the weekend, and Hunter remained in the NICU, Barry and me beside his Isolette, me nursing Hunter frequently. He was wrapped like a burrito—one with wires. His heart monitor beeped when the sensor pulled free, his pulse oximeter yowled when the miniscule cuff fell off his finger. Barry fed me, I fed Hunter. I was discharged after twenty-four hours, but Hunter remained hostage. We camped out mostly on the

NICU glider rockers, my feet in Barry's lap, our tiny baby cradled on my chest. Days and nights merged. A sympathetic nurse suggested we ask the attending physician to write an order dictating Hunter's feeding instructions during our brief absences, then taped Barry's pager number and the note to the cot: "No supplemental formula. Mother will come."

Hunter's plight worried Barry and me, but intuition nudged us away from deep fear. Barry's medical understanding of Hunter's so-called symptom, observed by one nurse only once, and the compounding normal test results reassured him. He also knew how easy it was for doctors to start patients down the garden path of tests meant to rule things out. On that path, each negative result prompted the next test, then the next. No one wanted to miss something, especially in a newborn.

My thinking leaned more toward magical. I felt as if nothing would harm Hunter or be truly wrong if I was with him. The few times Barry whisked me home to shower, I leaked tears and breast milk under the hot stream, fighting panic because Hunter was not in my arms. I was being indoctrinated into motherhood, and I reached for the strongest tools I had: my growing love for this new human being and my fervent trust in my own powers of benevolent control.

Finally, six days after Hunter's normal speedy birth, our entrapment in the NICU ended. "Your baby is fine! Take him home! Enjoy him!" the jocular neonatal cardiologist someone had finally unearthed assured us. "Not a thing wrong with him!"

It didn't take me long to realize that my first plan of having baby Hunter live in a basket under my desk at work was ludicrous. I vaguely pondered looking for a nanny, going back to work managing the subscriptions office when my maternity leave was over. Several women who worked with me had babies, and one, Katherine, disappeared into the glamorous gold-trimmed ladies lounge that served theatergoers by night and our staff by day, breast pump in hand, emerging twenty minutes later with pouches of milk she tucked into her special basket in the staff refrigerator. Working without ending a baby's breastfeeding experience was possible, I'd seen.

Hunter was intense in every way. Besides the constant breastfeeding, he was wide awake and active in our arms, distraught when put down. I responded with intensity of my own. I held him. I held him all day long, most of the night, and Barry spelled me when he was home from the grueling hours of his residency.

I was exhausted but beguiled. Hunter and I were settling into our groove. When he remained alert after hours of nursing, I held him against my knees, inventing things to talk to him about. Sometimes, talked out, I'd prop a book behind him on a heap of pillows, smiling and nodding to Hunter while gobbling up a few delicious pages for myself.

As my maternity leave ticked down, I felt increased misgivings about what was supposed to come next. I could pump milk for him, I thought, and hire a nanny to feed it to him. But what nanny would agree to hold him in her arms all day? I didn't know yet that this kind of round-the-clock connection had a name, attachment parenting, and that most parents who practiced it relied on slings or wraps to keep their babies close, freeing the parents' hands for other tasks. I felt as if I were learning to understand Hunter's cues and that only I could mother him as I felt he wanted and needed to be mothered. When maternity leave ran out, I simply couldn't leave my baby, and I resigned.

I wonder now whether Hunter's early misadventure in the NICU, our unconventional introduction to early parenthood, influenced my decision to stay home with him. I think I might have been afraid to leave, scared someone would take him from me all over again. I craved the feeling of control that came with giving this project every bit of my effort and the release I felt when I held nothing back for myself.

In hindsight, I see that in this choice for me to quit my job, like most of our decisions, Barry and I opted to do things the hard way. Barry's residency still had eighteen months to go when I walked away from my income, so this was a serious challenge. We crunched the numbers, realized that if he started moonlighting emergency room shifts on his free weekends and we economized drastically, we could almost limp through to the residency's end. My parents patched the remaining hole in our financial boat with a small but essential monthly check.

Barry worked all hours, condemned by our decision to see Hunter and me almost never. I made Hunter my full-time, twenty-four-hour-a-day job, days spent almost entirely alone with him, feeding him, taking him to the little park up the block from our apartment building, slowly making friends with the few other mothers who were home with their kids in nonstop, power-focused Washington, DC.

Once a week, I borrowed a car and loaded Hunter in, along with the barrels of soiled cloth diaper covers our pint-sized stackable washer could not handle. Because Hunter refused to lie still for diaper changes, I usually scrambled after his bare bottom clutching diaper covers fitted with my careful diaper origami, trying to slip-lift-fasten before cloth exploded from cover. The bulky diapers were so thick I had to stretch the crotch of Hunter's onesies to make the snaps catch. Sometimes the diapers came undone and went rogue, slithering down Hunter's leggings in a bumpy mess.

Despite all this, I'd been indoctrinated to the merits of Team Cloth by *Mothering* magazine, which I'd furtively perused in Poor Richard's Feed and Read during college, hiding the wholesome grinning baby covers inside *Ms*, hoping none of my ardent fellow feminists would smoke me out. Cloth diapers supposedly caused less diaper rash, and children who wore them potty-trained more readily. The gel in disposables was suspect, according to *Mothering*, maybe even toxic, easily absorbed through tender skin. So Hunter and I hit the laundromat, Hunter sitting in front of me in the laundry cart, me stuffing diaper covers into the washer and cringing at the wrinkled noses of my fellow patrons.

Once Hunter had turned a year old, we used the car to get to weekly Mom-and-Me swimming lessons at a public pool. Winter days, we rode the bus to the National Building Museum in downtown Washington. The cavernous Great Hall, nearly as large as a football field, weds grace with a monumental scale that allowed me to let Hunter stretch his little legs without disturbing other visitors. I'd put him down at one end, and he'd toddle blissfully across the full length with me in his wake. I'd scoop him up, turn him around, set him down, and we'd repeat: back and forth, back and forth, safe from the elements.

I wouldn't have said so at the time, but I was lonely. I was imbuing my small son with power to control our days. Lacking adult company, with its pressure valve of stress-releasing conversation and activities, I filled the gap with vibrant, dynamic, baby Hunter.

I also missed the pleasure of actually being alone. Hunter was with me always. No one in my whole life had ever been so present, so constant, as my little boy. I grew accustomed to the thin fatigue of never-aloneness, learned to sublimate that hunger with the pleasures Hunter brought: the salty-milky smell of his neck when I blew raspberries there to tickle him, the way I felt his simultaneous relaxation and focus as he sat on my lap paging through board books with me. The perfectly ripe peach, cold from the fridge, that I bit and then pressed to his mouth, sweet sticky juice running down his cheeks as he sucked and gummed. It was his first peach. I knew there would be many firsts, and I was glad to think I would be there for all of them.

When Hunter was a year and a half old, Barry's residency ended and we moved to Seattle. Settling there had been a goal for a long time—since we first visited the city in the late 1980s. It had seemed then like a wonderful secret we'd discovered, a misty, grey kingdom of hills and coffee and cafes that served fresh fish alongside eggs and toast at breakfast. We'd wandered through Pike Place Market, Capitol Hill, Belltown, Seattle Center. This was pregrunge, pre-Starbucks national expansion, pre-Microsoft-as-common-knowledge, pre-Amazon Seattle. The city glimmered with magic and promise, and even as we had moved from Dallas to DC, we'd felt that our eventual future would happen here.

Barry found work at the Seattle Indian Health Board, a large community clinic near downtown. We rented a house in the Ravenna neighborhood north of the University of Washington. Soon, Hunter started co-op preschool, and we began to make fast friends among the other families. Hunter met Alex Shaffer, who became his best friend, the person who taught him what those words meant. Alex's mom, Melissa, was pregnant, as was I. We found we had many other commonalities, as Barry had with Alex's father, Brad. Hannah, Alex's older sister, was ringleader to the boys, and our families formed what would become an enduring alliance.

During this year, just before Hunter turned three, Sawyer was born at home, and the tight triangle of our Mommy-Daddy-Hunter love expanded into something rounder, more organic. Sawyer's birth broadened the spotlight that Barry and I had trained on Hunter during his earliest years, cued full illumination that washed over all of us, better equalizing everything.

We lived those first Seattle years to a Guy Clark soundtrack. I'd heard the iconic Nashville-based singer-songwriter at the Kennedy Center's Texas Festival in June 1991, a few weeks pregnant with Hunter, not even knowing it. Of all the music Hunter heard as a baby and toddler, Guy Clark was his hands-down favorite. We kept cassettes of Clark's first two albums, *Old Number 1* and *Texas Cookin'*, in constant rotation as we drove around the city. Guy Clark was all Hunter wanted to hear, although he made occasional exceptions for Jimmie Dale Gilmore and Townes Van Zandt after I told him the two were friends of Guy's.

When co-op preschool ended, Hunter started attending a busy, happy traditional preschool fitted into the basement and backyard of a small house on a quiet street near our own. He made new friends, learned to socialize, enjoyed the class's walking field trips through the neighborhood. When the time came to choose a kindergarten, Barry and I began to seriously discuss homeschooling as an option. We didn't like the formality of the public school kindergarten programs nearby, and nothing else we found seemed to us like a good fit for Hunter.

Hunter was able to focus deeply, submerging himself in his interests with creativity and flow. For example: he learned, and we with him, all there was to know about the *Titanic*. His play revolved around it: constructing the ship with his smooth maple building blocks, creating Duplo models, turning the Cozy Coupe car upside down so that to him it became oceanographer Robert Ballard's submersible, and he was Ballard finding the long-lost liner.

Barry and I suspected that public school kindergarten would hobble Hunter's ability to access this kind of self-directed authentic play, force him to conform. We considered Waldorf schools, but they seemed esoteric and too eccentrically focused on fairies in the garden and playing with diaphanous silk squares. We thought hard about Montessori. I'd been a Montessori assistant for two years between high school and college, and the well-ordered, pleasingly color-coordinated classrooms appealed to me especially. I could imagine Hunter there, carefully counting the golden beads, ironing with a child-sized electric iron that really worked. There was a great Montessori school five miles or so from our house, but we balked at the tuition. I was pregnant again, and the thought of bundling Hunter, Sawyer, and a new baby into the Volvo twice a day felt daunting.

And there was something Barry and I sensed in Hunter, some quality we felt demanded the reinforcement of our presence. It was the look he had in photos when he wasn't smiling. Slightly worried. Concentrating hard. As if he were trying to understand a foreign language. There was a yearning unsettledness in him that we couldn't exactly place but felt our family's togetherness could quell.

We chose to homeschool. I learned all that I could about how other people taught their kids at home, planning a loose curriculum and plotting out our days and weeks. Our homeschooled kindergarten was a round of family field trips to dinosaur museums, zoos, parks, and outdoor adventures. Hunter's passions—trains, building, reading—guided our outings. The boys had structure, and within that structure, freedom. They had each other, and their relationship as brothers was unwavering, strong, playful, and deeply kind.

Our friends Brad and Melissa decided to homeschool too, so Hunter had Alex and Hannah, and Sawyer had their younger brother, Sam, who was his best friend. Melissa and I and all the kids spent every Friday together, alternating households. The kids dove instantly into their play, delighted in one another's company, while Melissa and I effortlessly picked up whatever conversation we had dropped the week before. Fridays, for all of us, were the most important day of the week.

The homeschool treatises I read stressed the importance of socialization. To me, that meant enrolling the kids in lots of group activities—T-ball, classes at the Log Cabin homeschool co-op. I didn't worry about the fact that in all these groups, we gravitated toward the other families most like our own. Although I didn't understand this at the time, we sidestepped the part of socialization that toughens kids by teaching them to endure a variety of personalities, including unpleasant ones.

When Hunter was nearly six and Sawyer nearly three, Lillie was born, tumbling into the world in our warm house one cold December night. From the very beginning, she seemed to click perfectly into place in the family puzzle, in the big middle of everything. Family photographs document the three of them bent over books, games, puzzles: Hunter intent, Sawyer wise, Lillie engaged.

Soon after Lillie's birth, we bought a house in Seattle's Maple Leaf neighborhood, a mile or so from the house we'd been renting in

Ravenna. The new house was half the size of the rental, a cozy 1920s cottage originally designed as a two bedroom but with an attic that had been coaxed into two small, slope-ceilinged additional bedrooms. One bathroom. A tiny, sweet original kitchen into which I shoehorned two folding stepstools so that the boys could help with meal preparation. A patch of front yard that I edged with shrub roses and lavender. A small back yard in which Hunter, Sawyer, Alex, and Sam immediately began to dig, turning up old coins and rusty toy trucks and other treasure.

The other houses on our street were much like ours. There was a park nearby and a bus line. Down the hill, our library branch. Up the hill, a friendly, family-oriented video shop, a hardware store, a coffee place. Sidewalks connected these businesses to us, promising a safe web for the children to explore as they grew.

It was a handmade life, a hands-on life. My hands, my children: holding them as I read aloud, showing them how to squeeze the cookie dough just so and shape the balls, stirring the milky oatmeal, making it perfect. We were old fashioned, but it was our choice to be so. The work was hard, also by choice: no dishwasher, so dishes were washed by hand. No fast food, but chopping, cooking every meal from scratch. We held modern life largely at bay, forbidding television and the then new Game Boys.

This was the life that I had always wanted. I had a few role models, families I'd encountered in my late teens, whose homes felt both secure and like magic portals, as if the back of any closet might open into Narnia. These parents produced kids who struck me at the time as extraordinary. My classics professor's five-year-old son, who spent the end-of-term student brunch curled in a padded window seat, bent over *The Complete Shakespeare*. The sisters I nannied for one summer: eight-year-old Priya, who woke each day at dawn to settle at an old garage-sale manual typewriter, producing stories she showed to no one. Her younger sister, Rachel, who walked me through the tangled back garden pointing out her favorite flowers by their common and Latin names. I want that kind of kid, I'd thought. I want to craft a place where children's creativity can flourish.

As a child, I'd liked old-fashioned books, books where Mommy was waiting when the kids got home. My mother taught school and rehearsed plays into the evening. The key I wore around my neck to elementary school opened a calm house, in which, somewhere, one in the series of women my parents hired as housekeepers labored quietly. I tortured my mother yearly with the request that she volunteer as room parent at my school, but she required room parents in her own class. "Why can't you be like Carla Hall's mommy?" I'd wail, naming my Brownie leader, a placid homemaker and constant volunteer who taught Carla to sew and bake, and whose sanguine demeanor was the polar opposite to my mom's theatricality.

Barry had had a mom at home, but he would have been perfectly happy to make a different life with me, something more midpath. I was the one drawn to extremes: cloth diapers, extended breastfeeding, family bed. Extremes felt more inherently virtuous to me, as if by making soup from scratch instead of opening the can, I'd won a point. I wanted deeply to be blameless in my parenting choices, and doing everything the hard way, the old-fashioned way, was the pair of magic spectacles I'd happened on as I picked my way through the transformation into motherhood. I was my own exacting arbiter, my goal nothing less than manifesting for my children the perfect balance of structure and wildness. In Montessori terms, I thought of myself as preparing an environment in which they could safely be free.

There was another reason to homeschool: doing so let me define mothering as my work. All this busy activity was why I was not running some theater's box office, rising through the administrative ranks at Seattle Rep or Pacific Northwest Ballet. Homeschooling was what we did and who I was. Making this work my full-time job carved out a way in which I was at home but could still consider myself to be ambitious. I'd gone from hiding *Mothering* magazine inside *Ms* to cloaking it in *Home Education*.

Hunter's progress gratified me. He was so bright—his eyes strong, his body fearless. By five, he could both read easily and ride a two-wheeler. I was relieved that the amorphous hours of his babyhood were long past. I summed this up in a haiku:

Now Hunter whose birth
abducted me from chronos
has learned to tell time

Every summer and some long weekends, we packed our red Volvo with tent, stove, Thermarests, and headed out across the West. We camped our way through Washington, Oregon, Utah, Montana, Idaho, Colorado, New Mexico, imagining that our car was an Oregon Trail covered wagon. We stopped at every interesting roadside attraction, from the blimp hangar and cheese factory in Tillamook, Oregon, to the Durango and Silverton narrow-gauge railroad ride in Colorado, to the fossil dig at the Wyoming Dinosaur Center in Thermopolis. If we found a carousel in Missoula, we rode it. If there were hot springs down a dirt road outside Taos, we soaked in them. We traveled repeatedly to Ashland, Oregon, so that the kids could see reliably great Shakespeare productions, listening to books on tape as we drove.

An average summer weekend, as documented in the homeschool journal I kept the year Hunter was seven, included a camping trip to Thorp, a small town in Washington's Yakima Valley. "Woke to warm sun. Boys explored campsite, picked wildflowers, and watched butterflies and crickets. After breaking camp we hiked down to a stream where the boys floated flowers. Watched a swallow catch insects on the fly, then loaded up and took the short drive to Ellensburg, where we had delicious fresh ice cream at Winegar's Dairy. Toured Olmstead State Park, an old farm homestead—boys very interested in gardens, old farm implements, and household goods. Hunter *shocked* at the state of the breaker box. Drove to Zillah for family-style lunch at El Ranchito, then to Yakima to the Fruit Grower's Museum where we learned new things about the Washington state apple industry." There was a tour of the Yakima Valley Museum, a folklife festival, camping at The Dalles near Mt. Rainier. "After breakfast and car-packing we went to see a 700-year-old Douglas fir which is in the campground. Holding hands, we five reached halfway around its nine-foot diameter." On the way back to Seattle, we sang along to Woody Guthrie's *Columbia River Collection*.

Home, in my memory, usually smelled like buttermilk pancakes. Every day started with what we called Breakfast Poetry, a literary vitamin. Say it was Robert Frost's "The Road Not Taken." We might read about Frost's home state of Vermont in the encyclopedia, talk about snow and fields and covered bridges. We might take the bus to the little store that sold maple sugar candy, using the bus schedule to calculate which route, then visit our favorite bookshop, All for Kids. Back home, after grilled cheese, Hunter might use his math workbook, then spend twenty minutes on the computer doing Mavis Beacon Teaches Typing while Sawyer and I worked on reading skills and Lillie colored or assembled puzzles. Perhaps later we followed a recipe and baked banana bread. Perhaps we drove to the Pacific Science Center to meet the Shaffers and watch the new Imax version of *Beauty and the Beast*. Perhaps we went to fencing, and I kept Lillie and Sawyer busy on the sidelines while Hunter thrust and parried, his white fencing jacket fresh from the dryer, face obscured completely by his stiff mesh mask. Every day was different, and each day was rich.

In parenting, as in the garden, Barry and I trusted natural shapes. We saw value in the children's organic beauty, pruned their behavior gently, pinching a leaf off here or there, eschewing shears. They were like heirloom tomatoes, valued for their individuality, the interestingly unsymmetrical way their minds seemed to work, their authentic natures.

We were a certain kind of liberal-arts-school-graduate cliché. We valued books, reading, creativity, curiosity, and being kind to one another more than anything. We didn't recognize that many other parents did the same. We were sincere and, I realize now, smug. We were sure we knew exactly how to parent, and we weren't interested in outside opinions on that point. Being the first of any of our siblings to have kids, we rendered our brothers and sisters silent, at least early on. Our parents were our cheerleaders and maybe knew us well enough to know their thoughts on altering our tack would be rebuffed. It wasn't that we had specific ideas about what the kids would grow up to be— doctor, lawyer, teacher. We wanted them to be happy grown-ups, secure human beings, able to care for themselves and others. Those were our only goals.

When Hunter was young, I never questioned my assumption that my love and good care were checkmarks on a balance sheet, deposits in a bank account from which he and even I could later draw. I tried to be my best, trusting that if I did my mothering job extremely well, he would flourish forever. It was naïveté, hubris, but I thought that my choices were a currency, that making them well would purchase predictable results, for me, for my children.

Hunter drew constantly. He created superhero identities for each of us and decorated our house with pictures depicting our superpowers. Mommywoman carried heaps of concrete garden blocks without flagging beneath the load. Sawyer was Screeching Shark and possessed sharklike abilities. Barry was Silver Streak and received special energy from the single shock of prematurely white hair that streaked across his head. Lillie was Purple Power, purple on the inside (from drinking grape juice) and on the outside (decked out in shades of violet, lavender, and lilac). And Hunter—Hunter was Ultrastrong, most super of the superheroes, able to do anything.

I felt so sure of what we had, sure that I knew my children well, that I understood all of their individual lovable and frustrating aspects. I felt, based on familiarity built from thousands of hours spent in each other's company, that I knew Hunter completely, could forecast his reactions to any given situation. I was certain I knew all his likely pitfalls. That Barry's and my guidance was something Hunter would always take.

My deep conviction that I knew all there was to know about my son muffled the early warning bells that should have hit me like a screaming smoke alarm, shattered my equanimity. By the time I finally awoke to what was happening, we were engulfed in flames.

Didn't Know Anything

When Hunter was twelve, Sawyer nine, and Lillie six, we stopped homeschooling. The decision to do so was complicated, different for each of us, but in the end, clear.

Barry had resigned from the Seattle Indian Health Board by this time and joined a family practice group near our house. During the last year we homeschooled, he left that job and started working as an independent contractor in far-flung rural emergency rooms around the state.

The work was intellectually challenging but often brutal. Leaving Seattle, Barry would drive at least three hours and then work twenty-four or forty-eight hours straight, often at breakneck pace. He was the only doctor in these ERs and spent many hours trying to arrange transfer for critically ill or injured patients to more thoroughly equipped facilities, all the while working to keep those patients alive. He'd be gone for days, then drive the long miles home, dodging the fully loaded logging trucks that fill the back roads of the Pacific Northwest. On the occasions when he managed to sleep for a few hours at the hospital, he'd arrive home tired but ready to engage with the family. Usually, though, he drove home exhausted and sleep-deprived, and went directly to bed. The need for quiet while he slept clashed with the children's busy schedule, adding to his already considerable stress.

When Barry was working, I was with the kids around the clock, with little time to catch my breath. Even so, I'd started working for pay again, slowly at first. Writing for *ParentMap* and a local monthly blossomed into freelance work for HistoryLink.org, an exciting small organization that was breaking new ground as the nation's first original-content online encyclopedia of state and local history. The more assignments I completed, the more work I craved, and *HistoryLink* offered me plenty. Carving out the time for research, let alone writing, while teaching three kids at home and ferrying them to activities was becoming more and more difficult.

This frustration became less tolerable when I turned forty. I felt, fairly suddenly and with intense conviction, that it was time for me to fully reclaim paid work, work that was not driven by my identity as a mother. It also felt important to me that the kids knew I could earn money, that I could model economic agency for them. I often roped them into my research outings and talked with them about my projects, trying to expand my work-driven activities into teachable moments. Hunter wrote well, and when I finished a piece, I usually asked him to proofread it.

I'd missed the camaraderie of working in performing arts organizations since I'd quit the Kennedy Center. It was a running joke between my mom friends and me that when we all met up at the Seattle Children's Museum, someone else would need to oversee the kids while they played in the little theater space. To reach the stage required passing through a space marked "Box Office," which unfailingly triggered me to burst into tears.

I did not miss the low pay and long hours that working in the arts entailed, however, and I still wanted to be more involved with the children's activities than working full time would have permitted. Barry and I talked about possible options—as long as he was practicing medicine, he was always going to be the primary breadwinner. I didn't want to take a job that might sometimes force him to juggle work and kid duties, but he did not want me to feel thwarted. It was obvious to us that if I was going to continue freelancing, I needed more available hours. Outsourcing school seemed like the obvious solution.

The children's needs were changing too. Hunter remained content in homeschooling, but Sawyer had gone from being engaged in the learning process to spending hours stretched dreamily across the couch, obviously at a loss. Lillie, at six, was ready for first grade, eager to be with other kids all the time and to settle into a formal classroom situation. Keeping her at home started to feel wrong, cruel even. My younger two clearly needed something different.

In the six years since we'd moved to the neighborhood, we'd walked past the modest complex of St. Lucy's parish and its pre-K through eighth grade school without giving it much thought. The campus was two blocks from our house, making it our closest school of any kind. Our first visit immediately convinced us that this was a warm, caring community. Plenty of other school families were not Catholic, the vice-principal assured us. Sawyer and Lillie were interviewed, spent time in the classrooms, and were accepted for the fall of 2004.

I suddenly noticed that I could hear St. Lucy's church bell peal from the house. The families we met at back-to-school gatherings were welcoming, and several moms immediately planned play dates for their kids and Sawyer and Lillie. St. Lucy's families, like our middle-class neighborhood and indeed most of North Seattle, lacked ethnic diversity almost completely. Economic diversity was better represented. There was a coterie of families whose living circumstances indicated wealth and a handful of families that appeared to struggle, with most families skewing to the middle. Most of the parents had college educations, and perhaps a quarter held advanced degrees. In keeping with Seattle Archdiocese policies for parochial schools, tuition was relatively low and discounted according to how many kids a given family enrolled. There were many months, to my great satisfaction, where my earnings as a freelance writer covered tuition.

The school did not feel overly cliquey to me, at least not in the beginning. Each grade had only one class. Many kids started in kindergarten or, as Lillie was about to, in first grade, so by the time they reached middle school and the boys exchanged the blue chinos dictated by the lower school uniform for khaki, they had spent many thousands of hours in one another's company.

So Sawyer traded his tie-dyed T-shirts and comfy sweatpants for slacks and a white polo shirt. Lillie exchanged her dreamy storybook-like April Cornell frocks (gifts from my mother) for a James plaid pinafore and white cotton blouse with Peter Pan collar. For the first time in their lives, mornings began with alarm clocks and hasty breakfast, the scramble for book bags and lunch boxes, and a five-minute walk with Barry or me to the two-story red brick school.

I volunteered at the school several times a week, reading aloud to Sawyer's third grade classmates during the weekly staff meeting and helping the music teacher herd members of the lower school choir, which Lillie had joined. The teachers referred to parents formally when speaking to their students: I was Mrs. Brown, despite protesting that I didn't use Barry's last name and would be happy to have the students call me Paula.

Our plan had always been to have Hunter begin school in Grade Nine, when Seattle kids enter high school. When Sawyer and Lillie started at St. Lucy's, Hunter was homeschooling Grade Seven. He was self-motivated, wrote extensively and read voraciously, was making his way easily through the math textbook we used, had a good growing understanding of history and science. We'd signed up with a correspondence course, Oak Meadow, so in addition to working with me, Hunter submitted assignments online to a teacher with that program. Hunter was also learning daily living skills—cooking, doing his own laundry—and taking aikido. I balanced time with him with writing for *HistoryLink* (that fall, a corporate history essay about the PACCAR truck company) and *ParentMap* (a bimonthly series about Seattle parks and their histories, features on birthday parties and kid-friendly coffee shops).

As autumn turned to winter, though, Hunter began to talk about going to school. He wanted to go to the private school his good friend Max attended, a quirky institution where he likely would have flourished but with what felt to us like a jaw-droppingly high tuition of around $20,000 per year. Barry and I were willing for Hunter to transition into school midyear but urged St. Lucy's. Interviewed by a panel of seventh- and eighth-grade teachers, Hunter was quickly offered a spot. He would join the seventh-grade class after the mid-January semester break.

I was mindful of the transition Hunter would experience as he began school after so many years of homeschooling. He hadn't been in a classroom since preschool, unless you counted the individual classes he'd taken with other homeschooled kids at the Log Cabin co-op. Kids at Log Cabin hadn't really formed social bonds, maybe because the classes were task-oriented rather than collaborative or maybe because the homeschooled kids were encouraged to be such fiercely independent learners.

I wasn't worried about Hunter's interactions with teachers. He had always been comfortable with adults and had no problem talking with them and connecting. I was more concerned that he wouldn't know the rules, written and unwritten, of being a classroom student. I tried to remember from my own school experiences what he might need to know. I had been studious but somewhat shy, confident when performing on stage but timid at sticky-floored middle-school dances. I had been insecure about my appearance, but what seventh-grade girl wasn't? Hunter, who had already had a growth spurt and was beginning to need to shave, had in the past shown no difficulty making friends. I knew the social side of school would have a learning curve, but I was confident that he would muddle through.

Sawyer and Lillie were thriving at St. Lucy's, making good grades and friends. They basked in the warm nurturing school community. As Hunter joined them, I paid close attention, and he too seemed to make the shift from homeschooling to school with ease. Soon Jeremy and Brent and sometimes Pete were walking the two blocks home from school with Hunter, hanging out in the basement eating cookies, playing guitar. Hunter started learning bass, formed a band, practiced for hours. He watched *Lost* at Brent's house with Brent and his mother, spent the night with various new classmates at our house or Jeremy's. Hunter seemed happy.

So I relaxed, made my own transition from full-on mom and homeschooling facilitator to researcher and writer. It was a major shift, but one I relished. My schedule was my own, allowing me to do my work and still drive for school field trips, teach Sawyer's class to knit, be Cookie Mom for Lillie's Brownie troop, drive Hunter to guitar lessons. I took increasing freelance work, writing a *ParentMap* cover story about creating holiday traditions, taking on *HistoryLink* biographical essays documenting winners of the Seattle Board of Real Estate's First Citizen Award. I planned my days around the children's schedules, doing my work with speed and focus when they were gone. Barry's schedule had some flexibility too. He had days when he could volunteer in classrooms, drive for field trips, be with the kids. We seemed to have achieved a balance.

Hunter even joined the St. Lucy's baseball team, surprising us because he'd shown no interest in baseball, despite his good friend Alex's loving the sport. Alex and Hunter didn't see each other as often as they used to. Alex's family had stopped homeschooling before we did, and Alex was often busy with Boy Scouts and sports. Barry and I were thrilled to see Hunter take to the field—it seemed brave. Although untutored, he had good hand-eye coordination and got some big base hits. A fellow St. Lucy's dad told Barry, "When Hunter hits the ball, it stays hit!"

But by the end of Grade Eight, despite the friends, the good grades, the pursuit of interests such as music and movies and books, something we did not pick up on at the time was starting to go wrong for Hunter. He felt, he said in anguish years later, as if he wasn't blending into the culture of his age-mates. Socially, he felt he didn't know anything. Nothing at all.

Part of this was directly attributable to our having fetishized oldfashioned ways. Hunter started school essentially illiterate in many aspects of popular culture. He'd watched no television, with the notable exception of *The Simpsons*. Tapes of that show had been my secret weapon: when I was writing on deadline, I'd let all three kids watch until their eyes rattled around in their sockets. Hunter knew massive amounts about the parts of pop culture our family liked—They Might Be Giants, The Beatles, *Zoolander, Star Wars*—but lacked common ground with his peers on such things as commercial jingles, what songs get airplay on the radio, how DJs talk, the evening news. By focusing on NPR instead of NBC, on the Marx Brothers rather than the Wachowski siblings, on the songs of Fred Astaire and Ginger Rogers instead of Belle and Sebastian, we had unwittingly deprived Hunter of certain experiences that can be talismans of commonality among teens. We'd also left sports—Mariners, Seahawks, Sonics—almost completely off the table. Hunter had not been forbidden these things, but he had not encountered them within our bubble.

Another aspect of this breakdown in Hunter's self-confidence, I now think, started earlier, and sprang from our take on that old homeschool trope: socialization. Socialization, which we'd thought we were handling so beautifully through encounters with store clerks, librarians, kids on the soccer team, the ballet/circus/fencing/gymnastics classes, chess club members, fellow summer-campers.

But Barry and I ultimately controlled most of these encounters. Kids in school learn to deal with, experience, and tolerate much more diversity—diversity of style, opinion, behavior. They toughen up in ways it pays to toughen up. Hunter, who had no older sibling to emulate and who homeschooled longest, had none of that. And he was Hunter, which, as we knew increasingly well, meant he was in many ways inexplicable.

People who knew Hunter as a child described him as extremely likable and equally intense. Intense meant this: Hunter had the quality of a lost person, of someone without a map, even when he should have had one. Even when he was experienced in a situation, he often acted as if it were new or unknown. He seemed to be aware of this. He was not routinely unhappy. He was socially perceptive, sensitive to emotional nuance in others even as a young child. But he often had difficulty projecting his mind into the future or outside of his interior self. He was not physically volatile, but he could be emotionally so. When thwarted, he could become despondent. He bypassed middle-range emotions: disappointment took him to a deeper, sadder place than similar encounters with daily life seemed to take Sawyer, Lillie, or the Shaffer kids.

Hunter's intensity gave him tremendous ability to focus but made him serious, especially compared to other children. His intensity put him outside the norm of most of the other children we encountered, and while Barry and I didn't see this quality as something troublingly abnormal or as something that needed fixing, it had guided our decision to create a homeschool environment that supported rather than questioned what we saw as personality quirks.

Plenty of kids homeschool for part or all of their education with great success. Plenty gracefully jump from home to classroom. Hunter, however, did not ultimately turn out to be one of these. The self-possession he'd had going into St. Lucy's had dissipated by the time he graduated, but not in any way that seemed clear cut.

There were a few things that gave Barry and me pause. During the school music recital, Hunter looked gloomy, disappointed, almost surprised to find himself in that group, in this place. He never spoke to us about his deep desire to have a girlfriend, although Barry and I sensed it. He seemed proud that several of the girls in his class confided their problems to him. The early teen boyfriend-girlfriend issues were familiar territory for Barry and me. I'd been, at thirteen, totally convinced that I was more grown up than my classmates, had wanted boys to notice me—but older boys. Barry was short at that age, and the girls at his school found him darling, made him their mascot. Hunter's St. Lucy's classmates seemed to find him odd and cast him in the role of class jester. He complied, his sense of humor darkening. Asked on a personal statement what he brought to the classroom, Hunter replied, "Carbon dioxide."

There were also three instances when storekeepers suggested they'd seen Hunter shoplift. The first time, Hunter had ridden his bike to Wizards of the Coast, a game shop at our nearby mall. Barry met up with him there, and as they left, the owner said he'd thought Hunter might have stolen a set of cards. Hunter denied this, and the shopkeeper let them go. A few months later, I was at the corner store, San Marco, and the owner, who knew us by name, said, "Hunter was in here last week, and my new clerk said she thought she saw him take a soda. She wasn't sure, so she let him go. I told her he was a good kid and I didn't think he'd steal, but I wanted to let you know." Again, Hunter denied stealing.

Then, as St. Lucy's graduation approached, my father offered to drive Hunter and three classmates to a volunteer project at a migrant farmworkers camp an hour north of town. They stopped for gas, and when my dad went in to pay, the clerk said, "Do you know those boys who were just in here? I'm pretty sure they stole candy, but I was ringing up a customer and I couldn't stop them." My father said he didn't want to embarrass Hunter in front of his friends but reported the incident to me. Hunter, incensed, denied it.

This was risk-taking behavior. Hunter had always been physically fearless, diving past the play equipment at Maple Leaf Park to clamber into the treetops. At ten, alone, he rode the rattling wooden roller coaster at Belmont Park in San Diego, his hands clamped to the safety bar and his grin ecstatic. On his eleventh birthday, Hunter had parasailed. If he was stealing, however, that was a totally different kind of risk. We had not foreseen that he might be capable of such behavior and told ourselves that those shopkeepers must have been mistaken.

Puberty increased Hunter's appetite for intense sensation. Barry and I noted this but were not initially alarmed. Hunter became increasingly fascinated by the idea of altered states of consciousness. He read the book *Exploring the World of Lucid Dreaming* and began trying to induce that experience for himself. He began to experiment with the effects of highly caffeinated energy drinks, canned sweetened beverages containing many times more caffeine than is in coffee. He liked the shaky buzz the drinks provided as the stimulant coursed through his system. He approached his caffeine experiences with an intellectual curiosity, making a chart, buying different drinks each day, and posting the results. We talked about the caffeine, its risks in such a concentrated dose. His fascination seemed basically harmless, like a homeschool science project. He was using a substance that was not illegal for kids and that Barry and I consumed daily in the form of coffee, Seattle's trademark beverage.

At the time, these new enthusiasms just seemed like ways Hunter was testing his world. Barry and I saw his fascination with caffeine and lucid dreaming as new aspects of our son, of this boy's becoming a young teenager. We watched and guided him as we had always done, pruning behavior gently, our faith in him and in our parenting unquestioned. In our view, our job as parents was to steer Hunter's natural impulses, through open communication, away from dangerous and destructive paths and onto more productive ones.

Hunter entered Seattle High School. Against his will and at his teacher's urging, he had halfheartedly applied to the nearby Catholic high school to which many St. Lucy's students matriculated and had been wait-listed. His classmates' mothers urged me to push for his admittance, but Hunter did not want to go. Barry and I saw no point in paying the tuition, which was far higher than St. Lucy's, to put him someplace he didn't want to be. Seattle High School was newly renovated, highly regarded among local public high schools, and a fifteen-minute walk from our house. Barry and I had gone to public high schools very like Seattle High, and our experiences had been good.

Hunter started settling in, did homework, hung out with friends from St. Lucy's, although few of those kids were current classmates.

He was still sweet, helped out around the house, asked our permission to go places. He rarely saw Alex, who was at another public high school and more involved with baseball than ever. I encouraged Hunter to join a club, of which the school had many, or to explore a sport, but he was not interested. He'd loved his Grade Eight teacher but felt lukewarm about his many teachers at Seattle High, although he did like French. His grades were good.

A film of normalcy so obscured our vision that I cannot put a finger on when it started, but gradually the Hunter I felt I knew began to fade away. Around Thanksgiving, Hunter started asking to stay home from school. He did not say this then, but his feelings of inadequacy were beginning to manifest themselves in what he felt was social awkwardness. This low self-image, this social anxiety, left him eager for the approval of his peers but unsure how to get it. He soon discovered the stoners and misfits who highly approved of one another, even if no one else approved of them. Theirs was an easy social circle to penetrate. Which Hunter did.

Signs were still good. Hunter's grades first semester placed him on the honor roll. The school's parent portal, The Source, let me track Hunter's test results, which remained strong through second semester. But by spring break, he routinely came home smelling like cigarettes. He talked increasingly about the kids in his web-design class, older kids who asked him to hang out with them on the small strip of lawn across the street from the school. Soon he was going late to the class after lunch, sometimes skipping it entirely. On those days we would learn of his tardiness or absence through the school's robocall system, which activated in late afternoon. We explicitly forbade his ditching school, and he sulkily more or less complied.

Puberty was now in full force. He was much moodier, more volatile, and often angry, especially with Lillie and Sawyer. "Grow up!" he'd shout at them with little provocation. His emotions were big and running roughshod over him. They always seemed to take him by surprise. This was consistent with his childhood, when he had been unable to let little frustrations roll off his shoulders. "Don't let that get your goat," we'd tell him when a brotherly power struggle overwhelmed him. Or later, "You are GIVING Sawyer your goat. Just walk away." Barry and I used the metaphor of Hunter's emotional horse galloping out from under him. As a child, he'd trotted along with no hands on the reins. When puberty set the horse at a mad gallop, he was clueless about how to steer.

As Hunter's freshman year drew to a close, mornings became a massive struggle. He stayed up late into the night, reading and playing music. Waking up was his responsibility, but when he didn't wake, I made it my job to call down to him—finally, shriek down to him—to come and eat his breakfast, go to school. He grew evasive, goofily happy sometimes and withdrawn at others. How much of this was normal teenage moodiness, we wondered? I read the parenting books, attended all the special lectures the Seattle High School Parent-Teacher Association sponsored. Hunter still seemed within the realm of average teenage behavior. His teachers liked him. After his English teacher urged him, he even read one of the stories he'd written aloud to the audience at Parents' Night, his amplified voice echoing through the school's big atrium. When I went to the school with him, other kids greeted him by name, lots of them. He seemed to fit in fine.

Often, Hunter rode the bus or walked into Seattle's University District, a sprawling urban neighborhood about three miles south of our house. Home to its defining feature, the University of Washington, the University District—or U District, as it is commonly called —provides off-campus student housing options ranging from old 1920s-era apartment houses and group houses to high-rises featuring tiny apartment pods the size of walk-in closets. Retail is centered along University Way Northeast, a north-south ribbon of ethnic restaurants, bookstores, head shops, and resale clothing operations. Known to everyone as the Ave, University Way serves students but also draws a wide array of homeless people, teenage dropouts, drug seekers, and dealers.

The land that became the U District was recently logged forest when the University of Washington relocated there from its first location in downtown Seattle in 1895. The neighborhood that grew up around the school was vibrant, and up until the 1960s the retail core was healthy and varied. Thereafter, like so many other urban retail centers, the U District lost customers to shopping malls. During the 1960s, the Ave was Seattle's version of Berkeley's Telegraph Avenue or San Francisco's Haight-Ashbury district. As UW students' wants expanded from textbooks and spiral notebooks to grass, hash, acid, and other substances, the Ave became a place where those desires could be satisfied.

Merchants and the district council fought to keep urban decay at bay, pressing the absentee landlords who owned the properties along the street to make repairs, repaint, keep up appearances. Despite these efforts, the Ave grew seedier during our first decade in Seattle. I went there fairly often, and the kids went with me, even as bedraggled waifs sprawled on the broad sidewalk panhandled us for change. By the time Hunter was going there alone as a teen, the Ave was gritty in some spots, funky in others.

Hunter's first brush with the law was for shoplifting two candy bars from the University Book Store. Writing these words, I still feel mortified. My children and I had shopped there for years. It was a place to hang out, as Hunter asked to do one Saturday late in his freshman year.

He took the bus, his weekly allowance fresh in his pocket. Barry and I worked around the house, the peaceful afternoon rolling slowly by. I thought of how much Hunter must be enjoying the luxurious experience of hours in a bookstore, nothing to do but soak it in. At four, just as the thought of summoning him home whispered across my mind, the telephone jangled.

"Yes, this is his father," Barry told the caller. "Oh, no. I am so sorry. Okay. Okay, I'll be right down."

Barry hung up the phone and turned to me, his jaw clenched, nearly shaking. "That was the bookstore," he said. "Hunter was caught shoplifting. The staff thought he looked suspicious, and they were watching him. He took two candy bars, ate one, and then about an hour later left the store, but they detained him as he exited. The police have been there, and Hunter's waiting to be picked up by a parent."

It was embarrassing and tawdry—and troubling. Shoplifting at the U Book Store legitimized the earlier incidents we'd disbelieved, confirming what we had refused to accept: Hunter was choosing to steal. For the first time, Barry and I allowed ourselves to consider that Hunter's character might have a fundamental difference from our own. We had raised him with the best possible values, and in this incident he'd cast them off.

Barry drove down, signed papers promising that Hunter would pay the $4 he owed for the candy, plus a $200 fine. "Oh, and he's banned from the store," Barry told me when they got home. "Usually they ban shoplifters for life, but because he's so young, they're only banning him until he's eighteen."

Hunter gushed apologies, heaped coals of shame and blame onto his head. "I'll pay the fine myself," he said. "I have some money saved, and I'll work doing anything you say to pay the rest off. I'll never, ever do anything like this again. I know it's wrong. I shouldn't have done it. I am so sorry."

He worked around our house and for neighbors earning money to pay the fine, two dollars here, five there. He was grounded for several months. During those months we got a call offering Hunter the chance to be diverted from the juvenile justice system into a community-led program where kindly volunteers mete out the consequences rather than a judge doing so. Having no prior record in the overworked King County juvenile court gave him a second chance. He was required to sign a form admitting guilt. One warm spring twilight, Barry and I accompanied him to the low-slung Congregational Church in the U District where the diversion board held hearings. We all met with the diversion board, then Hunter met with them alone, then Barry and I did, and then we all went back in together.

The three board members smiled as we settled again onto our folding chairs. "Hunter has convinced us that he's truly sorry, that he comprehends the mistake he's made, and that he's made amends to the extent that we are going to do something we almost never do," the diversion board chairman explained. "We're going to make no further recommendation and set no community service. Hunter, lesson learned, we trust. Go out and start fresh. Appreciate your supportive parents. Best of luck to you all."

I felt relieved. Hunter had learned from his mistake. We'd grounded him, he'd paid the fine, and this diversion board had in their expertise closed the case. I remained unsettled by Hunter's choice to steal. But I allowed myself to trust that, with the exception of Hunter's banishment from a place our family shopped frequently, the incident was past.

By the end of his freshman year, Hunter seemed to us fully a teenager. He'd turned fifteen in February, he was shaving, was taller than Barry or I. He looked older than his age, could probably pass for a college student. He's gotten handsome, I thought to myself, physically powerful, his brown curls charmingly refusing to be tamed. His chin was cleft by a deep dimple. He wore dark jeans or cords with a carefully curated collection of interesting T-shirts. One of these showed the cross section of a bird's digestive system. One featured stylized glow-in-the-dark aircraft silhouettes against a black background. He topped these shirts with tweedy or wide-wale corduroy jackets carefully chosen from the Value Village salvage store. Although his deep-set eyes were frequently accented by slightly mocking raised eyebrows during our interactions and his full lips pulled into a tight line of disapproval, I hoped the summer would bring us time together, time to reconnect now that he'd grown apart. Instead, the summer slipped away, and he slipped further from us, unwilling to participate in family dinners, cross when we forced him to accompany our extended family on a long-planned trip to my hometown, El Paso, Texas.

I was now working steadily as a freelance writer. Barry had given up the ER work for a job in the urgent care department of the Everett Clinic, a large health care organization with multiple sites around Snohomish County. He was much fresher and happier. One or both of us was at home every day, and Hunter came in and out, seemed calmer than he had during the school year. We thought he'd tried pot, although he denied this; knew he'd sometimes smoked a cigarette, although we forbade it. We made the argument that at his age, smoking anything was illegal and would harm his health, hoping that giving him good reasons not to smoke would suffice. We did not at this point threaten consequences.

For someone who had grown up in the freewheeling 1970s, I was a super straight arrow as a teen. I had never taken drugs of any sort, never drunk more than a beer or two in high school. The thought that Hunter would experiment with drugs, even pot, felt unfamiliar. But I was not a risk-taker, and I was sure I knew my son. I valued these two qualities as strengths. Both blinded me.

Chasing It

The first night Hunter did not come home was November 2, 2007. Barry was out of town. Hunter had spent the day with his friend Harold, a wealthy, shifty kid whom Barry and I did not much trust but at whose sprawling four story house in Seattle's Central District we had occasionally dropped Hunter. Small for his age, cute, nonthreatening, and nonaggressive, Harold had learned over time that he could fake his parents out on nearly every point. A smugness at that fakery, contempt for the naïve adults who were so easily fooled, flickered behind Harold's harmless façade. We knew his parents only slightly—they seemed like kindhearted earnest Seattle liberals, much like ourselves.

As dusk rolled in, I laid out pieces for two bright baby quilts. Ten days before, my sister Susan's twins had been born nearly three months early; now they struggled for life in a neonatal intensive care unit in Illinois. The quilts were for them, hopeful claims toward two futures. Lillie and Sawyer settled down to bed, and I called Hunter's cell phone.

"I'm at the movies, it just got out. Can I spend the night with Harold?" Hunter asked.

"I want you to come home, Hunter. Your dad is out of town, and I'll feel better having you here."

"Okay," he said reluctantly, "but can we watch one more movie first? I can still be home before eleven."

"I guess," I said. An hour and a half ticked by as I cut and pinned. Just before eleven, Hunter phoned.

"I really, really want to spend the night with Harold," he said. "Is that okay?"

"No, Hunter, you can't, and we had a deal," I said, feeling peeved. "Where are you now?"

"I'm at the Metro Theater. I really want to stay with Harold, and I'm going to, Mom."

"You are absolutely not!" Outraged, I slipped my shoes on, grabbed my purse and keys. Sawyer and Lillie slept upstairs. Forcing myself to ignore the fact that they'd be left alone, I locked the front door, headed to my car. Still talking to Hunter, my cell phone wedged between my ear and shoulder, I began to drive, bending another of my steadfast rules. Hunter talked on, trying to justify his case, to convince me. Five minutes later, I was at the theater. It was dark, box office shuttered, and no Hunter.

"Where are you, Hunter?" He didn't know I'd left the house.

"I'm at the Metro Theater," he said testily.

"Hunter, I am at the Metro now and you are not here. Where are you really? I'm coming to get you right now."

"Oh, I'm in Fremont, I think, I'm not exactly sure." He sounded like he was just making it up as he went along. He's no more in Fremont than he's at the Metro, I thought, scrambling to formulate my next move, but too late. "I'll see you in the morning," Hunter concluded swiftly, and hung up. Instantly I called back, to be greeted by his voicemail message.

I drove home, frightened and furious. I checked Sawyer and Lillie, who were fine. I'd been gone less than fifteen minutes, not that I felt that justified my leaving them. I tried Harold's home phone, but there was no answer. Sleep was impossible. I worked on the quilts and cried and paced all night, leaving Hunter periodic voicemails.

"You are grounded," I spat when he walked in the next morning, sheepish, but offering no further explanation of his reasoning or whereabouts. "I don't know for how long. Barry and I will decide when he gets back from Portland this afternoon."

I had embraced the learning curve for mothering babies and then ridden that wave into the strong good work of mothering my growing kids. Now I was learning to be the mother of a teenager and finding it infinitely more difficult. This task asked more of me than all the years of baby/toddler/childhood combined. I resisted these new demands. I hated the way they made me feel.

A week or so after Hunter had refused to come home, I woke in sudden inexplicable terror, rushed down to his room, and found it empty. "He's gone," I moaned to Barry after climbing the narrow stairs back to our bedroom. "He stuffed a pillow under his sheets to try and fool us. That is the oldest trick in the book!"

We waited in the living room until the creaking basement door signaled Hunter's return. "What the hell are you thinking?" Barry asked angrily as we descended into Hunter's room. Hunter hung his head, looking not exactly sorry, but sorry to be caught.

Barry and I had made a nonauthoritarian household built on trust. We believed fervently in persuasion as a parenting technique. We now redoubled our efforts to persuade Hunter not to misbehave and to convince him that being trustworthy was his best path.

The next week, Hunter snuck out again, this time not bothering to leave a pillow-Hunter under the covers. "What would have happened to you if you'd snuck out?" I asked Barry despondently as we shivered in the gaping basement door. Hunter might or might not have pulled it closed as he slipped out into the chilly night. Now it yawned open.

Barry shrugged and shook his head. "I never thought of trying."

I knew that if my father had caught me sneaking out at Hunter's age, there would have been physical repercussions, but Barry and I were not going there. We had been spanked in childhood but had never raised a hand or felt we'd needed to with our own kids. We were not willing to mete out physical consequences now. That was not our way.

Barry shut the thick door and slid the deadbolt. Hunter would have to use his key and come through the front door rather than slink back into the basement when he returned.

The concrete floor was cold beneath my bare feet. "I thought we knew what we were doing," I said. "We reason with the kids, and they get it. They always have. We've barely ever had to ground them or even hold back allowance. I just don't understand why Hunter seems to have lost all sense of how to keep an even keel."

Barry sighed as we passed through the dark kitchen. "I keep waiting for him to come around," he said, "to self-govern, if that's the word. He knows how we feel, but how we feel doesn't matter. He acts like he has nothing to lose."

We grounded him, gave consequences, lectured. Hunter nodded, apologized, and then he did what he wanted, primarily by sneaking out at night. We could keep him home while we were awake, but eventually we had to sleep. Repeatedly, he left the house by the basement door, immune to confrontations when he returned.

Hunter's grades slipped. Barry and I talked with him about expectations, encouraging him to meet with his teachers, make a plan, turn in late work. I watched for results of these efforts on the parent portal. His grades did not improve. Barry and I emailed the teachers, met with them, met with Hunter's guidance counselor. He loved history, in which he'd earned an A the year before. Now his AP Euro class was tracking at D.

Even in English class, Hunter floundered. Barry wrote to Hunter's English teacher. "Hunter had not mentioned any difficulties in Language Arts thus far this year, so I was unpleasantly surprised to see a No Credit in Language Arts on his recent report card, which came in today's mail. Hunter was not able (or perhaps not willing) to tell me very much. He said he thought that he'd turned in most of his work and that he could not explain the poor grade. He says he is enjoying the class."

Photography, which we'd thought would be a fun break in Hunter's academic schedule, became an all-out war. He loathed the teacher and made no secret of it. We met with her several times but again with no results. One Saturday, knowing Hunter had contact sheets due Tuesday and had not taken any pictures, I forced him into the van and drove along the Ballard neighborhood's working waterfront. "How about here? What about there?" I babbled. "Okay, Mom, all right!" Hunter said angrily, framing a shot or two, obviously placating me so this ordeal could be done with. I tried not to give way to panic. Hunter would fail the class, not I. But Hunter's failures felt like mine.

One Thursday in early December, my cell phone rang as I drove home from the University of Washington library. The afternoon was unseasonably bright, the sun low in the sky but, for the moment, not obscured by clouds.

"Hang on, hang on," I answered. "I'm driving, let me pull over."

"Is this Paula Becker?" a woman's voice inquired.

"Yes, who am I speaking with?"

"This is Officer Williams of the Seattle Police Department," she replied. "I have your son Hunter here and he's not hurt, but I need to release him to a parent."

I felt the blood rush to my head. "Where can I meet you?" I asked quickly.

"We're in the alley near Northeast Sixty-Third Street and Twelfth Avenue Northeast," Officer Williams explained. "Not far from Seattle High School."

"I'm two blocks away. I'll be right there."

Hunter was sitting with his back against a grey garage door. Another boy, slightly shorter than Hunter and wirier, wearing neat jeans and pine-green hoody, slouched next to him. A tall police officer, her black curls closely shorn, handgun holstered, stood nearby. I shook her hand.

"A neighbor on this block called to report that these boys were drinking and loitering," she explained. "I've talked with them. I'm going to let them go with a warning. They've poured the vodka out."

"Thank you," I stammered. I looked more closely at the other kid. I couldn't place him, but he looked familiar. "What's your name?" I demanded.

"Jess Masterson," the boy replied, barely suppressing a sneer.

"Do I know you?" I pushed.

"Jess was on my soccer team for two years, back when we homeschooled," Hunter explained. "He's a year ahead of me in school."

I burst into a lecture. "You guys know better than this! This isn't some minor thing. I'm going to call your parents, Jess, so you'd better tell them yourself first and save yourself some trouble."

I led Hunter to the car.

"Don't call Jess's parents," he begged as I drove. "Just stay out of it."

I snorted, unmoved. When we got home, I dug into the back of the junk cabinet and found Jess's listing on an old soccer roster. Jess's dad answered the phone.

"Oh, Hunter's mom," he said ruefully. "Yep, when Jess sneaks out at night, it's usually with your son."

I was now waking multiple times each night, as sleepless as Hunter himself had been as an infant, frightened for him and furious that Barry and I had not found means of controlling his behavior. "I love Hunter so much, you know," I told Barry one morning as I packed Lillie's lunchbox and drained my second cup of coffee, "but lately he's getting pretty damn hard to like. I feel like nothing I say to try and reason with him works. It's like a bowl I use every day has suddenly sprung holes and turned into a sieve. Every bit of wisdom I pour into Hunter now drains right out."

At least Barry and I agreed—consistently, repeatedly, nearly unwaveringly—on what our response to Hunter's behavior should be. Like any couple, we had differences to be fought and negotiated through. But as Hunter's misbehavior tested us, we presented a unified front.

Agreeing didn't keep us from going round and round trying to understand why this was happening by comparing Hunter with ourselves at his age. We spent lunch at nearby Than Brothers, bent over steaming bowls of aromatic pho, repeating the same lines. "I never acted out like this," Barry would start, and I'd say through gritted teeth, "But Hunter is not you." "When I was his age," I might say a few bites later, oblivious to that contradiction. "It doesn't make sense," Barry would continue. We did this often, sometimes daily.

It was a drawn-out version of the brief parenting crisis we'd plunged into years earlier, visiting Hampton Court when Hunter was nine. I carried Lillie in the sling. The boys danced ahead of us, eager to reach the center of the famous hedge maze. "Can we find our own way out?" they'd bubbled when we were well inside. "Well . . . okay," Barry allowed, and they were gone, laughing. Within thirty seconds, Sawyer began to scream. Barry and I stood rooted, frozen, right in the middle of the maze. "Where are they?" I cried. The screaming continued. "What's happening? Oh, God, how do we get out of here?" I turned on Barry wildly for not knowing. He blasted me back for panicking.

We found the boys soon enough, still together, Sawyer's heel nicked and bloody, the pair of them otherwise unharmed. My trauma lingered. Barry and I vowed never to venture into a hedge maze again, but Hunter was leading us now into a deeply threatening enclosure.

Disoriented, desperate, bent over our bowls of pho, the maze surrounded us.

We felt alone. Friends, peers, especially parents whose kids were younger, really didn't want to know what was happening with Hunter. When your child veers off kilter, people assume the blame lies at your parental feet. I do not resent people who think this way. I thought that way too, and then it happened to me.

I didn't want to keep what was going on in our family a secret. Hunter's sneaking out was now a constant. He was skipping school. He'd almost certainly smoked pot, and I'd smelled alcohol on his breath more than once since the incident in the alley. Worried deeply about where this might be heading, I reached out to Dina, the mother of Lillie's St. Lucy's classmate Wren. Wren's father, Jay, was a local rock musician. Wren was their only child, but I figured Jay and Dina's social history might give us some common ground. When I described Hunter's situation to her as we filed out of the Saturday afternoon mass at which the children's choir had just performed, though, Dina froze and physically pulled away.

People with several children were sometimes more tolerant, more alert to the fact that rebellious behavior is not necessarily contagious, more sympathetic to the difficulties of supporting two kids who flourished while coping with a third kid spinning out of control. Still, Jane, mother of Sawyer's close friend Danny, tilted her head and sighed a kind of tsk-tsk when, picking Sawyer up from her house one afternoon, I blurted out a bit of what was going on. "You might just be stressing because of perimenopause," Jane said. "You should ask your doctor about medication."

Was I overreacting, I asked myself? Rebellious teenage behavior isn't really considered unusual, although to me it was unexpected and unacceptable. Or might Barry and I be underreacting? Should we be considering something drastic, like Barry's taking a job in rural Australia or the Outer Hebrides and moving us all there? Was getting Hunter away from Seattle until he was out of puberty an answer? What, then, of Sawyer's life, Lillie's, mine?

Our closest friends, Alex's parents, Brad and Melissa, did not pull back. They had divorced around the time we stopped homeschooling, but each listened supportively when Barry or I called to vent. Their extended family's backgrounds gave them some insight, and they, like us, believed in Hunter's essential goodness. Also, a handful of St. Lucy's mothers told me they prayed for Hunter.

I was worried. Also angry. This anger overwhelmed me sometimes, blanketing me like thick, hot vapor in a steam room, choking, blinding. I was furious with Hunter, incensed and hurt at what he was doing to himself, to our family unit, to Barry, and to me. Infuriated that he refused our help. Each figurative safety line we tossed to him, he used against us, not climbing to safety but rather lassoing us and pulling the entire family off balance. It broke my heart that Hunter was not succeeding academically when I knew he had so much potential. I saw him throwing away his present chances, and with that, his future options. And although I strongly resisted this idea, I knew it must at least be possible that during the midnight hours when his bed was empty and on those afternoons when he was absent from Seattle High, Hunter might well be experimenting with drugs. This was my greatest fear, my deepest dread.

By midyear, Hunter was skipping at least one class every day, often more. The phone rang every afternoon with the dementing robocalls these unexcused absences generated: "This is the Seattle High School Attendance Office. Your student, Hunter, was marked absent or tardy in one or more classes today. If this was an excused absence, please contact the attendance office immediately. Goodbye." Barry, Sawyer, Lillie, and I soon had them memorized. I must have called the school thirty or forty times to tell them Hunter's absences were NOT excused or sanctioned by me before I gave up. It mattered to me that they knew, though their knowing it apparently changed nothing.

I did not understand why Hunter was not suspended or expelled. We were constantly expecting that to happen, threatening him that expulsion was a likely consequence of truancy. The school's enrollment was about 1,700, and, like most public schools, it was understaffed. While truancy was against the rules, it did not weaken the school community. The school staff doubtless had their hands full dealing with more pressing problems, such as fighting, property destruction, drug possession. Hunter was well groomed, white, and unfailingly shyly polite to adults. Those qualities worked in his favor when it came to skirting the school's stated consequences. I was learning now that neither Seattle High School nor Barry nor I had any magical way to force Hunter back into line.

Barry and I walked the three-mile loop around Green Lake one blustery early January afternoon. It was too cold for my comfort, but at least, for the moment, it wasn't raining. "This endless sneaking out, all this ditching class!" I fumed. "I just can't help but take it personally. It is so disrespectful of us, and we have always, always shown him respect. I feel like Hunter is stomping all over the whole moral system we've taught him and operated under since he was born!"

"It's confusing," Barry agreed. "I mean, he loves us. We know that, we have to know that. But the more he rejects his social and family and moral obligations to us, the more I feel like he's starting to use us instead of love us." He grimaced. "It feels like shit to say that, even to think it."

"Yes," I said. I pulled my scarf tighter against the wind. "But Hunter's actions feel like a pretty aggressive betrayal. He isn't just breaking rules, he's burning the rule book."

I spoke at length to Hunter's guidance counselor, strategizing on the phone and in person. Because Hunter obviously hated high school, we planned that he would enter Running Start if he could pass enough classes to gain junior status. Running Start is a program that lets Seattle Public Schools students with at least junior year status take some or all of their classes at community college, receiving both college and high school credit. Some students earn a two-year associate's degree by the time they graduate from high school, and many students transfer their community college credits to a four-year college, saving themselves as much as two years of college tuition. Running Start promised Hunter the chance for more self-directed learning, which we dearly hoped would help.

The guidance counselor also put me in touch with other parents at the school who were struggling with defiant teens. I tried to stitch their desperate fragments of advice into some cohesive whole. One mother suggested a program called King County At-Risk Youth. This would involve petitioning the juvenile justice system to step into our family, assess our parenting skills, assess Hunter's mental health and test him for controlled substances, and ask a judge to set the rules for Hunter's and our behavior and interactions.

We considered this option with great trepidation. Asking for such intense intervention felt shameful to us. We worried that putting our household under judicial scrutiny would disrupt and further damage Sawyer and Lillie, who seemed increasingly traumatized by what was happening with Hunter. We were not even sure that Hunter would qualify. The program defined an at-risk youth as a child under eighteen who met at least one of three criteria:

Absence from home for at least seventy-two consecutive hours without parental consent.

Being beyond parental control to the extent that his behavior endangers the health, safety, or welfare of the child or any other person.

Having a substance abuse problem for which there are no pending criminal charges relating to the substance abuse.

Of those three, only the second criteria seemed likely to apply to Hunter. Despite my worries about Hunter's possibly experimenting with drugs and with the whiffs of alcohol I'd smelled, "substance abuse problem" seemed like a giant reach.

I spoke with other mothers of defiant teens. "Hunter is blackmailing you emotionally," one said. "Traditional parenting techniques don't work when a kid is acting out or using drugs," another offered. One weary mom advised, "Consequences are a good thing. You want them to experience legal consequences before they age out of the juvenile system." This excellent advice made little sense to me at the time.

After months of robocalls, Seattle High sent a letter scheduling a meeting with Hunter, an assistant principal, and Barry and me. We all gathered in the assistant principal's office a few days later, and she asked us to sign a Seattle School District Student Attendance Agreement, a contract promising no future truancy. Hunter's summation of what the form termed his "nonattendance problem" was this: "I made poor choices regarding attendance because of stress and disregard toward the consequences." The assistant principal's stated opinion:

"Student made some poor choices regarding attendance and education." The day after the form was signed, Hunter skipped classes, and I called this assistant principal. An office worker told me she'd be on sick leave through the end of the year. "Who is handling her students?" I asked. "No one," was the reply.

We decided to move him to a different school, but when I called, Seattle Public Schools had no openings for his immediate transfer. In any case, I had little faith that another public school would be much better. The school he went to was the district's most desirable, the jewel school, staffed by the city's most experienced teachers. Still, I called the enrollment center several more times, trying for a spot in one of the two other schools that were fairly close to our house. One long conversation with the school district's enrollment specialist yielded a sheaf of notes, including "he needs to learn to count his blessings" and "every time you do something wrong, you put a dagger in your mother's heart."

We looked at private schools with smaller, more alternative student bodies where we thought Hunter might fit better, but none had spots, or those that did were so expensive as to seem out of reach. These schools cost upward of $20,000 per year. Barry and I drove old used cars, neither of which had cost more than $10,000. We shied from debt, paying off credit card balances monthly. After nearly a decade in our house, we were closing in on paying off the thirty-year mortgage. Expensive vacation trips were extremely rare and crafted with as much painstaking frugality as we could muster.

Increasingly desperate, Barry and I decided to put our faith in therapy.

We found a therapist who saw Hunter twice and told us that he was a good kid with good insight going through a rough patch and that he didn't need professional help. Barry and I were unwilling to accept this therapist's reassurance that Hunter didn't need counseling, so we found a different therapist. Hunter, always polite and deferential with adults, charmed and disarmed him, then started blowing off appointments. I started driving Hunter to his therapy slots, juggling Sawyer and Lillie's schedule, ignoring my own work. I wanted to facilitate the process, to ensure Hunter gained insight and help him learn to make better choices and to help himself.

Barry and Hunter and I had a few sessions of family therapy together. The last session unhinged me. The therapist advocated for Hunter's right to act out, to leave the house late at night without permission, even to skip school.

"He's processing what it means to grow apart from your family unit," the man explained—I thought—smugly.

"Those actions are against state laws, at the very least!" I responded, clutching a tissue I didn't need for tears because what I was feeling was sheer rage. In the car a few minutes later, as Barry navigated our way out of the parking lot and past a Chinese restaurant, I lost control completely.

"I should have hired a nanny or left you at day care from day one!" I screamed at Hunter. "I gave up my career to raise you and for what?! Look at what you are doing to yourself and to us. You are killing me. I should never have bothered nursing you! I should have stuffed a fucking plastic bottle of formula in your mouth! You're making what I've done for you NOTHING!"

Later that evening, when I'd calmed down, Barry and I talked. "These family therapy sessions make coping so much harder," I confided. "I certainly don't want to see that guy again."

"It's like he's trying to erode our conception of ourselves as parents," Barry agreed.

We were surprised and delighted when, early in his sophomore year, Hunter had expressed an interest in joining his French class on a trip to France. We helped him set up a savings account, into which he deposited money he earned doing odd jobs for us and for my parents. He asked relatives for checks for France rather than Christmas and birthday presents.

His desire to travel with his class and the advance planning he did to prepare seemed to promise that Hunter might be turning a corner. But as the year and his truancy wore on, we entertained misgivings about letting Hunter go. We wondered whether, in light of his truancy, the school officials would object, but they were silent. The monthly meetings we attended with the French students and their parents showed us a group of nice, eager, well-adjusted kids, a marked contrast to the louche group Hunter now gravitated toward, the line of smoking, slacking kids who hung out across the street from school. We hoped that traveling and bonding with the French class kids might help Hunter shift onto a healthier path, cement better relationships. It was a gamble, but things had been fairly calm in the weeks right before the trip. Calm enough that we kept walking toward the thought of Hunter's finally applying himself, flourishing as we believed he could. And so we pushed our fears aside.

The Squat

I was writing, deeply absorbed, when the call came from King County Youth Diversion. Mentally surfacing, I thought the volunteer on the line wanted to survey me about Hunter's experience going through diversion for the bookstore candy theft. I pulled my thoughts together, ready to rate the diversion process—tell her how well it had all gone for Hunter and for us. Hunter was doing better, I planned to say, in fact, he was in France at the moment with his class from school.

"I'm calling about the incident on March 1," she said. The date was six weeks past, not ten months. "Wait," I said, "the incident when? I thought you were calling about Hunter's 2007 diversion." I focused on the woman's words.

"No," she replied, "this was the March 1, 2008, incident, when Hunter was removed from the squat house in the U District by the Seattle police and the University of Washington police."

I felt like she had bashed me on the head. A squat house? The police?

"I don't know what you're talking about! What squat house?" I nearly shrieked.

"I don't know all of the details, and I'm sorry to have to tell you this," she said. "I guess Hunter never mentioned it. There is a house at 4308 Twelfth Avenue Northeast that is owned by the University of Washington. They used to use it for office space, but apparently it is going to be demolished fairly soon, and so they had it boarded up and posted

No Trespassing. For some reason they never had the power turned off though, so it had heat, and of course that attracted vagrants."

The woman told me what she knew from the police report that had prompted this second opportunity for diversion. It wasn't much. After weeks of phone calls, research, and tearful visits to the University of Washington police headquarters—where Barry and I separately spoke to officers who were there that night—we were able to learn more.

We had thought Hunter was sleeping over at his friend Jeremy's house that night. He left Jeremy's house around midnight, bused to the U District, and was wandering around when he ran into someone he knew—someone he later described to us, under duress, as "just a guy I know from the Ave," who told Hunter he wanted to show him a cool place he and some friends had found. So Hunter followed him. The house was mostly dark but easily entered by moving boards covering the back door. Hunter followed his Ave "friend" into the house, greeted the others, and began to look around.

Suddenly, eight Seattle and University police officers burst into the house, guns drawn, shouting, and shining lights. It was a planned raid. The officers had expected to find the squatters—homeless street kids of varying ages—expected to find squalor and drugs. They had not expected to find my barely sixteen-year-old son, fairly clean cut, among this handful of the unwashed, barefoot, lost souls who panhandled and dealt drugs on the U District's main thoroughfare. He was not a familiar face in this pack of what some unkindly called the Ave Rats.

"We were shocked," one officer told me, "really surprised to find him there."

Hunter was sober when the officers confronted him, and he was the only minor, so they took him out before searching the property. Another officer who participated in the raid helped fill in some detail. "If we had found the drugs while he was there, he would have been charged with a felony. He could find himself in a world of trouble if he continues hanging out with people like these. They steal things, they are all into drugs. Hunter is not grasping that these are very bad people."

The officer who had removed Hunter from the squat house asked him for his phone number to call his parents. The number Hunter gave was not our number.

The officer told Hunter he would transport him to someplace where an adult could take charge of him, because the juvenile detention facility was full. Hunter gave him a friend's address and the officer drove him there and left him with the friend's father.

"They were pissed," Hunter told us later. "They were not happy to have me show up at their door at two a.m. with a cop. But they let me in."

"Where did you leave him?" I asked the officer in headquarters. "I want to talk to the dad."

"I didn't note the address," he answered, "it was north, up around 125th Northeast."

Hunter would never tell us who the friend or the father were or where the house was. The officer had noted the man's name, but it must have been wrong or false—I could not match the name to a real person.

Barry tried to obtain a police report, determined to find more clues about the frightening evening, but the clerk at Seattle Police Department headquarters denied his request.[1] Although Hunter's name appeared in the report and even though he was a minor, the other people charged were named and described and the case was still under investigation. "I can tell you some of their dates of birth," the clerk told Barry. "There were seven of them. Three I don't know, three were born in 1986, one in 1987." This meant they were in their early twenties, significantly older than Hunter.

I could well imagine Hunter's following the "friend" to the squat house. He was intrigued by things others might find disquieting or even repulsive, and he was not afraid.

Hunter had demonstrated this dispassion recently. Barry and I were horrified to read one morning in the paper about the death of a teenager who had been skateboarding down the Ave, hit a rock, and tumbled into the path of a city bus. Hunter, listening to us discuss the tragedy, was buttering the sesame seed bagel he'd just toasted. "Oh, yeah, I saw that happen," he offered. Later, he told Barry that he had gone over to take a look.

By some quirk of my interest in history, especially my work researching and writing about Seattle's history, when bad things happened with Hunter, I found comfort in drilling down into the genealogy of place. Researching and unfolding other events, mostly benign and commonplace, that had also happened in that place calmed me. Having other stories helped me put things into perspective, somehow.

I knew the squat house was University-owned and slated for demolition. UW routinely bought up U District properties as they became available, using the existing structures to house various departments or student organizations, sometimes for years. When the school had amassed enough contiguous parcels and had funding in place, these little houses were demolished, often to be replaced by fancy dormitories.

I soothed myself by driving to the squat house. I had determined that the house was built around 1909, an era in which I was currently steeped because of my ongoing research for a book I was cowriting, a history of the Alaska-Yukon-Pacific Exposition. Good things have happened in that house, I told myself. I imagined workers building the house, materials brought to the site on horse-drawn wagons. The exposition had been held on the then barely developed University of Washington campus, three blocks east of what was now the squat house. I thought of fairgoers, maybe fair employees, rooming in that then new house, walking to the fairgrounds. I imagined a professor and his family living there in the years after the fair or college students boarding. Contextualizing the place this way seemed crazy maybe, but it helped me calm myself.

Hunter, in France with his French teacher and fellow students, of course knew nothing yet of what we'd learned about his new interaction with the police. During this week, Hunter's bank statement arrived. My name was also on his account, and I opened the statement.

Hunter's beginning balance was $550, the money he'd saved for France. Almost all of the money had been withdrawn in $20 or $50 increments in the days before his departure. During the week in France, he had spent less than $150. I wondered how exactly he had fed himself—some meals were covered but certainly not all.

What did he spend the money on? A notebook page ripped from a spiral notebook and discarded on the floor of Hunter's room gave clues. One side—labeled with his name, Biology 106/p. 2,—contained a lovely detailed sketch noting his observation and dissection of a frog, dorsal and ventral views. Brow spot, nictitating membrane, tympanum: each part was marked. Beautiful, I thought, he can really draw.

The flip side of the paper was labeled "Folklife Shopping List." It detailed substances he planned to use during the upcoming Folklife Festival, an annual Memorial Day event: "1 g $45, ¼ oz. $60, 2 fifths R&R $20, 4 hits A $40, 4 packs cigs (2 Lucky Strikes, 2 Camel Reds) $24 = $189 + food and additional drug money = about $250."

Here it was, finally: my lingering fear that Hunter was experimenting with drugs, confirmed. I felt my teeth, stomach, even my breathing clench. The list was confident—and was so Hunter. "Additional drug money." I read the phrase again. No way to obfuscate that one, I thought. It's like that story about the thief apprehended with a to-do list stating, "Rob bank."

I showed the page to Barry, and he stared at it awhile. "Well," he finally said, "he sure as hell can't go to Folklife." We decided to send Hunter to Barry's father in Carmel Valley for the holiday weekend. Maybe long discussions with Grandpa Stuart would bring Hunter some perspective. We also planned to talk with Hunter about this evidence of his alcohol, marijuana, cigarette, and "A" use. Barry thought that "A" was Adderall, which would explain Hunter's recent loss of ten or fifteen pounds. He had carried a little extra weight since age ten or eleven, something our many discussions about nutrition and healthy eating habits had not changed. Adderall is a stimulant that is widely prescribed to treat Attention Deficit Hyperactivity Disorder. An internet search informed me that it was sometimes prescribed off-label as a weight loss aid.

Finally, the morning came when I drove to the airport, parked, and went in to wait for Hunter's plane. The kids emerged from the arrival area in clumps and groups, teacher chaperones herding them a little. Hunter was with a group, actually socializing. He hugged me. Two girls hugged him goodbye.

In the car, he looked so happy, talking about how he'd had lunch with my expat cousin in Paris, telling me about the side trip the group made to a perfume factory in Grasse. I wanted so much not to have to talk about the squat house, wanted it never to have happened, wanted this revitalized Hunter to have the chance to grab the rope, finally, to start the climb out of the pit he'd been slipping steadily into throughout the last year. I wondered whether I should wait until Barry and I could confront him together, factoring in that Barry was at a medical conference in Vancouver, Canada, for the next two days. Each moment I withheld our knowledge from Hunter, kept silent, felt like a bigger lie, a betrayal.

"Hunter," I finally said, "I have to tell you that we know now about the squat house, the trespassing. The people from Diversion called. This is a huge thing."

His mouth tightened. Shaking his head, he slumped into the passenger seat. "I didn't think they'd call you," he said. He seemed embarrassed to have been caught and angry because he'd thought he had gotten away with the events of that night.

Hunter was charged with criminal trespass in the first degree, a misdemeanor. He went again through King County Youth Diversion —the board of volunteers, less happy with us now, telling him this was strike two, suggesting we approach King County At-Risk Youth, the social service program another struggling mother had suggested earlier in the year.

I made the call. But At-Risk Youth, the woman on the phone explained, was for low-income kids. Hunter would never qualify, not while he lived at home. Many years later, I learned that either the woman misunderstood my question or I had mistaken her answer. There was no income cutoff. There never had been. At the time, though, we felt that door slam shut.

Get him a mentor, everybody said, involve him in activities. As if mentors were for sale at Target. As if facilitating classes in anything— yoga, fencing, aikido, guitar, tightrope walking, fire juggling, knife throwing—was as easy as discovering the class and signing him up. What do you want to do, I begged him, I will set up any lessons or anything—you need to get involved in something, plough into anything. We love you, we want to help you. If you find something you enjoy and focus on that, high school will go by faster, and then you'll have college, which is so much better, we promise, I promise, let us help you help yourself. Please, Hunter, please.

But there was nothing he would agree to do: not things he'd been good at but hadn't formally pursued, such as drawing; not activities he'd enjoyed as a child, such as fencing; not joining a group with whom he might have affinity, movie enthusiasts, for instance, or booklovers or mountaineers or backcountry skiers.

After Diversion, things got worse. Soon, worse was all there was.

The Accident

As the end of sophomore year approached, we assessed our options for Hunter. Letting him spin his wheels over the summer—or trusting, given his behavior at school, that he would find a job—would obviously be foolish. We made a plan for him to go to Outward Bound for a six-week wilderness course, and he reluctantly agreed. It was not a course for kids at risk—that seemed like a bad idea. Better to have him mix with teenagers who were on track and who were glad to be on Outward Bound.

It was early June, the weather cool, about a week before Hunter was due to finish school and head for Outward Bound. The afternoon was unusually still. Barry was at work, Sawyer at a friend's house, Lillie at Girl Scouts. Final deadline on the Alaska-Yukon-Pacific Exposition book was fast approaching. At my desk, I wrote into the peace of the clean, quiet house, pushing words into the document, spinning the thing together. I was aware, physically, of the stillness, the pause for breath in the usually busy household, and I filled it with my work.

Sound seemed to carry on the silence. I heard barking dogs that sounded as if they were blocks away, heard them stop barking. I heard a UPS truck, not near. And far away, south of me, from the U District, I heard the thin wailing of a siren. I registered the sound, still working. It did not stop, the wail went on. It was an ambulance.

The phone rang then, sharp, breaking the suspended moment. "Hi," the man said, "is this Hunter's mom?"

"Yes," I said, "this is Paula Becker, what's going on?"

"This is Joe in the Medcare Ambulance, and I have Hunter with me."

I gasped. "He's okay," Joe said quickly, "but he was hit by a car and we're taking him to University Hospital. Can you meet us there?"

My knees had buckled. People say that happens, but I'd never felt it. I knelt, clutching the phone. "Yes, yes," I said, "University Hospital, I'm on my way."

I tried to breathe, stand, pull myself together. The phone rang once again.

"University Hospital emergency is full," Joe said, "we're heading to Northwest instead."

"I'll meet you there," I blurted.

I was shaking. I could barely stand. Hit by a car? The ambulance guy had said Hunter was okay, but what did that mean? How could he be okay if he was heading to the hospital? I heard that siren, I thought suddenly, that siren was the ambulance coming for Hunter. It was happening right then.

I called my parents, and my father answered. The ambulance, the call, Northwest, I'm shaking, I don't think I can drive. "I'll be there," he said, "hold on, I'll be right there."

I grabbed my shoes, coat, purse, called Barry's cell phone. "Hunter has been hit by a car," I told him. "They say he's all right, but they're taking him to Northwest Hospital."

"I'm leaving right now," Barry said. "I'll meet you there as fast as I can."

My father drove up and whisked me quickly to the hospital. "Should I come in?" he asked me. "Should I wait?"

"Yes, please," I said, "can you?"

Emergency entry doors are all the same, ushering desperate families and patients in pain into a busy triage area, a waiting room with a nurses' desk, and forbidding doors marked Medical Staff Only. Northwest was no different: antiseptic, relatively small.

"My son is here, Hunter Brown, he came by ambulance," I stuttered to the nurses.

"Okay, come this way," one of them said immediately, leading me toward the double doors.

My dad sank back into the waiting room. "Barry is coming soon," I called to him.

The nurse led me down the sparkling corridor, paused before one door. "He's in here," she said. "He needs to stay lying down, but I don't think he'll try to get up. We're pretty slammed this afternoon, so it might take the doctor a while to make it in to see him. You can stay with him, of course."

I pushed into the small procedure room. Hunter was splayed out on the low exam table, eyes closed, covered with scrapes and just-dried blood. "Hunter!" One step took me to his side. I touched his face gingerly, recoiling slightly as the waves of alcohol fumes rising from his pores, his breath, reached my nose. "My God, Hunter, I'm so glad you're all right. Are you all right? What happened?"

"Mom," he moaned, "I'm sorry, Mom, I'm so sorry, Mom, I'm sorry."

"What are you sorry for, Hunter? They told me you got hit by a car, what happened?"

His words were slow, slurred, interspersed with apologies. He'd been with friends, waiting to cross Fiftieth Street in the U District, heading toward the bus stop to come home. They'd been "hanging out" together—that handy all-encompassing euphemism—and they were laughing, pushing one another as they waited for the light to change. Hunter had stumbled, or a girl had pushed him, jokingly, he couldn't remember which, and he had fallen backward into the busy thoroughfare, clipping the side mirror of a moving truck, rolling up and over the truck's hood, then hitting the pavement.

The truck had stopped, the driver distraught. Police arrived, the ambulance. Hunter was loaded in, disoriented. He'd blacked out, he thought, "for a while." The quiet afternoon, the screech of tires, screams from his friends, the lonely siren, and here we were.

"Hunter, I am so grateful that you are alive. You could easily have been killed, you know that, don't you?"

"It was an accident," he moaned. "It was an accident."

"Yes," I said, "I know that. But Hunter, you absolutely reek of alcohol. You guys were clearly drinking—you are drunk. You were horsing around right by a busy street. So it was accidental that the truck hit you, but in a way it was predictable that something bad would happen. Do you see that?"

"Can we not talk about it now?" he asked. "Please? I feel really terrible."

I sighed, held my tongue, dragged a chair close enough that, sitting, I could rest my hand on Hunter. We sat in silence, a quiet impinged on only slightly by muffled voices, gurneys in the corridor. I kept my hand on Hunter's upper arm, willing my strength into his battered body, trying, as I had tried when he was a child with croup or fever, to let my love help heal him.

An hour passed. Finally, a knock, the door swung open, and a young male doctor entered, introduced himself. I was relieved to see him but also, as part of a medical marriage, mortified. Barry's years working in rural emergency rooms during our homeschool years flashed through my mind. He had been the one in charge of managing crisis after crisis. Now our drunken, battered teen placed Barry and me on the wrong side of the equation. During his ER years, Barry had controlled the chaos. To this time-stressed young physician, we were the chaos.

The doctor asked me to step out while he examined Hunter. I stood in the hallway, awkward, the nurses glancing at me briefly as they walked busily by. After a few minutes, Barry burst into the corridor, hugged me.

"The doc is examining him," I told Barry. "He looks okay, a little beat up, but he reeks of booze."

"Really," Barry said, "are you sure?"

"Ah . . . I'm sure," I said. I wondered why he questioned it.

The doctor opened the exam room door and invited us in. Barry hugged Hunter gently, sizing things up.

"Hunter is okay," the doctor said, "but his hand is sprained, and he has a mild concussion. He needs to rest. You should keep an eye on him for twenty-four hours." Small talk, chitchat, the doc withdrew to write up discharge orders. Hunter hobbled into the hallway bathroom, leaving Barry and me alone.

"I don't smell alcohol," Barry said, "I don't believe he's drunk."

"What?" I said, uncomprehending. I'd spent the past hour breathing the fumes. It was impossible that Barry didn't smell them.

"I don't think so," he insisted. I shook my head, confounded. Hunter and the doctor returned, Hunter moving slowly, the doc with forms to sign. We said goodbye and thanked him, moved toward the lobby.

My eyes caught the doctor's summary of the visit: Diagnosis: alcohol intoxication, mild concussion, sprain, abrasions. I tilted the form toward Barry.

"See the diagnosis? He was drunk," I said.

"No," said Barry, shaking his head. "I still don't think so."

It was denial, certainly. Hunter was drunk, I saw and smelled it, and the doctor diagnosed it. Perhaps Barry's own experiences during the long shifts he'd worked—twenty-four hours here, forty-eight there—and all the distraught families and drunken teens he had dealt with through the years made it too painful for him to see plain truth. We did not want—no parent ever wants—to carry that stigma, the visit to the emergency room that tells the doctors and the world: My kid is uncontrollable, beyond my grasp. This might be doubly true for doctors.

As we crossed the parking lot, Hunter said, "Please, will you buy me cigarettes? I need a cigarette!"

I was appalled. I'd never seen Hunter smoke at that point, although I'd smelled smoke on him and asked about it many times.

"No way," I said. "There is no way on earth we are buying you cigarettes."

He grumbled as we made our way toward home, refusing offers of food, popsicles, ginger ale. Once we got to the house, his agitation grew. He stood in the front yard clutching his cell phone, telling friend after friend that he'd been hit by a car. When a man ambled up the sidewalk smoking, Hunter dashed down the steps, bummed one, smoked it standing in the grass.

Finally, it seemed he'd settled down. Retreating to his bedroom, he lay down, cell phone still in hand. I did the dinner dishes, Barry checked email. Suddenly, Hunter burst into the room, pulling on a jacket.

"I'm going out for a little while to see a friend," he said quickly.

"What? No!" Barry and I both moved toward him, Barry blocking the front door.

"Hunter," I said, "you have a concussion, and you are not going anywhere."

"Just for a while," he asserted, "I'm just going for a while!"

"Absolutely not. You should go back to bed."

He dodged around Barry, made it through the door. Barry surged after him, grabbed his arm. I saw them arguing in the front yard. Finally, spent, they came back in together. Hunter stomped through the kitchen, down the basement stairs. "I told him that if he left, I'd call the police and report him as a runaway," Barry said.

That night, Barry slept in front of Hunter's bedroom door, guarding him, ensuring he'd not leave, keeping him in and safe, keeping the world—as much as it was possible, for that one night—away.

The next night, just after Barry descended into Hunter's basement bedroom, I heard Barry begin weeping, sobbing deeply and inconsolably. I'd never heard him make that kind of sound, that hopeless keening. I nearly flew from our second-floor bedroom into the basement, sliding down both flights of stairs, screaming back, "What? What's happened?" I thought of the stout iron ring Barry had drilled into an old-growth beam to hold Hunter's punching bag, conjured an image of Hunter dangling in a noose.

But Hunter sat calmly on his black metal single bed, looking concerned and perplexed, gently hugging Barry.

"Oh, Dad, what's wrong? Dad?" he said softly. As if he really didn't know. As if his actions and our fear for him were wholly disconnected from his father's intense distress.

To Barry, our efforts to keep Hunter from flinging himself into the arms of every kind of danger culminated with that night. Barry felt, suddenly, and even though Hunter sat calmly before him, as if some part of his child had died. He knew, he told me years later, that Hunter had broken him. Thereafter, Barry stepped back from the belief that he could truly control Hunter.

I felt differently. Hunter's behavior was teaching me many unwanted lessons. I could begin to see that physically controlling him was impossible, but I still trusted my ability to make him see reason. Hunter's actions terrified and beleaguered me. But I was certainly not broken.

We held out hope that Outward Bound might change Hunter's outlook. Barry, especially, had great faith in the program. When he'd been eighteen, doing poorly in his first year at UC San Diego and unsure of who he was, a three-week Outward Bound wilderness course had clarified his thoughts, galvanizing him into improving his grades and transferring to Colorado College.

Hunter still had to make it through one more week of school before the Outward Bound trip. He was enthusiastic about taking community college classes through Running Start and knew he had to be a junior to qualify. But by the last week of his sophomore year, Hunter had skipped so many classes that, unless he went to class every single period and passed all his finals, he would be forced to repeat the second semester and forgo eligibility.

All that last week, we drove Hunter to school in the morning rather than having him walk the fourteen blocks. At lunch time, Barry returned, watched Hunter leave the school and cross to the stoner's row across the street. As lunch ended on the last day of school, Hunter headed away from school rather than toward it. Barry confronted him, Hunter threatened to run. Barry told Hunter that if he ran, Barry would report him as a runaway. Once again, this threat stayed Hunter's impetuous momentum. He eventually agreed to return to class, Barry following him at a distance. Hovering in the hallways all afternoon, clutching a visitor's pass, Barry ensured with his physical presence that Hunter attended each class. Finally, his exams were finished, his sophomore year complete. For Barry and me, it was a small, sharp victory in the midst of so much sadness and confusion.

Hunter's determination to skip classes even though he knew he had to go to gain access to Running Start was inexplicably self-destructive. It shook my hope that Running Start would be the answer to Hunter's lack of engagement with school. We recognized that Hunter was trying to navigate the transition from child to adult by seizing power—from the school, from us. He needed to gain serious traction in managing himself over the summer.

We did not trust Hunter to make it to Outward Bound on his own by train. My parents drove him across the western states and checked him into the program office in Grand Junction, Colorado. Barry and Sawyer flew to visit my brother in Dubai, a long-planned trip. I powered through the final stages of the Alaska-Yukon-Pacific Exposition book while Lillie played with friends or stretched on the sofa listening to music. Having Hunter safely out of town and productively engaged was an immense relief, although the rest of the summer loomed, and then Hunter's third year of high school.

Hunter's tumultuous sophomore year had brought Barry and me to a stark confrontation with the limits of our power over him. We had perceived a crisis and tried to take action. We were legally responsible for his health, safety, and security until he turned eighteen. We had legal authority over him, but how to exercise that? He was not a recalcitrant toddler being forcibly buckled into a car seat. In terms of strength, he was a grown man.

Hunter hadn't engaged us in physical struggle, although once when he was fourteen and arguing with Barry in the kitchen, Hunter had picked up a cast iron skillet and brandished it as a weapon. Barry burst out laughing, which had the effect of embarrassing Hunter into setting the skillet down.

We were determined that in saving Hunter we would not sacrifice our marriage. We knew that we needed to be functional to provide for Sawyer and Lillie and for each other. Friends of ours, faced with a similar situation, took out a loan that was larger than their home mortgage and used the proceeds to hire interventionists to kidnap their troubled fourteen-year-old daughter and whisk her to a religious-based therapeutic boarding school on a remote island. Three years and $150,000 later, their reformed daughter graduated and was doing fine. Her parents' marriage fared less well.

We shied away from the thought of putting Sawyer's and Lillie's college savings on the chopping block, and the thought of taking on such extensive debt felt like being held for ransom. We were determined to keep Sawyer's and Lillie's lives as normal as possible and to make sure that they knew that each of their lives mattered exactly as much as Hunter's did. We fought against allowing Hunter's unacceptable behavior and our anguished response to become the axis around which our family revolved. This struggle was ongoing, but Barry and I continually reassured each other that we were succeeding, sometimes just barely.

When Hunter's Outward Bound program finished in late July, he spent a night alone in a motel, then caught the Amtrak train home to Seattle. Sawyer and Lillie and I waited for him at King Street Station. He looked older, deeply tanned, better, I thought.

Weighing profit and loss, Barry and I decided to compromise our standards. While Hunter was at Outward Bound, we had begun a process of assessing his past actions, figuring out what we could tolerate and what we could not. Of all Hunter's infractions, the most exhausting issue had been his repeatedly sneaking out at night. Now Barry and I sat down with Hunter and tried a different approach to resolving that issue. "We need you to not leave the house at night without telling us, never to do that again. We cannot live with how it felt to wake and worry so intensely, to look for you and find you gone." He seemed to understand and promised that if he was going out at night, he would wake us up. It wasn't that we wanted him to leave. But we had learned that he would do it anyway. This was a way, one way, to manage that fact.

For a while, the new plan seemed to work. Hunter's break from us and ours from him during Outward Bound, coupled with his experiences in the rigorous program, had given us a sort of reset. We hoped the crisis had passed and that Hunter was starting to straighten out.

Weeks after Hunter's return, I gave up on his unpacking the giant duffle that held his clothes and gear and did it for him. Two empty bottles of Jack Daniels clinked against each other in the tangled dirty shorts and T-shirts. Someone helped Hunter get ready for the train trip home, I thought cynically, and Barry and I remained in a permanent flinch as Hunter's junior year began.

Totally Fucked

To our immense relief, Hunter now qualified for Running Start and so could take some of his classes at Seattle High School and some at North Seattle Community College. Hunter's Seattle High guidance counselor helped us decide which Running Start classes he should take and registered him. We bought the college textbooks, and Hunter headed ten blocks north of our house for several classes each day, then south to high school for the classes he took there.

With the freedom of Running Start, Hunter's acting out became less intense. After the horrible spring of sophomore year, he didn't skip high school quite as wholeheartedly, keeping his truancy just under the level that seemed to trigger the school's concern. Hunter went to classes he enjoyed or those whose teachers somehow succeeded in connecting with him personally. He read books, took tests, turned in assignments, and passed most of his classes. He often got an A, or an A knocked down to B or C because of poor attendance.

With no new crises every week, Barry and I began to breathe again, settling into an uneasy equilibrium. Running Start was college, and parents were not in the attendance loop. Hunter mentioned taking tests and writing papers and left the house each day in time to get to class, so we were surprised, when college grades arrived in the mail, to find that Hunter had received no credit. He sheepishly admitted that he'd only gone to class for a few weeks, then stopped going.

"Where were you when you were supposed to be at class?" I asked him.

"Oh, just hanging out. Getting coffee."

I lectured. We met with his guidance counselor. "Maybe let's try different Running Start subjects this time," she suggested. "How about an English class instead of the chemistry, which you can take here?"

Second quarter, we tried again. This time I drove Hunter to the college when I could manage, reassured when he loped toward the bunker-like concrete buildings. I felt more satisfied that he was going to class, but there were warning bells that I refused to hear.

"I saw Hunter on the bus midmorning last Tuesday," my friend Amy mentioned over coffee. "I was surprised to see him during school hours, but he seemed pretty relaxed about it."

"Hunter," I asked him that afternoon, "Amy said she ran into you on the bus last week when you were supposed to be at North. What were you doing on the bus?"

"I wasn't on the bus," he replied, "but you know, it's really strange, people tell me all the time they've seen me places where I haven't been. There must be a guy out there who looks just like me."

I called Amy. "Did you actually talk with Hunter when you saw him on the bus?"

"Sure, we chatted for several minutes," she replied.

"Amy says you two spoke when she saw you on the bus," I said to Hunter.

"Well, I can't explain that," he replied. "It wasn't me."

Did I then call the college to at least try and verify whether Hunter had been in class? I didn't. I should have, of course. But this, like many other incidents, unfolded over days crammed with the flotsam of our busy lives: Girl Scout cookie site sales at which Lillie and her troop mates sold while other moms and I hovered nearby. Judging a regional History Day contest. A research trip to Tacoma. A half-day off for Sawyer and Lillie, a birthday dinner for my dad, Lillie's usual thrice-weekly ballet classes, her Thursday voice lesson, my weekly *HistoryLink* staff meeting, Barry's several twelve-hour shifts at Urgent Care, an eye appointment for Sawyer. No action of Hunter's took place in isolation.

Everything played out against the whirling backdrop of our family activities.

Hunter had been an erupting volcano during sophomore year. Now he was dormant. Barry and I monitored him, volcanologists. There was still smoke, there were occasional rumbles, but for a while Hunter put out relatively neutral readings.

Hunter's voracious reading continued: Frank Herbert's *Dune* series and other intellectual science fiction, Katherine Dunn's *Geek Love*. He liked his English Comp class and wrote A+ essays on Machiavelli's *The Prince*, Scott Russell Sanders's essay, "The Men We Carry in Our Minds," Langston Hughes's story "Salvation," and Dave Barry's "Red, White, and Beer," among others. He was taking psychology and finding it fascinating, engaging Barry in detailed discussions about the collective unconscious.

Hunter was interested in the graffiti artist Banksy and in graffiti art in general. He listened to the Gorillaz and a lot of hip-hop, plus a wide range of old and new music. When he was eleven and twelve, Hunter had made me mix tapes. I loved hearing the songs he chose—he understood my musical taste well. It had been years, and so I asked for one. He rolled his eyes but slipped me a just-burned CD labeled "Mix for Mother" a few days later. The playlist synthesized where we'd been, filtered through the lens of what Hunter knew I'd like: "It's the End of the World as We Know It" by R.E.M.; the Ramones' "Sheena Is a Punk Rocker"; "Such Great Heights" and "Nothing Better" by the Postal Service; Jimmy Eat World's "The Middle"; "She's an Angel" by They Might Be Giants; the Shins' "New Slang"; "Some Postman" by the Presidents of the United States; and Guy Clark's "Baton Rouge," the perfect finale.

Hunter seemed more settled for the most part. On this veneer of normalcy, we tiptoed onward. It was better than it had been: we were not in constant crisis. We were relieved at the relative peace, too grateful for it to notice that Hunter's rebellious behavior had not stopped but had gone underground. He had become better at hiding it too and at obscuring his friends from us. Barry and I failed to factor in how closely Hunter had bonded with, imprinted on, the group of stoner friends he'd started hanging out with the year before. Some of them went to his and other local high schools, and some, although we didn't know it yet, came from the street.

Hunter's associates, the few I met during his junior and senior years, were full of a righteous self-assurance and hostile inner energy. The boys were smug and never met my gaze. The girls were sleek and knowing, as if they'd seen too much, too soon. He brought the flock of them into the house twice or three times at most. I'd given up on trying to shape Hunter's social group, and I was relieved that these friends of his kept their distance, that Sawyer and Lillie were not exposed to them.

Countless times, Hunter watched Gus Van Sant's 1989 film, *Drugstore Cowboy*, the story of a ragtag gang of Portland, Oregon, drug addicts who rob pharmacies to satisfy their cravings. He seemed even more entranced by the filmmaker's 1991 film *My Own Private Idaho*, about two Portland street hustlers, one born in poverty, the other the wealthy mayor's son. Hunter watched Gus Van Sant's films as if he were cramming for some dark examination. He seemed to crave the seamy. He was not in the least put off by people or behavior I found repulsive. "They're not bad people, Mom," Hunter told me when I voiced concern about these characters.

"Okay, maybe, but Hunter, they do bad things," I tried to explain. Still, we were talking about all these films. I was reassured to realize that Hunter was not just intrigued by storylines but interested in casting choices, camera angles.

Perfumers know that some people are attracted to the smell of rotting flesh or feces. Of dank spaces, vomit, dirty feet. Figuratively, these odors drew Hunter, or so it seemed to me. Danger—and those who promised it—seduced and captivated him. I saw glimmerings of this, and it worried me, but Hunter brushed my concerns aside. No part of Hunter seemed to experience squeamishness. All his life, he had walked fearlessly into the dark.

In the Grimms' fairy tale called "The Boy Who Went Forth to Learn What Fear Was," the younger of two sons can't understand why his older brother is frightened by ghosts, by dark and scary stories—in short, the things most children find terrifying. The younger boy seeks increasingly alarming situations, trying, the story says, "to get the shudders." That, we decided when he was a little boy, was Hunter. He was not personally frightening. He was sweet and kind and openly sincere. But he examined what other kids found frightening in a way that was almost clinical, studied it like a scientist, drew measured conclusions. And found it thrilling.

When Hunter had slammed into public high school in 2006, he was as unprepared for that confusing universe as it was possible to be. He floundered, grasping for something, some kid who was kind or at least not cruel. Then, at the beginning of his sophomore year, he found Tamlin. Tamlin was one kid Hunter did bring home, although not often. He mentioned him, hung out with him. Now, Hunter spent much of the summer between his junior and senior years in Tamlin's company.

Tamlin and his mother, Lana, welcomed Hunter into their world. At the time, I saw Lana as another version of a familiar type, the Seattle hippie mom. Hunter told me he thought I'd like Tamlin and Lana's charmingly decrepit house, accessed by pushing through overgrown fir trees. I picked Hunter up a few times early on, spoke with Lana, peering up the twisting staircase or peeking inside from the heavily shaded front porch. The place seemed fine, Lana and Tamlin like variations on the homeschool/Waldorf school families we'd known. Hunter was increasingly navigating the city without my help by the time he and Tamlin became friends, and the city bus linking our neighborhood with Tamlin's became Hunter's most frequently used route.

I learned, much later, that Tamlin had been brought up in a household where ongoing addiction was accepted as a possible norm. Lana's mother had struggled with drug addiction during Lana's youth, and Lana's boyfriend, who was often at the dark fairytale-like house, used heroin.

Many years after these events, reading an old journal entry of Hunter's written the summer between his junior and senior years, I found these lines: "I met Tamlin and them the first day of sophomore year and that was that. And we ALL fucked up in the months after, to varying degrees. I kept doing so for a pretty sizeable fuckin' chunk of time. We all had fucking fun, though. Fun beyond belief." A few pages later, this phrase, which would in time prove telling: "Jess likes corrupting innocent minds." Jess was the boy with whom Hunter had been caught drinking in an alley near Seattle High.

Junior year had ended with enough high school credit to give Hunter senior status. He passed one Running Start class and got no credit in the other. At the suggestion of his guidance counselor, we transferred Hunter to Running Start at a different community college, Seattle Central, in the hip, multicultural Capitol Hill neighborhood about five miles from our house. Seattle Central offered a wider variety of classes than North, and students there skewed younger. Hunter's counselor thought it might be a better fit.

As senior year began, Hunter seemed more guarded and less often at ease. He stayed away from home, always with explanation. "I'm going to a coffee shop to study after school." Or "I'm taking the bus to the downtown library." The conversations about film and psychology petered out. Hunter was often terse. Barry and I felt as if he saw us as adversaries.

I often snooped through Hunter's room, drawers, backpack, even journals. Keen for information, I broke whatever rules I thought I'd have in terms of my teen's privacy. I hate that I had to do this but felt that Hunter's past actions warranted my intrusion.

Sometimes Hunter's journals were sad revelations, sometimes completely puzzling to me. He practiced writing a script that wasn't English, filling pages and pages. Were these tags, rehearsals for something he'd spray-paint across a bridge someday? Or was the scribbling hallucinatory? I didn't know.

The backpack, the goddamned fucking backpack. Hunter carried his backpack with him everywhere. "Why do you need that?" I'd ask.

"Oh, I need my books to study."

"I'm spending the night at X's house."

"I'm in the middle of a good book and I might read it in the park."

I blahblahblahblah.

Lies.

I came to hate and fear the sight of the pack slung on his shoulder. That this particular backpack was the deep-purple, three-pocket Jansport we'd purchased at REI to serve as Hunter's diaper bag during our first months in Seattle layered ironic nuance onto my antipathy. Often, I'd make him open it before he left, enduring his anger. Harder to manage was searching it when he came home: he slipped in quickly or left the backpack outside the house to be retrieved later. Sometimes when he showered, he took the backpack into the bathroom with him. When he forgot to do so, I pawed through.

What did I find? Cigarettes, lighter, liquor bottles, baggies, loose pills, rolling papers. What would I do? Confront him, talk to Barry, confront Hunter together, cry, obsess, lecture, threaten, ground, reason, explode, implode, flush things away. Naïve as I still was then, no part of me believed that taking away this particular backpack would make one bit of difference. What was inside the bag was what mattered. There could be many other bags.

There were more counselors and therapists, agreed to in the beginning and then quickly dismissed, appointments blown. Hunter never saw any of these practitioners more than a few times. One therapist called and said, his voice literally shaking, "I cannot tell you anything because of patient confidentiality, but Hunter *is not taking care of himself.*" What the holy fuck? Um, right, that's why he's seeing you, and yes, I'm wild with terror, but what do I do with that cryptic call to action?

There was one therapist who saw them all, all Hunter's Lost Boys, and it is this man I remember best. Hunter told me later that he and his friends laughed about how, at various times, they had all been in therapy with the same man. He was the go-to guy for troubled, troubling male adolescents. He let them howl, meaning he had no rule or contract that said Just Say No. His group sessions drew a ragtag gang, ranging from disgruntled teens to entrenched drug abusers. In theory, everyone learned from everyone else; in practice, none of it was good. His office was equipped with the requisite couch, chairs, Kleenex, and with a circle of large rocks arranged on the woven rug. Rainsticks, wolf skulls, Native American drums. It was Robert Bly for the young millennial, Iron John meets Bart Simpson.

But Hunter did not see even this therapist for long, maybe four sessions, before blowing an appointment he was supposed to get to on his own by bus after school. The therapist called me, explaining that we'd still be billed. I apologized for wasting his time and then drove Hunter to the next appointment.

"I don't want to do this," he said, and when I told him he had no choice in the matter, he walked into the building and out the back door. Fifty minutes later, no Hunter. I waited awhile and then went in and knocked on the therapist's door.

"I'm sorry to bother you, but I'm waiting for Hunter. Are you guys done?"

"Hunter no-showed again," the man replied. "I'm going to have to bill you again. Given his reluctance, I'm probably not his best option."

Somehow, the days rolled on. We tried to help Hunter, keep him from slipping down the slope that was rapidly becoming a glass-slick log flume, a glacier, the edge of a sheer cliff. We tried to focus on Sawyer and Lillie, who seemed engaged in their own lives, doing fine. We did our work, knowing some emergency could yank our attention away at any minute but holding the tiller steady until that moment.

Hunter's behavior still sometimes looked to us as if it were just about to turn a corner and improve. He was often surly with Barry, rarely with me. He hugged me, thanked me for meals, made jokes, talked politics. We still hoped that Hunter's intelligence would help him see the picture clearly, help him wake up, if we could only get through to him. This faith allowed us to be optimistic, despite the signs. But there were other times, like the birthday dinner when he showed up clearly high, his eyes half-focused, that mocked that hope.

An undated to-do list found on Hunter's floor, headed "Friday's Itinerary," included reminders to study for his biology final, turn in his AP Euro book, take finals, talk to his French teacher, make up two biology tests after school, and to "GET IN TOUCH with JR + get money, go meet, back by end of lunch." "The Evening," the list continued in two neat columns. "If meet up with JR: take one, go find a party, get a fifth, buy cigs, maybe jam with Graham. If not: Talk to Henry about Rafa, facilitate acquisition, get some money, get some bud, wander around."

"Who is JR," I asked Hunter when I found the list. "Is he your drug dealer? Who is Henry? Who or what is Rafa? Who is buying you liquor?"

"Oh mom," he scoffed, "those are just guys I know. I didn't do any of that. No one bought me anything. That list is old anyway, it's from, like, months ago."

One late afternoon, Hunter was caught stealing beer from a grocery store. Summoned by my cell phone's vibration as I did research in the Seattle Public Library's archival collections, I heard the news from the officer filling out the police report. "You tell him," I said shrilly, my voice carrying to the library patrons on levels below, "that he is NOT going through Diversion this time, because Diversion has not *diverted him!*"

For whatever reason, this police report was never filed, and we heard no more from the police about the incident. Hunter was banned for the next year from entering that particular grocery store, and Barry and I, as his guardians, received an invoice for a $200 fine. Hunter had not received an allowance from us since the squat house incident. Did we ground him? I hope we did. We were worn down by how ineffectual we felt, incapable of successfully enforcing any consequences we set for Hunter.

A decade later, Sawyer told me that when he was in high school, one of Hunter's old friends had told him that Hunter was famous for shoplifting beer at that particular store. The employees knew he did it, and they were all just waiting for the chance to catch him.

A few months after the beer incident, the phone rang late, jolting us from sleep. Hunter was in police custody, found on the Ave with an open container, one of a crowd of many. The officer brought Hunter home, his cruiser pulling silently to the curb in front of our house. I watched from behind the curtain as the officer helped Hunter from the patrol car's back seat and removed the handcuffs from his wrists.

For two hours we clustered in the living room, Hunter silent, the officer lecturing him and giving us advice. The cop seemed to understand Hunter's potential, to see a boy who could be reasoned with, motivated to turn his life around. "If my kid was screwing up like this," the officer said, "I'd take the door off his bedroom. Do you know what a lot of parents in your folks' situation do? They put up with it until the kid turns eighteen, and then the kid comes home to changed door locks, and, if they're lucky, some of their clothes in the front yard. Do you want that to happen to you, Hunter?"

Hunter performed contrition, hung his head. "No, sir, I don't," he said. "You're right. I screwed up. I'm sorry. I won't do it again."

I thought about what it might feel like to lock Hunter out. It would feel desperate. It would feel cruel. And on some deeply exhausted level, I admitted to myself, it might feel something like relief.

Another evening, late, Barry's cell rang: the police had Hunter on the Ave again, this time with a stolen bike. Barry should come and pick him up, the officer said. Filing no charges—they'd seen Hunter remove the bike from a rack but didn't know whose bike it was—the officers delivered Hunter into Barry's custody. Hunter was very drunk. They'd walked along the Ave as Barry tried to convince Hunter to return home, but to no avail. Eventually, he ran off down the street.

What would have happened in decades past? There were boys' homes for the wayward, which Hunter was. Would he have jumped a train, ridden the rails, gone hobo? Left town with a traveling carnival, become a roustabout? Learned to breathe fire, walk on hot coals? It was the twenty-first century. Those paths were closed.

Barry and I, in spite of what was right in front of us, still hoped that Hunter would pull out of this nosedive. We still envisioned him entering college with his age-mates, imagined that if the school were right, that sweetly quirky person would once again present himself. That he would flourish. We believed the narrative we'd invented for and with him in childhood, denying the story he was screaming at us now.

The eighteen months between Outward Bound and the middle of Hunter's senior year had felt like a series of small, incremental declines in Hunter's functionality: cops bringing him home, drunk in the U District, stealing beer. We were certain he was experimenting with drugs but saw no signs of actual addiction to any substance. So Hunter's senior year proceeded, with weeks of relative calm periodically interrupted by crisis. Barry and I were no longer the same parents that we had been two years before. We had diminished expectations of what our relationship with Hunter looked like, little idealism, only a great desire for pragmatic results. We were settling, buying relative peace by ceding confrontation. We would not spring into action unless some event pushed us past our greatly lowered limit. Since Outward Bound, no single incident had been dire enough to do that.

Hunter had dabbled enthusiastically with pot, with Adderall, with alcohol, maybe with acid. Now, in the first months of 2010, around the time he turned eighteen, he turned to opioids. Hunter responded to this new substance with the same enthusiasm he'd shown when he embraced trains, chapter books, and the *Titanic*: he was all in.

The first thing that happened was this: I couldn't find the Reynolds

Wrap. "Where is the foil?" I asked Sawyer and Lillie. "Did either of you take it for a craft project?" They had not. I wandered through the house, puzzled, ended up in Hunter's room. The box of foil protruded from a heap of laundry. Huh, I thought, that's odd, as I returned it to the kitchen.

Later, we started finding bits of foil, burned on one side, sticky and black on the other. Cheap ballpoint pens, the ink part missing, their empty plastic exteriors strawlike. Sometimes I'd wake in the night, smelling smoke, feeling the terror of an unknown something, somewhere—the house was not safe, something was not right. Barry or I or both of us would descend to the basement, sniffing, quiz Hunter. "I lit incense," he'd sometimes say. Or, "Nothing, there's nothing burning, what are you talking about?" We never saw him burning whatever it was, but evidence piled up: the broken pens, the foil. Notebook paper covered with doodles I could not read at first but that resolved themselves as "PhenPhenPhenPhen," forever, again and again, a love song.

The details of these days are clouded, full of holes. I know I was working on my second book. I know Barry was working three or four twelve-hour urgent care shifts each week. Now cash began disappearing from my wallet, five dollars here, ten there. Barry ran almost every day, leaving his wallet in our bedroom closet where, more than once, I stumbled upon Hunter. When did the evidence become undeniable that Hunter was stealing money and that he was using one drug consistently, not "just" pot (bad enough, to my mind), not "just" alcohol (again, not good)?

Self-deception is a powerful urge. Smelling liquor on his early morning breath sophomore year, I'd told myself it couldn't be. Stumbling onto the foil now, my mind flipped, spun, through every possible reason it might be there except the truth. Trying to unsee the evidence. Feeling the pull of fear's deep inescapable well.

Around the time we started finding the burned foil, around the time my eyes decoded the scribbled word fragment, I googled "Phen." Phen/fen/fentanyl, the screen whispered, a powerful synthetic opioid used to control pain in cancer patients, used during surgery, fifty to one hundred times more potent than morphine. The drug of choice, my googling informed me, among anesthesiologist substance abusers. Expensive, very. Extremely deadly if misused. The drug, when abused, is often heated to release its vapors, which are then inhaled. That was the purpose of the disassembled pens. Their shells were straws, conduits for vaporized fentanyl.[2]

The afternoon we finally figured this out was brightly sunny, mid-April. Barry and I hovered, whispering, in the living room, Barry describing to me fentanyl's potentially deadly risk. I felt as if I'd been smashed down by a giant wave, that something enormous, overwhelming, had flattened and disoriented me. We heard Hunter's steps coming up the basement stairs. He'd said earlier that he was going to Tamlin's house, and here he was, his backpack with him, as always.

Barry blocked Hunter's path. "Open the pack and show us what's inside."

"I'm not going to do that," Hunter refused, bumping against the old upright piano as he tried to squeeze past us and reach the door.

"We know about the fentanyl, Hunter. This is really, really serious. You need help," I said. "Oh, Hunter, this is so scary. Please take this seriously. I love you. I am so frightened for you . . ."

Yanking the backpack away from Barry's grasp, Hunter fled the house.

"You cannot live here if you're using drugs," we shouted after him, and then collapsed into each other's arms.

This was new territory, and I had no idea what came next. I remembered the police officer who'd brought Hunter home from the Ave, his lecture and warning that once kids reached legal adulthood, parents sometimes changed the locks. Hunter was eighteen, barely. But I didn't want him back in the house while the fentanyl issue was unresolved.

Barry rekeyed the locks on the front and back doors. Two days passed and two long nights. Hunter did not come home. I felt as if my skin had been flayed off. When I drove past homeless people sleeping in doorways, a common sight on the U District's main streets, I craned my neck, scanning the heaps of blankets, wondering whether Hunter was wrapped in them.

The third night, about midnight, soft knocking on the front door roused me from fitful sleep. I rushed downstairs, looked through the curtain. It was Hunter, bedraggled. His eyes met mine through the glass. "You changed the locks," he said, his words muffled. "That didn't take you long."

"Hunter," I said, opening the door. I put my arms around him. "I cannot let you in unless you are ready to go into a rehab program. You cannot live in this house if you are using drugs."

"I will, Mom. I will go to a program. But I'm so tired now, I just want to sleep. Can we figure it out in the morning?"

I let him come inside and go downstairs to his bedroom. Barry and I agreed that time was crucial, we needed to get him into something right away. He was soft tonight, vulnerable. We suspected that this openness to entering rehab might be temporary. We knew there was a concept called "hitting bottom," that it was a step in the recovery process that many people grappling with addiction had to proceed through. Maybe, we thought, Hunter's brief stint on the street had helped him hit bottom? But how long would that last?

The next two days were a sheer blur, like standing in front of a full-on fire hose. Endless Google searches for rehab: drug rehab, 12-Step rehab, non-12-Step rehab, affordable rehab, instantly available rehab, inpatient rehab, anything remotely promising. Families seeking drug rehab programs are always desperate. Google search results weight programs that purchase advertising right at the top, and these programs are expensive, often dizzyingly so. They are the names everyone recognizes from the newspaper: Betty Ford, Hazelden, Pine Grove, Morningside. All want your contact information before quoting you a price. When Barry and I were looking for rehab for Hunter, few of these name-brand rehab facilities accepted insurance, a situation that seems to have shifted in recent years.

The 2010 Affordable Care Act, signed into law about a month before we started looking for rehab, includes substance abuse disorder services among the mandates that every insurance plan in its marketplace must cover. This was not an issue for us because we had good insurance through Barry's workplace. That insurance, Premera Blue Cross, covered inpatient drug rehab services under certain circumstances. But finding the right program was daunting.

There is no Cyndi's List for rehab facilities, no Good Housekeeping Seal of Approval, no governmental rating system.[3] An unbiased vetted list that compared and rated facilities based on success rates would go a long way toward helping parents make an informed choice. Rehab center websites feature reassuring photographs and make many claims that are impossible to substantiate, although some, such as that of The Clearing, a facility on Washington's San Juan Island, provide what looks like good information. As for price, according to The Clearing's list of more than fifty facilities across the country, a month of inpatient treatment ranges from $8,000 to as much as $111,000. Programs that are not based on the Alcoholics Anonymous/Narcotics Anonymous 12-Steps generally command higher prices.

We weighed taking on substantial debt against a possible chance, certainly not a guarantee, of our child's well-being. Barry and I knew that Hunter's future, even his life, might hinge on our decision, but in spite of the stakes, we could do no better than take a wild guess at which program to choose. We wanted a program designed for young men, and there were plenty. I waded into the search, trying to filter out the bad or dangerous programs—the one that promised sweat-lodge treatment for ten or more hours daily, the ones whose names yielded news stories about frequent suicides—eventually becoming overwhelmed. It was like staring at a row of identical doors. Barry stepped in and finally stumbled on Pacific Recovery. The pictures were beautiful and the facility looked safe. They billed insurance for the first thirty days; they'd check our coverage. Draining our savings account, we could just do it.

Pacific Recovery strongly urged a minimum of three months' treatment, but our insurance covered only a portion of the first month, the fully locked-down inpatient part of treatment. The two additional months were $10,000 each. Barry was scheduled to receive a bonus—we'd devote the whole toward the rehab. My parents lovingly and without judgmental comment ponied up the rest. They loved Hunter and they loved me, they said. They wanted him to have this good chance to get better. I was faint with gratitude—and fully aware that this was a one-time deal.

The program sent a packing list, like summer camp. Five T-shirts, two long-sleeved shirts, shorts, sandals, swimsuit, pajamas, clothing suitable for yoga. Hunter packed a bag, I got his passport from the strong box. Hunter had taken driver's ed but never pursued a driver's license. His passport was his only legal identification. We would need it, along with his insurance card and a substantial check to start his intake process.

I called Hunter's high school guidance counselor to tell her what was happening and that he would not be back to Seattle High School or Running Start. "He isn't graduating next month," she said.

"I know, I know that—you already made it clear he wasn't graduating—you and I spoke about it and you sent a letter." I tried to tamp down my stress-fueled frustration. The stakes were much higher than graduation. I tried again. "He has an opioid addiction and we are sending him to an inpatient rehab program."

The counselor—who was a caring person and, like her peers, massively overworked—put me on conference call with the community college registrar, who suggested we withdraw Hunter from his classes. "That way, when he comes back, his record won't show failure."

"That sounds good," I said, thinking, right, when he comes back, no failure, let's hope for that, why not.

Hunter had his own list of things to finalize before he left for rehab. "You won't like this, Mom," he said, "but I owe money to someone, and I want to pay it off before I leave town, so I don't have to see him again when I come back."

"Is it for drugs? Is he your dealer?"

"I don't want to talk about it," Hunter answered. "I know if I don't pay him now, he'll add to what I owe him while I'm gone. I'll have to settle it when I get back, and it will be worse by then."

Barry and I talked about it, about this one more straw on our figurative camel's back, finally deciding just to do it and pay the debt. We didn't want Hunter leaving the house by himself, now that we had secured the rehab situation. "I'll drive you there," I told him.

Hunter said he didn't want me to know where the dealer lived because this knowledge might be dangerous for me. He suggested that I drive to the grocery store across the street from Seattle High School and wait while he walked to the dealer's house nearby. Feeling entirely uneasy, I complied. I pulled five twenties from my purse and gave them to Hunter. "How long will it take?" I asked.

"I should be back in fifteen minutes," he replied, striding away toward the school.

A man was cooking kettle corn in a giant pan in the corner of the grocery parking lot. The melted sugar smell drifted in my window as I waited fifteen minutes, twenty, half an hour. I am a total fool, I thought. I gave him a hundred bucks and sent him to a dealer. He is not coming back.

An hour after Hunter left, he returned, breathless. "The guy wasn't there, but I called him, and he told me to wait on a certain corner and he'd be by in five minutes, but he didn't come, not for a long time. I'm sorry you had to wait, thank you for waiting."

Early the next morning, less than two days after he'd agreed to treatment, Hunter and I were on our way to SeaTac Airport, bound for Orange County, California, where he was scheduled to begin Pacific Recovery's three-month drug rehab program.

Flying South

I flew with Hunter to Orange County on Southwest's first morning flight. The plane was nearly empty. We started out sitting next to one another, but when the fasten seat belts sign turned off, Hunter shifted to the row in front of me, lay down, pulling his sweatshirt neck over his eyes, and fell instantly asleep. He looked exhausted, rough, frightened, younger than he'd seemed over the past months.

I stretched out across three empty seats, pulled my eyeshade on, and started sobbing silently. My eyeshade blocked out all the light and soaked up tears, perfectly accessorizing the moment. I let my thoughts drift back to little Hunter, to that bright lively person we had encouraged, treasured, nurtured, believed in. I felt the reversal of our long-ago arrival in Seattle viscerally, how I had clutched Hunter's tiny hand and carried his car seat to the baggage claim, where our friend Peter was picking us up, as Barry and his sister, Lauren, and their father drove cross-country in the moving truck. Now Hunter and I shared this somber, desperate journey.

Grasping to somehow structure the pain, I willed the words and feelings washing over me to fall into a pattern:

> when all the pens have become drug straws
> dollars and coins palmed
> purse rifled through,
> we fly away

high, literally, our nearly empty plane
careening south
we stretch across the
seats—aisle, middle, window—
a row apart
reaching for slumber

this is not family
bed or the pair of us approaching
a new beginning so
long ago, car seat and diaper bag
in tow—

another journey.
when you were small you pointed
to a picture of the earth taken
from space. "like a moon,"
you said.

tell me again, tell me
this moment's metaphor

The plane landed, taxied lazily toward the terminal under the sunny Southern California sky. Please let this be the place, I whispered to myself, where Hunter regains his senses. Please let this fog of self-destruction lift from him here. Please let him be again that boy with a firm grasp on his own narrative. Let him be trustworthy again, that kid whose words I could believe without events proving that choice delusional. We grabbed our carry-ons, moved off the plane, and into the terminal.

Hunter was edgy. I tried to exude calm as we exited the secure area, started down the escalators. "I want to buy some cigarettes!" Hunter said suddenly, "I need them . . . ," and he turned to climb up the stairs as they moved down.

"Wait, Hunter, this is an airport, you can't smoke in here, so they don't sell cigarettes," I called. He hesitated, and the escalator delivered us to the baggage claim, where a burly giant in his midthirties held a sign that read, "Hunter."

"I need to buy cigarettes," Hunter said again.

"Are you Hunter?" the tall man asked. "I'm Josh, I'm here to drive you to the program."

Josh's presence reassured me. I felt as if he would be my ally in case Hunter changed his mind about entering rehab. Not that Josh could have legally forced Hunter out of the airport terminal, but he was physical reinforcement for our next few hours. He knew the way, literally and metaphorically. He was our guide to this new planet.

"Can we stop for cigarettes?" Hunter asked him.

"Oh, I'll be making a run later for all the guys. You can tell me what brand you want, and how many packs." Hunter's eyes widened. I gritted my teeth. "Are you Hunter's mom?" Josh asked. "Smoking comforts a lot of people working through addiction." He shot me a half-smile. "I know, it's an addiction too, but . . ."

The van was large enough to transport twelve, and Josh said they used it to take residents on outings. "We don't go many places in the first month," he added. "The first month happens at a place we call New Chance Ranch. The Ranch is tough, the guys have meetings every day, and we drive them to NA and AA meetings in the community. We do a sunrise walk and a meditation and graduation when a resident completes thirty days. We work on the property, clearing brush and stuff. There are wildfires here, so it's important, but the exercise is also good, distracting."

Josh locked the van doors. We pulled out of the airport parking lot and passed a large complex of aged warehouses. The road became more rural, winding through scrub and sand. The Ranch, where we were heading, wasn't in Orange County, where the main program facilities hugged the tony Newport Beach seashore, but out in the eastern LA basin. We pulled up to a manicured front lawn and low-slung ranch-style buildings. It could have been a retirement community or a Western prep school but for the locking gate across the driveway.

Josh led us in. About a dozen men in their early twenties were scattered across armchairs and couches, balancing lunch plates. Several men chopped vegetables in a large kitchen. "You can join us for lunch if you'd like," Josh offered. I declined. I was heading back to Seattle later that day, and time was tight.

"Let me give you both a quick tour, and then we'll start Hunter's intake," Josh said. We peered into Spartan bedrooms, each outfitted with two twin beds, all neat and antiseptic. "The residents do their own laundry," Josh said, pointing to a washer and dryer in a hallway closet. "Self-care is something many people in recovery have to learn—or relearn."

"That sounds great," I murmured.

One bedroom door was closed. "The guy who lives in there isn't feeling so good," said Josh. "We let them sleep sometimes if they really need it. People who need medical detox do that in a clinic down the road, but sometimes people feel pretty bad here for a while."

Hunter and I were ushered into an office, where I handed over Hunter's passport, wrote out an enormous check, and accepted a stack of Pacific Recovery materials. These looked like high-end real estate brochures, the kind full of attractive, expensive-looking houses photographed at dusk, their windows glowing invitingly. Clients in the photographs—or maybe they were models—smiled knowingly, straight into the camera, clear-eyed. We've learned our lessons here, the pictures said. We're all better now, back on the straight and narrow. Boy, close call, good choice, your kid is going to be A-OK soon too, just like me.

The brochures made me hopeful but also nervous. They pictured surfboards, bike rides, yoga on the beach. In one image, five grinning kids in caps and gowns waved rolled diplomas. None of the people pictured looked as if they needed rehabilitation or even as I imagined someone who had so recently wrestled with addiction might appear.

We had chosen Pacific Recovery because its program was for three months instead of the thirty days most other rehabs we considered offered at the time. The first portion of Hunter's program at Pacific Recovery, New Chance Ranch, was bullet-pointed: CARF Accredited, Licensed by the State of California Alcohol and Drug Programs, Relapse Prevention, Individual & Group Therapy, Anger Management, Spiritual Retreat with Workshops, Men's Gym. After his thirty days at New Chance Ranch, the plan was two more months in what the brochure called its signature extended-care program. One day at a time, I told myself.

"I'm going to talk to Hunter now alone and go through his bag," Josh said. He sent me on a tour of the grounds—horses grazing in a paddock, small bunkhouses that were used as offices.

I met briefly with the resident physician, a harried-seeming man in a small cluttered office in a former stable. He grilled me about our family, seemed surprised to hear that Barry and I were still married and had been for so long. His eyebrows flew up when I told him fentanyl was Hunter's "drug of choice," a term I was learning for the first time.

"Wow, that's unusual, really expensive. Dad's a physician, huh, is he an anesthesiologist? Did Hunter steal the drug from him? And it's really dangerous, high risk of overdose. Hunter's only eighteen, you say?"

"Hunter told us he buys it on the street. I don't know. He's taken other stuff, I don't know what all, but at least LSD and pot, a lot of alcohol—I don't know what to say. Yes, he's eighteen."

"So young," the doctor muttered. "Well, it's a good thing you've brought him here. We'll assess to see if he is dual-diagnosis, meaning something else like depression, psychosis, ADHD, something like that on top of his primary diagnosis, which is opioid addiction. He'll go to 12-Step meetings, get a sponsor, work out in the gym. We'll let you know."

Back at the ranch house, it was time to say goodbye. Hunter smoked in the front yard—he'd bummed a cigarette from someone—but followed Josh and me toward the van. "Do I really have to stay here?" he asked.

"Hunter," I told him, "I love you so much and you can do this. You can do this. You can straighten out your life, and what you learn from this experience will let you help other people someday. I promise you."

I was thinking, maybe, about my own lessons learned during the week spent in the NICU after Hunter's birth, of how several times I'd had a chance to tell new moms in similar circumstances to have a doctor write feeding orders to be posted on the Isolette. I felt my experience had spared those other mothers and that this good thing had emerged from that difficulty.

I didn't know it at the time, but I was unwittingly espousing one of the 12-Step tenets: having had a spiritual awakening, the person in recovery vows to carry the message of recovery to others suffering from addiction and to practice the 12-Step principles in all their affairs.

I hugged Hunter close, pulling him down so I could graze a kiss onto the crown of his head. I was leaving him. I dreaded the wrench, but I craved distance from the chaos of parenting him, needed the separation and the rest. I felt relief as I slammed the van door and buckled myself in for the ride.

Josh sensed my struggle to hold back emotion. "I want to let you know you're doing the right thing," he told me. "I have to say I was surprised when I saw you coming down the escalator with Hunter this morning, because I've never seen a parent bring their kid in, and I've been working here four years."

"Really," I said, "never?"

"I've seen the clients come with interventionists," he told me, "but never moms or dads."

"I can't imagine that," I said. "For one thing, I'm not sure Hunter would have made it through the process alone, but also, he's my kid, and I know having me come along helped him do this."

"As part of the intake I ask clients who supports them, who is always there for them emotionally," Josh said. "When I asked Hunter that question, he said, 'My mom.'"

Hunter's answer made me feel close to him, even as Josh's van carried me away. I did try to be there emotionally for all my kids. I tried to feel each one's essential nature, to listen to that inner Hunter, Sawyer, and Lillie. I valued my commitment to doing this but also feared that this aspect of my parenting style had made it harder for me to recognize and admit to Hunter's mounting difficulties over the past few years. His inner self was perfect and complete to me, and this had led me to normalize Hunter's behavior and discount warning signs. I sighed.

"You've worked here four years," I said, "what all do you do?"

"I do the driving, help with intake, hang around. Sometimes it's hard for residents to deal with counselors and therapists, but I'm kind of like a friend. I was like them for most of my life, since I was younger than Hunter. I drank. I took all kinds of drugs. I stole from my family, scammed them, so bad that even though I've been clean for six years now, I've got a sister who won't talk to me, won't take my calls. She's just—done. I understand that. I burned through everyone who loved me. But the great thing now is that, finally, I've rebuilt a relationship with my mom. She's widowed, and she lives near here. I stop by every day or so, take her to lunch, hang out. It's the best thing in my life, something I got back. I never thought I'd have that. Lots of people in recovery choose to work in the recovery industry," Josh added. "We see them coming in, so messed up, and we have to tell ourselves, that was me. That could be me again. It keeps us honest."

The little airport offered few food options and no distractions. I cleared security, bought a salad, and hunkered down far from the other travelers. I was drained, exhausted, but even the short distance between Hunter and me felt balmlike. I had done what I could do. It was someone else's turn to help him. Maybe, finally, my heart could rest.

Waiting

The day after flying Hunter down to enter rehab at New Chance Ranch, I felt an intense need to connect in some way with what my son was going through. I decided to sit in on a Narcotics Anonymous (NA) meeting, just to see what they were like. I knew that NA is to drug addiction what Alcoholics Anonymous (AA) is to alcoholism, but that was all. I didn't know that there were rules, that I was breaking them—that NA meetings were for people struggling with addiction, not their bruised and battered mothers.

I want to call this moment the beginning of my long apprenticeship in what it means to be the parent of a person with addiction, but that's wrong. In this, as in all other aspects of our parenting, Barry and I were autodidacts. Apprenticing ourselves to no one. I knew there were Nar-Anon family support groups. I barely considered attending one before quickly turning the thought aside. I now see this as a fault, as one more example of finding a harder way to deal with even the hardest things, but at the time going at it alone was my natural impulse. I am stoic by nature, and stubborn. Asking for help felt like a weakness, a vulnerability I could not emotionally afford. Still, I wanted to understand Hunter's new world.

And so I drove to the Fremont neighborhood, intent on observing NA rather than participating in Nar-Anon, and climbed the front stairs of an old church. Fremont, a former streetcar terminus flanked by turn-of-the-last-century buildings, calls itself the Center of the Universe. The high Aurora Bridge stretches over Fremont's eastern edge, and under the bridge the famous Fremont Troll sculpture clutches a battered Volkswagen. The church was near the troll. Upstairs, chairs ringed the room. We were welcomed, then one by one the people gave first names, summed up their stories: two days clean, a week, two weeks. Waiting for a bed at King County Detox. Grateful to a sponsor. Clean four years. (Applause.)

One emaciated man in his thirties, hours clean, he said, from meth, chanted unceasingly to the group and to himself about the places he now must not go—primarily the Jungle, an infamous unlawful homeless encampment under the I-5 freeway near downtown—to keep from using. A beautiful young woman with long dark hair fingered a thin chain around her neck, smiling ruefully after admitting a relapse with heroin. "I know what I've got to do, I'm on the list at detox and I'm waiting for a bed, but 'til then . . ." There was a row of five or six young men about Hunter's age, bused in from a local outpatient rehab, getting their so-called 30-in-30: thirty meetings over thirty straight days.

My palms grew moist and my breathing shallow as I listened to these people sharing their triumphs and their darkest stories. When it was my turn, I stuttered, "Hi, I'm Paula, and I'm the mother of an addict. I just took my eighteen-year-old son to a residential treatment program yesterday, and I know he'll be going to a lot of NA and AA meetings, and I just wanted to know a little what that feels like."[4] People nodded, and the person next to me started his story. After another half-hour, I felt my sorrow building, and I fled.

An older man who had been standing in the back of the room followed me out. His frame was wiry, his dark hair streaked with grey and gathered in a low ponytail. "You said your son is eighteen?" he said. "That's really young. It's good he's in a program, but sometimes it takes the young ones a while to come around. On the other hand, sometimes it turns out that the drugs they're doing are just experiments, and they move past that phase. It just depends. I will say, though, that a person can get sober anywhere, with a program or without. When your son—what's his name?"

"Hunter," I said softly.

"When Hunter comes back here, tell him to go to a meeting with other young people. There's several—the Alana club up on Aurora is a good one. It's hard when they're so young. They think they are invulnerable, the guys especially. Young men . . ."

His words trailed off. It touched me deeply that he'd taken the trouble, sought me out, given advice. "Thank you," I said.

Sitting in my car, I spent a while just breathing, trying to pull myself together, reaching for calm. The thought that Hunter might be at the beginning of a struggle that, based on what I'd experienced in that meeting, might last the rest of his life felt overwhelming. I understood, even as I sat grieving the loss of what I'd thought of as a normal life for Hunter, that what I'd seen at the NA meeting was normal life for so many people. What the vantage point of my enormously privileged life had taught me to call normal was just one sliver of a million shades.

I wasn't even thinking of my economic privilege, of what my education or skin color had given me. I was thinking of a life untrammeled by the kind of compulsions, the struggle with them, the concurrent acceptance of and distancing from them, that seemed to be what was meant by recovery. I realized that, because of Hunter, I might be learning, probably viscerally, addiction's brutal spectrum.

A few days later, New Chance called and set the program. Hunter's case manager was Javier. His sessions with Hunter would be Wednesdays at nine a.m. and Thursdays at two p.m. Hunter had signed full release of information forms for Barry and for me, so Javier would call us every Wednesday at ten a.m. to report.

Javier's other function was to convince our insurance company to pay their portion of Hunter's treatment. It was unusual, apparently, for coverage of drug rehabilitation out of state to get approval. Javier would need to call the Seattle headquarters every week, report on Hunter's progress, make the case for the following week's treatment to be covered. He did this expertly, securing the full month's treatment week by week. We'd been required to pay the whole first month in advance, so any coverage Javier got approved would be applied to the remaining months that insurance wouldn't cover.

We kept a little notebook to record key points from our conversations with Javier. My first note read: anger and resentment, low self-esteem, guilt and shame, encouraged other young kids to use, wants to be a better role model, mild depression, ruled out any personality disorder, no dual diagnosis. Past drug use: THC, using a variety of drugs for years, heroin once but never has injected, trying many things once or twice. He's very open.

I assumed Hunter felt anger about being in an inpatient program, resentful that the program's rules controlled his time. I thought it was natural that he felt guilt and shame about encouraging other young kids to use. I was glad he wanted to be a better role model. I hoped he realized that Barry and I were making huge financial sacrifices to give him this opportunity and thought it was appropriate if that was one of the things making him feel guilty. I felt sick to my stomach to hear that he had been using a variety of drugs for years.

Week Two: Hunter staying engaged, tired of being away from home, anxiety—environment changes all the time—hard when new people are always coming in. The group climbs Mount Rubio once a week. Softball against other treatment programs. Mild mood swings, journaling, focusing on things that are important. Participation is good, no denial. Plan to attend Family Week during his second month in treatment.

Week Three: Doing very well. Still having trouble with the "higher power," but participating in all aspects of treatment. He's still working through some cravings, gets these feelings that go in and out. Triggers: old friends, boredom. Still having mood swings, feeling anxious, knows he's going to have to go to meetings for a long time. Javier told him he'll need a support group. Part of recovery is giving back. Doing Fourth Step—moral inventory.

Javier said Hunter told him that he used drugs because he felt the only way to be accepted was to use. He was introverted but found he could socialize when he was high.

I thought about this statement. I could see that, among the people Hunter had gravitated toward beginning in the latter part of freshman year and particularly sophomore year, using drugs would equate with fitting in. There were so many other groups of kids at Seattle High, though, with whom fitting in had widely differing criteria. If he had thrown his lot in with the literary magazine kids, the newspaper staff, the film club, the tennis team, I did not see how using drugs would have been the bar set for inclusion. Looking back on those recent years, I contemplated whether what Hunter was describing was having lost his sense of belonging, not just with his peers, but with the world. He no longer knew who he was, on a deep level. I allowed myself to see now that this had made him anxious in school settings, but the root problem seemed more like alienation than anxiety.

Javier gave us contact information for the woman in Newport Beach who ran a group for kids who wanted to get their GED. Going to high school had never worked for Hunter, but maybe, after a successful rehab experience, college would work for him. The GED was key to that. Hunter agreed.

I remember this first month of Hunter's treatment as a time of total numbness, of putting one foot steadily in front of the other, as much as I possibly could. I stood at my computer, writing steadily, willing my thoughts away from Hunter. The book—a history of the Century 21 Exposition, Seattle's 1962 World's Fair, cowritten with Alan J. Stein, as was my first book—had a strict deadline. Commissioned for the fair's fiftieth anniversary, its release date was October 21, 2011—the forty-ninth anniversary of the fair's closing day. The book would be an elaborate volume with scores of color illustrations and would take months to edit, design, and produce. I was committed to the project and determined not to let this crisis in my personal life make me blow my writing deadline, which would have forced my colleagues to blow theirs and violated *HistoryLink*'s contract with the client. Breaking the momentum to work through the wrench of Hunter's addiction and removal from Seattle was unthinkable, so I worked on, all day every day, standing at my desk and pausing only when Sawyer or Lillie needed me.

Frankly, I am glad I had the deadline, the distraction. It was good to have absorbing work that demanded my attention. The book's massive to-do list—traveling to archives and libraries, interviewing the remaining world's fair employees and VIPs, submerging myself in the writing process—provided structure during this time of traumatized hope and uncertainty. Having to focus on the book kept me at least moving forward, creating something. All of that was satisfying, while things with Hunter hung unresolved.

When I was not working on the book, I thought of Hunter constantly, imagining him moving through New Chance Ranch as I understood it. I wrote him letters every week, telling him what was going on at home: Sawyer's eighth-grade camping trip to Dry Falls in eastern Washington, my helping out backstage during Lillie's ballet recital, my getting a year-long pass to the Space Needle to aid my World's Fair research.

In between everything I did—the work, the letters, spending time with Sawyer and Lillie—I felt numb hope for Hunter. I cried whenever I was by myself, usually in the car. *Women and Country*, a Jakob Dylan CD I'd bought on impulse at Starbucks the day after Hunter flew to rehab, comforted me and steadied my thoughts. It was almost the only music I could tolerate for months and months, my constant soundtrack as I drove and cried: soothing, protective, like artificial skin applied to burn victims. I cried all the time when I was driving, crying was boilerplate, but within the music I was cradled and protected, on my way somewhere, propelling my bubble, unlikely for the moment to be unpleasantly surprised.

I told friends what had happened, usually sobbing as I spoke. People who'd known Hunter all his life, people who'd listened to me strategize and vent: my hairdresser, Donna, who'd sometimes also cut Hunter's hair; Zoey, who managed Reckless Video a few blocks from our house and who'd helped shape Hunter's broad appreciation for film over the years; Rene, who'd managed All for Kids, the bookstore we'd visited almost daily when Hunter was young. All these kind souls were sympathetic, comforting me, withholding judgment. "Poor Hunter," Donna said. "Poor you, but also poor, poor Hunter."

Lillie baked chocolate chip cookies for a care package. I bought Hunter a blank book for journaling, drawing paper, good art supplies —presents for the person I hoped was still inside of him, the Hunter who'd filled journals with stories and art pads with drawings of superhero characters not so long ago.

Sawyer and Lillie seemed to cope. We offered counseling, and they considered this reluctantly. Sawyer began regularly seeing a gentle therapist who specialized in young teens. He kept their discussions to himself, but I felt relief to know he had an outlet. Lillie resisted, finally agreeing to try a child psychologist who brought her yellow Labrador to sessions, under the condition that I too participate.

Lillie answered the therapist's questions and stroked the dog. On the way home she told me she felt like she was doing fine and didn't need to talk to anyone. "I want you to know that talking with a counselor is always an option," I told her, "about Hunter or any other thing you might feel like talking to someone about." I wanted Lillie and Sawyer to see therapists as one of life's coping strategies, to think of counseling as a possible tool. I had not grown up knowing that. I wanted better skills for them.

Barry and Sawyer and Lillie and I did things together, enjoying each other, going to Red Mill for veggie burgers, walking around Green Lake once or twice on warm evenings. We all felt the relief of this respite from the drama, the trauma, that had consumed our home. The lyrics of Leonard Cohen's song "Anthem" became my mantra. Sawyer and Lillie were my bells, and spending time with them lifted the pain of Hunter's situation, the sad reason for his absence.

I told myself that it was okay to feel both hope for Hunter and deep relief at this break from him. I knew he was safe, so I could both miss him and be glad he was gone. Hunter's actions had stressed me beyond the point I would previously have thought endurable. Yes, there had been periods of relative calm in which the stress receded, but always, during those times, I felt the threat of the next possible explosion.

For three years, the daunting task of responding to Hunter's crises had absorbed Barry and me. Throughout that time, we had struggled to maintain our own healthy functioning, to keep the nourishing parts of our existence as a family on track. This had required massive reserves of emotional energy, all day every day, at work, at home. Hunter's removal from our house and the knowledge that he was getting help in rehab now gave us the chance to rest and recuperate from that Herculean labor.

Moving helped me, and each day I walked for an hour or went to the gym. After I exercised, I lay face down in the gym's sauna. The sauna's heat and the warm cedar smell reminded me of my desert childhood. I let myself sink fully into thoughts of Hunter for these few minutes, picture him, grieve for his pain, send him love. I modified a Buddhist

Metta meditation I'd read someplace, made it my own, whispered it in the heat:

May Hunter be at peace.
May Hunter be free from suffering.
May Hunter be healed.
May Hunter know the light of his own true nature.

My first impulse in any unfamiliar situation is to start research, read up, hope for breadcrumbs. I'd combed the parenting section of Elliott Bay Books and the University Book Store, looking for something to help me understand why Hunter was slashing away at all the safety nets his loving family had woven to protect him. I found little. The problems dealt with in these books, at least those I found, paled compared with those I was experiencing.

Once Hunter was diagnosed with opioid addiction, I left the parenting section behind and moved on to Addiction / Recovery. I bought a copy of the Alcoholics Anonymous "Big Book"—an updated version of the 1939 classic text setting forth AA's 12-Step plan for recovery from alcoholism—and read it. I had a hard time imagining Hunter earnestly embracing the philosophy, although I hoped I was wrong, hoped I was being too cynical. I thought about the NA meeting I'd crashed, and how my heart broke open listening to the stories. I could better imagine my son in such a meeting than I could see him bent over the Big Book, but it was all unfamiliar territory.

I read *In the Realm of Hungry Ghosts*, Gabor Maté's frighteningly frank book about working with individuals with entrenched drug addictions in the Downtown Eastside clinic in Vancouver, BC. Maté asserts that all drug users have a wound rooted in troubled childhoods and are self-medicating their internal pain.

I questioned this. I was grateful that I had been at home during Hunter's childhood. There were virtually no moments during those years in which I did not participate or observe or of which I was not at least aware. I saw Hunter's childhood, and it looked happy to me. He had a stable household, financial security, access to books and nature, to camping and kayaking, swimming, art supplies. Whatever he showed interest in, we gave him more of. We pushed him gently to take part in things he shied from, such as soccer, and he seemed satisfied when he gained mastery in activities he had resisted. Barry and I were unfailingly emotionally available to him. He knew that he was deeply loved. He was fully equipped for happiness—we gave him all the tools.

I understood, though, or was beginning to, that leaving the family bubble for school had challenged Hunter in ways I might never fully understand. I wonder now whether, if Hunter had followed a more traditional school path, some aspect of his makeup that made him vulnerable eventually to addiction might have been pinpointed in childhood. Many kids Hunter's age were diagnosed, for example, with ADHD. I saw no sign of the symptoms, as I understood them at the time, in Hunter, but then I was not trained to do so. Maybe a teacher, a learning specialist, would have seen something early on.

I read what books I could, finding them realistic, if not particularly encouraging. Debra Gwartney's memoir about her rebellious daughters, *Live Through This*, showed me another mother's extended struggle to concurrently parent functional and dysfunctional siblings. David Sheff's *Beautiful Boy*, which recounts his years parenting a son with meth addiction, drove home the reality that people in active drug addiction routinely preyed on their families and that recovery was not a battle that could be permanently and definitively won. People suffering from addiction relapsed, recovered, relapsed again.

These messages were not consistent with my quiet hope that all of this so far—these years of Hunter's flight into opioid addiction, of his racing away from a stable life—would prove an aberration. That three months in rehab would bring Hunter to his senses, senses I knew he'd had as a child and hoped he still had. That maybe he'd get his GED, get a job, stay clean and sober, spend a good year reading and working on college applications, then jump back onto the path his childhood friends—all of them—were walking.

Many years later, cleaning out a closet, I found the journal Hunter kept during his month at New Chance Ranch. He had indeed been processing. He had been trying. Barry and I had not been wrong to hope. "How can I ever get over my past when everything I am is built on its foundation?" Hunter wondered in one entry. The next day, wryly, "I bet that if you added up all the drugs my 'friends' and I have ever bought and ingested, the revenue from their sale could sustain some small African country for at least a few months." And on May 8: "I have an opportunity to make it instead of sitting on my ass waiting for my life to fix itself spontaneously of its own accord."

It was late spring, the season of high school graduations. Families we'd known, children we'd loved, were graduating from schools across Seattle, heading off to college. Invitations to graduation celebrations filtered in. We went, brought checks and fountain pens for gifts. These were children we'd carpooled to preschool with, kids for whom I'd made grilled cheese sandwiches and chocolate milkshakes on play dates, young people whose success thrilled me even as Hunter's absence of success broke my heart.

The families who invited us to parties knew us well enough to be familiar with our situation. Other guests knew bits—or felt they did. Was I meant to overhear the boorish father of a boy Hunter knew slightly? "Where's Hunter?" he asked Hunter's best childhood friend, the guest of honor. "He went to rehab," Alex murmured. "That's good," the dad exulted, "that kid is really fucked up." I turned away, my happiness for Alex subsumed in a tidal wave of grief. "Fuck you. Shut the fuck up," I wanted to scream at the man. I made my way into another room, explained to a concerned mom friend who'd been out of the loop why we hadn't planned a gathering for Hunter, felt several kids shift their eyes sideways as they saw me pass, threw out my paper plate and napkin, found Lillie reading in a corner, made my retreat.

At another party, we encountered a litany of success stories from the expensive private school where we sometimes wished we had sent Hunter. The older cousin of the guest of honor, her long ginger locks flying, laughingly finished her story with the punch line, "he was the bad kid, you know, the *rehab* kid!" as I walked by. She has no idea, I told myself. That was probably the case, but I was stripped of all ability to shrug things off. I could barely hold the thread from which my family and I seemed to dangle.

"Good luck, congratulations, we're so happy for you," I repeated. "College is great, I know you're going to love it. Hunter? Oh, thanks for asking. Hunter gets out in July."

Family Week

After a month at New Chance Ranch, Hunter was transferred to the main Pacific Recovery campus, blocks from the shore in Newport Beach. I studied the images I found online. White villas, unmarked, nestled seamlessly into the winding lanelike streets. The vibe was wealthy beach village, always sunny.

Javier had explained to us that Hunter would live in sober housing, which meant an apartment with several rooms, each shared by two recovering men, with another room reserved for the apartment manager. These managers were men with some recovery time under their belts, enough time that they could be trusted to oversee the newbies and enforce the rules: curfews, doing chores, and maintaining sobriety.

Hunter was issued a beach cruiser bike as transportation between the apartment and the complex of classrooms and offices where he'd spend his days. His schedule called for group therapy, one-on-one therapy, study for his GED exam, recreation. Every day or evening, residents were required to attend an AA or NA meeting—there were many to choose from. Hunter would find a sponsor, work the program, do the steps.

Hunter's coordinator at Pacific Recovery was a man named Jack. Jack would report to us, though less frequently than Javier. The first time he called, he told us Hunter had received a few minor write-ups at his sober house, nothing major, but he was having trouble in the morning getting up on time.

"Hunter is disappointed that his mental clarity hasn't continued to improve," Jack told us. "There's a syndrome, PAWS, it means Post-Acute Withdrawal Syndrome—it takes a while for most people's brains to clear, to recover. It's frustrating. Hunter'll have to be patient."

Jack said Hunter needed a California identification card that cost thirty dollars and also some shorts. Saturday was shopping day, so if we sent fifty dollars, the staff would take him to Target. "He'll need regular spending money too. Get him a debit card, or you can send a check to us and we will dole it out. The guys in each sober housing unit usually cook dinner together, but Hunter will need to get lunch, coffee, cigarettes, incidentals, you know. He'll need at least fifty a week for that."

We struggled to decide how to best handle this issue of spending money. We understood that Hunter needed money to buy lunch and incidentals but were reluctant to send Pacific Recovery a check to be doled out to him in cash. We finally settled on sending a prepaid VISA gift card every Monday.

Life on the Pacific Recovery campus was different from life at New Chance Ranch. The Ranch was a controlled-access facility, and residents there had no individual freedom of movement. At Pacific Recovery, residents biked or walked independently between sober houses and the main center. They were free to meet with their NA sponsors whenever and wherever worked best and to get themselves to therapy and caseworker appointments. Pacific Recovery residents could also make and receive phone calls, and Hunter called us soon after settling in. Things were okay, he offered, not as good as the ranch because "the people here aren't taking it seriously," an assertion Jack adamantly denied when we asked him about it.

"You know, Hunter," I offered, "you can absolutely take it seriously, no matter what other people are doing. This is your chance to build up good routines and habits that will help when you come home." Hunter agreed. We talked about the GED. Hunter was ready to be finished with high school and relieved that he could take the exam in California.

Our calls were brief—he phoned every few weeks. I filled him in on what was happening with us: Sawyer's eighth-grade graduation and the special dinner and baccalaureate mass that had preceded it, Barry's trip to Utah with fellow Everett Clinic leaders to tour an air-bag factory that used the lean-manufacturing waste-minimization philosophy the clinic wanted to implement, Barry's and my twenty-third wedding anniversary. Sawyer had his wisdom teeth extracted. Lillie and her friend Ruby and Ruby's mom took the train to Portland for a night.

Several weeks after Hunter moved to Newport Beach, Jack called to tell us that Hunter's cruiser bike had been stolen. "That's too bad," Barry said, "how did it happen?"

"Well," Jack explained ruefully, "Hunter left it unlocked behind the offices, and when he went back for it, it was gone. We'll need $200 from you guys, and we can give him a new one."

"Um . . . ," I said, "if Hunter didn't lock the bike and it was stolen, isn't the consequence that he now doesn't have a bike and will have to walk?"

"Well, yeah, but you know, this happens all the time. Hunter isn't the only one to lose a bike, not by any means."

"Do most parents just send the $200?" I wondered. "Are we the only ones to be surprised by this?"

"Well," Jack said, "yeah, I don't remember anyone reacting like that."

Barry and I talked with Hunter, who reiterated that lots of people had unlocked bikes stolen. Hunter's apartment, we discovered, was about five blocks from the offices: an easy walk. Also, he seemed to take the incident in stride. He wasn't sorry. Where was a glimmer of the bigger picture, Barry and I wondered?

It did not occur to us that Hunter might have sold the bike for drugs, although for a cynical moment I wondered whether Pacific Recovery might have a racket. Hunter was submitting to frequent random drug testing as part of Pacific Recovery's program. If he had relapsed, everyone would know.

Barry called to tell Jack why we weren't sending money for another bike. "Hunter's been riding around Seattle since he was ten," Barry explained. "He knows to lock a bike, even one he's only leaving for a minute."

Family Week was coming. This knowledge was like a cloud, dark but hopeful, carrying storm and rain toward parched farmland. Barry and I of course would go—I was nearly on deadline with the book, but for this, it would have to wait. Sawyer wanted to go too. Lillie did not and so would stay with my parents. Lillie always preferred to absent herself from Hunter's drama if she possibly could. Barry and I weren't sure what Family Week might entail specifically but reckoned it would be intense and saw no benefit in forcing Lillie to participate against her will.

We packed, steeling and centering ourselves in our different ways. I felt the need for something to hold, something physical to clutch that would tether me and comfort me through what I imagined would be a wrenching experience. I found sandalwood prayer beads strung on red silk and a small Hand of Fatima—protection from the evil eye.

"Call to tell us when you get here," Jack instructed. "Wednesday, you will see Hunter briefly, then be on your own for dinner. Thursday is a group session with other families but no clients, and then you'll be able to sign Hunter out, take him to dinner. Many families accompany the client to a meeting that evening, so you might think about that. Friday, clients will join their families for a large group session, and then you can have a family session with Hunter's therapist. I'll meet with you sometime Friday to plan the transition for when Hunter completes the program."

We flew to the John Wayne Airport in Santa Ana, pulled our suitcases past a large bronze statue of the actor, rented a car. Orange County in June had perfect weather—warm but not hot, with clear blue skies. We checked into the modest hotel I'd picked from the list Jack had emailed, then drove the few miles into downtown Newport Beach.

Newport's central streets twisted like those of a tiny European village. When we arrived at Pacific Recovery's white stucco complex and stepped into the shady entryway out of the bright California sun, a low-key guard at the front desk stopped us and asked who we wanted. "Hunter!" one of the staffers called into a back room. "Hey, Hunter, your family's here."

Hunter seemed years older to me, not months. My memory flashed on the confusion and anguish I'd seen in his face when we had said goodbye at the ranch. Those emotions were gone now. He wore a short-sleeved, button-up plaid shirt and loose-fitting, knee-length camel-colored shorts. He had a kind of confidence I hadn't seen in him for the past few years. He stood tall, looking us in the eyes, hugging us. "I'm so glad you're here," he exclaimed repeatedly. "I want to show you around. Would you like to get some coffee? There's a really good place the next street over."

We walked the half block, Hunter in the lead. Small talk was fairly easy—Hunter described his routine, clearly proud to have one. He also seemed resigned, a little jaded, as if he knew much more about other people's troubles than he had when we'd last been in his company.

"Does Josh help out at Pacific Recovery like he does at New Chance Ranch?" I asked Hunter, thinking of the gentle man's kindness to me on the day Hunter had arrived for rehab.

"Oh, that guy died," Hunter said nonchalantly.

"He *died*?" I asked, "How did he die?"

"He had a car wreck," Hunter said. "He always drove too fast."

"Was he driving the Pacific Recovery van?" I asked.

"No," Hunter said, "he was in his own car. It happened a few weeks ago. He was an okay guy."

I remembered what Josh had said as he drove me to the airport about his gratitude that his sobriety allowed him to take care of his mother. I knew how broken that poor woman must be by this loss of her son, regained from addiction, snatched from her now again. I had grasped Josh's story as a lifeline, taken maternal comfort. To Hunter, I guessed, Josh had been just one of many new acquaintances whose regulations governed his current existence.

When I met Jack, I told him I was sorry for the loss of their colleague. "Yes," Jack said, "that has been hard for all of us. But he died clean and sober, so that's something."

As Jack had explained earlier, Hunter wasn't free to join us for dinner. "I have to go to an AA meeting," he said. "My sponsor will be there." Sawyer and Barry and I drove to the boardwalk, picked the most classic-looking seafood restaurant. The focus of the trip was Hunter, as expected, but being with him remained taxing. We all had complicated feelings. When we were not with Hunter, we caught our breath, stored energy for the next encounter.

The following morning was devoted to lectures on the disease model of addiction. Barry and I asked many questions. Greatly simplified, the debate was whether addiction is a disease or a moral failing. Walking into the auditorium that morning, I didn't see Hunter's situation as a disease. But "moral failing" implied a sort of weakness, something almost accidental. Hunter's dogged pursuit of altered consciousness over the past three years looked to me more like a compulsion than a failing. Drugs were a solid wall at which he'd flung himself repeatedly, willing the wall to let him through, which, with fentanyl, it finally had. He had wanted, had chosen, the sensation drugs brought him. He'd seemed to be actively running toward something that fulfilled his strange, quirky expectations of what life should be. Seeking to find something rather than looking for an escape.

Listening to the addiction specialist lecture, though, I wondered what the relationship between compulsion and addiction actually was. If, in his youth and inexperience, Hunter, who had fed on risk all his life, had compelled himself toward the sticky web of opioid addiction, and was now stuck, might that very compulsion be considered the disease? And what was 12-Step abstinence-based rehab, really, except a more extreme attempt, once again, to reason with him?

After boxed lunch, we gathered with the program director and other families. We quickly found we were the only family whose addicted member was going through their first rehab experience. These families had seen it all, and they were battered by it, broken. The evidence of some families' extensive wealth—designer handbags, fine shoes, sleek clothes, a mention of a private jet parked at the airport—had not saved them from pain and would not. The brutal facts of our loved ones' addictions were grim equalizers.

I realized, of course, that all these families, including ours, were here because of privilege. This high-priced attempt to pull our respective family members back from addiction's cliff was inaccessible to the legions of families who had more limited means, although the fat checks we'd all written could not guarantee results. Hunter was only at this place, this rehab that had looked to us like his best shot at rescue, because of our excellent insurance, the funds that we had been able to put aside in savings over the years and were now willing to expend, and the savings that my frugal parents were able to contribute as well. Rehab programs cannot promise recovery, but having a family member in treatment fans families' flames of hope, reassuring them that they are at least doing something. I knew that we were fortunate to be able to experience that sensation.

Opioid addiction, at the time Hunter entered Pacific Recovery, was not widely discussed. Many middle-class families—most even—tried to hide what they were going through. People with addiction and their families experienced a level of shame that has eased somewhat as America's opioid crisis has become undeniable, mushrooming to epidemic level. The inescapable truth that opioid addiction cuts through every layer of socioeconomics has only recently been the topic of media examination. A day rarely goes by now without mention of this crisis in major newspapers.

Exhausted by the session, we met up with Hunter. We found the sushi place he had heard was good, lost ourselves momentarily in the delicious food. I watched Hunter dip his first piece of salmon nigiri into soy sauce and wasabi, knowing he'd pause and involuntarily close his eyes for an instant when the fish hit his taste buds, appreciating that moment as he had always done.

Hunter enjoyed the sushi but spent most of the meal focused on getting cigarettes. I knew he'd been buying cigarettes with the spending money we'd been sending, knew that the recovery community in general considered cigarettes a lesser evil, an acceptable vice. Dinner over, Hunter directed us to a nearby convenience store. Now, for the first time, feeling resigned, Barry and I physically purchased Hunter cigarettes.

After dinner we headed for downtown Newport Beach and the Narcotics Anonymous meeting. Several hundred people gathered in a sort of warehouse off a quiet lane, the light from the inside rooms spilling onto the dark street along with many smokers grabbing a last puff before the meeting started. Hunter joined them, and I saw a thin, dark-haired young man about his age bum a cigarette. Maybe Hunter's determination to get his hands on that pack of Marlboro Reds stemmed from a desire to share, I mused to myself.

Narcotics Anonymous, like AA, relies on the 12-Step process, a series of statements the person with addiction must claim, step by step, as his or her own. Working through the steps takes some people years, or a lifetime: the distance from Step 1 ("We admitted that we were powerless over our addiction, that our lives had become unmanageable") to Step 12 ("Having had a spiritual awakening as a result of these steps, we tried to carry this message to addicts, and practice these principles in all our affairs") is determined by everything the person working through them brings to the process.

Hunter melted into the crowd, greeting a person here and there, and Sawyer, Barry, and I found folding chairs. Many people welcomed us, shook our hands, told us their names. NA and AA meetings have varying policies. Some meetings are closed to outsiders, but this one was always open, regularly welcoming the families of the many people drawn to Newport by Orange County's extensive recovery industry. I spotted other family members from the Pacific Recovery program, perched on the hard chairs, holding their addicted family member's hand sometimes, looking grateful but ill at ease.

The meeting started. Each person who spoke—the middle-aged woman running the meeting, the older-looking man asking people to consider contributing to the coffee fund, the twenty-something young woman with bright cherry-colored hair—introduced themselves by their first name and addiction: an addict, an addict and an alcoholic, an addict. Each fervently thanked NA for saving them. I knew from reading through the Alcoholics Anonymous book that in 12-Step professing gratitude is considered a big way to keep the faith and maintain resolve.

This meeting was a speaker's meeting, which was a different format from the one I'd crashed in Fremont. In Fremont, everyone had gathered in a big circle and shared their names and stories (or passed) in turn. The Newport meeting had one main speaker, who told a fuller story that lasted about an hour. The speaker was tall and tanned and looked to be in his early thirties. He spun a long sad tale of using drugs and using people close to him to get them, of his slide into homelessness, run-ins with the law, and finally hitting bottom and finding redemption through working the program—following the 12-Step tenets. The crowd was with him. It felt like church to me, or theater. I watched Hunter several rows away, nodding in agreement, whispering to a friend, slipping out to smoke.

When it was time to hand out colored chips denoting benchmarks of sobriety, Hunter received his two-month chip. "Hi, I'm Hunter, and I'm an addict and an alcoholic," he told the crowd. "Hi, Hunter," they said in chorus.

After the meeting I asked Hunter about the alcoholic label—did he think he was one? He'd used alcohol, I knew, and we had seen him drunk on several occasions, but I'd figured that was because maybe alcohol was easier to come by.

"Oh, we have to say that. Saying it is part of the program," he replied. "We cover all the bases. It's the way it works." I wondered at his casual incorporation of this aspect of participating in the program. Had Hunter skewed his interpretation of what his counselors and sponsor had told him? He'd mentioned that he was hoping to work through the NA 12-Steps by the time he came home. I doubted that the fast-approaching end of rehab was the finish line for processing complex issues. I don't think you can work the program at a sprint, I thought to myself. I didn't want to step between Hunter and his sponsor, though, and stayed silent.

Before we parted for the evening, we spent an hour walking on the beach together. The night was starlit, the waves whooshed softly at the shore. Nature was healing, soothing. I lagged behind, trying to step in Hunter's sandy footprints, following him along, half-listening to his banter with Sawyer.

The next day, we had a group session: clients and families all together, taking turns talking to each other. When we checked in for the group session, we were required to sign a document stating we would not speak publicly or write about what happened in the room. So I will not. I came out feeling more than ever that being the loved one of a person with any addiction is brutal and perpetual, a cruel and powerless path.

The families in the room had had a month, two months, or three, to catch their breath while their addicted family member was in rehab. To sleep without waking in the early hours, grappling with their family member's doom. To hear the phone ring without fearing that the caller would be police, hospital, or morgue. Rehab may not help all people with addiction, but it surely helps their families. Rehab is respite care for the families of the addicted. It isn't billed as such, but such it is.

Once the initial shock of realizing that Hunter was smoking fentanyl and the scramble to get him into rehab had receded, sometime around the start of Hunter's second month away from home, the tight core of strangling fear that Hunter's past three years had wound within me started to unwind just a little. With Hunter out of the house and in a safe place, the crushing effort of operating within this constant fear for him had eased. I didn't know whether the relief I was experiencing would prove permanent or if I should gather my strength for more to come. I let myself acknowledge now that it had become difficult to be with Hunter. I loved him. And I hated the stress that came from living with him.

Those years had worn me down, but I didn't want Hunter to know this. I felt that revealing to him how deeply his behavior had taxed me would be cruel. I wanted him to believe that, in spite of everything, I was in control, that I could make him safe by teaching him to want safety for himself. That I would have infinite stamina to endure anything mothering him asked of me. I wanted, still, to be his Mommy-woman, that superhero image of me he had created and I'd believed in. That strong, that patient. But I admitted my exhaustion to myself.

After the session, we all met with Hunter's therapist. The two seemed to have good rapport. Hunter was as relaxed as I had seen him in recent years, stretched out on the couch, us nearby. "I don't think you all realize how traumatic the transition to school was for Hunter," she said.

"Right," Hunter said, "I know how much you love me, but I don't understand why we homeschooled. It made everything so hard when I started school because it made me different! I didn't know anything, not how to act or what to expect. I didn't really know kids could be mean or lie or make fun of me. I think that if we hadn't homeschooled, none of what happened to me would have happened, and I wouldn't be here."

We took this in. I wanted to be fair to Hunter, but I simply could not believe that our homeschooling held the seed of his fentanyl addiction. I appreciated the point he was making about how starting school after homeschooling had been stressful, although I questioned his inference that this stress went beyond a tolerable range. If he tells us that he experienced this as overwhelmingly stressful, I decided, I'm going to give him the respect of taking that at face value.

"Hunter," I finally said, "if homeschooling was part of what got you here, I deeply, deeply apologize to you that we made the decision to homeschool. Believe me, if we had thought for an instant that it would do you anything but good, we would not have done it. We decided to homeschool because we truly felt it was the very best thing for you— the best way to encourage the voracious interest in the world you showed with everything you did. We were afraid that school would dampen you, change what made you Hunter."

"But I was a cool little kid," Hunter replied. "And when I finally started school, having been homeschooled made me a weirdo."

"We can't undo it, Hunter," Barry sighed. "But you can know that we meant only to encourage your love of learning and of the world. We never, ever, meant to do anything to stunt you."

Walking from the cool dark office into the afternoon sun, we embraced, said goodbye. Hunter had three more weeks at Pacific Recovery. We left with templates for developing an aftercare plan, and Hunter had the same. His job during those last three weeks was to decide where in Seattle he would find support for his sobriety, and to pass the GED. High school was over for him, and the test would provide a bridge to college, sooner rather than later, we hoped.

We kept notes on our calls from Jack, as we had done with Javier. July 2, "Hunter doing great—went to noon outside meeting. He finishes the program July 18—Jack will send us something re: triggers, things to try and help Hunter avoid."

Late in his stay at Newport Beach, a staff member drove Hunter to Fullerton, where he took and easily passed the California GED examination. When the official transcript arrived months later, I saw that his scores had put him in the 98th and 99th percentiles in reading, writing, and social studies, and only slightly lower in math and science. "You have demonstrated the twenty-first century skills of communication, information processing, problem solving, higher order thinking skills," the test transcript stated.

We longed for Hunter's return but also braced for it. His room was clean, sanitized of all the things that had perplexed and terrified me in the months leading up to rehab. His clothes were laundered, folded into the wardrobe. Light filtered through the small window, emphasizing stillness, anticipation.

It seemed unwise for Hunter—fresh from rehab—to fly home solo, so Barry booked a ticket to Orange County. The second-to-last page in our Pacific Recovery logbook filled with Barry's notes: which flights, what times, where in Newport Beach to pick Hunter up, and how to sign him out of the program the final time.

Barry and I drove to SeaTac Airport. We held each other for a long moment at the curb on the departure level, sure only of what was behind us, hoping Hunter's months in rehab would make the future better than the past. I pushed the Jakob Dylan disc into the car's sound system one more time, pulling carefully back into the flow of traffic, and Barry headed into the terminal to start his journey and bring Hunter home.

A Hundred Needles

Shortly after coming home from rehab, Hunter began spending much of his time with Jess, Tamlin, and Jonah. Jess and Hunter had played soccer together when they were kids. Tamlin and Hunter had been friends since sophomore year. And Jonah, who was a year younger than Hunter and still in high school, was a new friend.

Jonah was the teenage version of a baby angel, his face still round, his eyes wide and laughing. Jonah seemed to lack malice, to be fundamentally good-hearted. Tamlin was pre-Raphaelite, a slight blond hippie-legacy child, proud of his countercultural roots. He carried himself with entitlement, a sense that the world's idle pleasures were his by birthright. Jess was shifty, foxlike. His neat appearance and formality with adults barely masked an inner surliness. He seemed lacking in compassion, not averse, perhaps, to watching others suffer. He was a skillful jazz trombonist, playing professionally in clubs while still in high school. Barry and I weren't keen on these friends, but we had no hard evidence that they were trouble. We were relieved, in fact, that Hunter had friends he was willing to bring home. Jess played our piano a few times, and Jonah joined us for dinner once.

I was trying to help Hunter maintain sobriety, driving him to NA meetings, swapping black sesame seeds for poppy seeds in baked goods. We had been testing his urine for drugs every few days during the first several weeks after he got back, but Barry no longer observed Hunter producing the sample.

Hunter had done well with the female counselor he'd met with during his last two months at Pacific Recovery, the woman we all talked to during Family Week, but he had not wanted to continue working with her by phone once he got home. Barry asked medical colleagues to recommend someone local and found a woman who practiced in the Green Lake neighborhood, about a mile from our house. Hunter agreed to weekly appointments and saw the therapist through late July and early August before no-showing. "I just don't think it's helping," he told us.

"What kind of person do you think might help?" Barry asked, but Hunter shrugged him off.

I started googling, looking for therapists who specialized in young men with addiction issues. I sent Hunter links to three people I'd vetted. "How do these people look?" I asked him. "You can totally try out all three, or someone else if you find someone who looks like a good possibility."

"Thanks, Mom," Hunter said noncommittally. "I'll read their websites."

Hunter had always asked us for money to pay for books, bus fare, food when he was out, art supplies, clothes. Once he was home from rehab, these requests steadily increased. "No," we said after a few weeks. "If you need money, you should get a job."

Instead, Hunter gradually began stealing cash from us, first so subtly that we assumed we'd been mistaken about the number of twenties in our billfolds, the ten-dollar bill left on the counter for Sawyer's or Lillie's camp field-trip fee. It was one ten at first, not all four I'd tucked into the zipper compartment of my wallet. After a few incidents, though, I couldn't deny that this was theft, not my own absent-mindedness. "Hunter, I had two twenties in my wallet and there's only one now. Did you take that?" I'd ask. But no, no—that was always the answer.

Why was he stealing money? I wanted bus fare, movies, burgers, books to be the reason. I didn't want to think ten dollars missing meant that Hunter had relapsed. Maintaining hope in the face of theft required denial. Relapse was such a horrifying possibility. Relapse would mean that Hunter's time in rehab, our efforts to make those months happen, had come to naught. We'd heard the phrase "relapse is part of recovery" at Family Week, but the reality of seeing that cycle play out was nauseating. We were determined not to expect the worst.

But my suspicions steadily increased. One afternoon in early September, after I'd transferred a load of laundry from washer to dryer, I started slowly searching Hunter's basement bedroom. Moving intently, methodically, I combed through drawers and backpack thoroughly but carefully, warily. There were pills, unidentified, scattered in the sheets. There were lighters, a bong, bags of herbaceous substances. No burned foil, no plastic pen casings, no evidence of fentanyl.

The pills, the pot, still signaled relapse, I knew that. I climbed the stairs and numbly shoved the kettle onto a burner, scooped a teaspoon of tea leaves. I wanted to unsee what I had seen in Hunter's room. The house was empty. I sat at the crumb-strewn pine table waiting for my tea to cool. I'll tell him later, I thought to myself, remembering all the crisis calls I'd made to Barry during Hunter's high school years, interrupting him during patient care. But that night, I kept silent, and the night after.

It took me nearly a week to summon the stamina to face reality. Barry shook his head a few times when I told him what I'd seen. "Show me." We went downstairs to Hunter's empty room. The backpack, where I'd seen the bong and the pot, was gone. The bed, unmade as always, yielded nothing. We decided to wait a few days, wait and see.

Why not check the backpack when Hunter returned? Why not confront him directly? Because we understood that confrontation would equal banishment. If Hunter was using drugs in the house and knew we knew it, we would have to follow through and kick him out. We were not sending him to rehab again if he relapsed—we had discussed that with him and with each other. The funds were gone, and anyway, if rehab failed to work once, why would the second try be any better? I remembered the advice the kind man at the Fremont NA meeting had given me: "A person can get sober anywhere, with a program or without." He'd meant, I knew, if the person wanted to.

Seattle's rain held off, and early October was bright and warm that year. Hunter, Jonah, and Jess lingered in the living room, laughing together, Jess playing the piano. They went downstairs "to get our jackets" and fell suddenly silent. Ten minutes later, they rattled out together, still laughing, into the sunny afternoon. Suspicious of what might have prompted their brief silence, I went downstairs and scanned the empty bedroom.

On the floor beside the old free loveseat Hunter had dragged home a few years before, not even hidden, I saw three bright sky-blue elastic bands, like strips cut from balloons, scattered. And on the 1950s inlaid pecan coffee table that had once belonged to my grandma, a bent spoon, its convex bottom charred. My heart was pounding.

I looked at the bulky aluminum heating vent that snaked across Hunter's ceiling, scanning the space between the top of the vent and the floorboards overhead, trying to tell whether something might be hidden there. Grabbing Hunter's desk chair, I peered into the space, but there was nothing. The storage closet's difficult sliding door was slightly ajar. Using all my weight, I tugged the door further open and reached inside, pushing aside the outgrown Candyland, Monopoly Jr., Dinosaurs: Survival or Extinction.

My hand closed on an unfamiliar gallon-sized plastic bag, and I pulled it from the closet. Inside the bag were what looked like hundreds of clear syringes. Most were capped with orange plastic protective tips, sharp needles at the ready. A plastic box, blood spotted, near the top of the bag, held syringes that had clearly served their purpose.

Hunter was using heroin.

This time I did call Barry. He found someone to cover the rest of his shift—something I couldn't remember ever having happened before—and came home. I showed him everything, and we settled grimly in the living room. We were united, though we barely spoke, saving our strength for what we knew was coming.

Reaching for some comparison, some way to understand this moment, I flashed on an experience I'd had years before when we'd toured *Titanic: The Artifact Exhibition*. The final room showcased a block of ice against which visitors were encouraged to place their palms. This simulated the frigid water in which that disaster's victims drowned or quickly froze to death. We'd counted the seconds, then, before pain impelled us to yank our hands back. I felt pinned, now, against that unrelenting, unendurable cold.

When Hunter returned an hour later, Barry and I confronted him directly: "Hunter, you are using heroin. You cannot do this in our house." Hunter's face paled, then quickly flooded with anger. Without admitting or discussing anything, he grabbed his backpack, turned, and strode down the front steps. "These can't be in our house," he parroted back to me, and then, turning toward Barry, "Fuck you!"

Fortuitously, Sawyer and Lillie were not at home during our confrontation. Barry began, again, changing the locks. I started clearing the paraphernalia out of Hunter's room and found bottles of urine stashed in the back of his wardrobe. Hunter must have been substituting someone else's heroin-free urine for his contaminated samples in the weeks after rehab when we had halfheartedly been drug-testing him.

We later learned that Hunter had relapsed five days after getting home. Hunter told us that it was Jess's idea for them to try heroin, huddling in Hunter's cavernous basement bedroom one sunny summer afternoon. They took a silver-plated spoon from our kitchen cutlery drawer, heated the drug with a cigarette lighter, and helped each other shoot up. The histories of jazz and heroin are intertwined: Charlie Parker, Chet Baker, Billie Holiday, and many other jazz musicians used heroin. Jess found that connection intriguing. Hunter was curious about how shooting heroin would make him feel. There'd been a friend he'd had at rehab, the son of a drag-race promoter, for whom heroin was the drug of choice.

Barry recognized immediately that the bag of syringes and the sharps box must have come from Seattle's free needle exchange program, which he said passed out those blue elastics as well. Needle exchange, a public health program for people who use drugs by injection, hands out new sterile syringes for free and safely disposes of used ones. Its purpose is to reduce the spread of HIV and other blood-borne diseases.[5]

The two days Hunter had spent on the street in May before agreeing to go into rehab had given me a taste of how it felt to live within the reality that, if homeless, he faced peril. The sight of people sleeping in U District doorways was common, and I knew from reading the newspaper that there were not nearly enough beds in Seattle shelters to meet the need. St. Mark's, the Episcopal church we'd sometimes attended when the kids were little, had transformed its daylight basement into a women's shelter every night. But I had no real under-standing, when we turned Hunter out of our house in October 2010, what being on the street in Seattle truly meant, except that it was by definition brutal.[6]

Many young people experiencing homelessness patch together var-ious places to spend a night or two, couch surfing, queuing for shelter beds, squatting in boarded-up buildings. The U District/Roosevelt neighborhood corridor, where one property owner has amassed hun-dreds of old homes and, over decades, poorly maintained them, has many of these houses. They sit, boarded over, awaiting redevelopment, often for years, as future light rail stops in the U District and Roo-sevelt are slowly constructed and, in response to related zoning and height-limit changes, the surrounding built environment alters. In the meantime, these squat houses offer shelter and privacy, albeit usually without sanitary services, water, or electricity. Young people also sleep in public parks, of which Seattle has nearly five hundred. City ordi-nances forbid overnight use, but this is only sporadically enforced. Young people are probably safer sleeping in parks than in doorways.

If we had not had younger children in the house, would Barry and I have drawn so hard and so immediate a line forbidding Hunter from living with us (once he was of legal age) while he was using drugs? I think we would have. I cannot be certain. This was not a decision we made lightly. We saw Hunter's drug use as a legal and moral threat to our family's well being. It felt absolutely essential to shield Sawyer and Lillie from the danger to which Hunter's drug use and eventual active addiction subjected them. Had Hunter been our only child, I cannot know what choices Barry and I would have made on this—on any—issue.

My thoughts looped endlessly: Hunter is using heroin. Hunter is on the street. Pushing through ordinary tasks felt like moving through glue. I forced myself to function, fulfilled a public-speaking event for the Pacific Northwest Historians Guild, toured Holy Names Academy with Lillie and compared it with other high schools she was consider-ing. Sawyer and I took the light rail, which had only opened recently, to the Columbia City neighborhood south of downtown to visit a farmer's market he'd heard was good. I took Sawyer and Lillie for flu shots, struggling to steady myself with all these familiar tasks.

I probed Sawyer on the issue of Hunter's drug use, asked him whether Hunter had ever given him drugs, which he denied. I believed this, mostly because throughout the years of rebellion, Hunter continued to value his place as protective older brother, certainly to Lillie but to Sawyer also. Although he did not want to discuss Hunter with me, I took comfort in the knowledge that Sawyer was still seeing a counselor.

Lillie's busy schedule, as usual, was a significant factor in organizing my time. As we drove from school to ballet to voice, I attempted to understand how Hunter's abrupt departure and its reason were affecting her. "I'm fine," she said repeatedly, convincingly. She seemed intent on holding herself aloof from all the messiness of Hunter's actions, on being able to do that, needing the separation. I pressed her again on seeing a counselor, and she again declined. "I'm fine, Mom, and I'm way too busy anyway. Yes, I'll let you know if I change my mind."

During the week after Hunter's departure, Barry and I realized that taking money from our wallets was not the only stealing Hunter had done. Some of our books that had been stored in the basement were missing, and a clutch of CDs that were not favorites and had ended up in the bottom drawer of the dining room hutch were gone. It especially pissed me off that Hunter had taken the books, but I was too worried about him to do more than briefly seethe.

My constant fear for him during the day transformed to terror when the sun went down. I woke at two or three each morning and lay imagining where my oldest son might be, reaching out to him with mind and heart. Cold rainy nights were worst, and there were many of them. I pictured Hunter in Ravenna Park under the Fifteenth Avenue Bridge in the deep ravine, thick with trees. In happier days, Hunter and I had often wandered through that ravine. He'd waded in the little stream, picked salmonberries, scrambled up cliff walls. Once, pregnant with Sawyer, I'd let us get too far for Hunter's little legs to make it back. Carrying him slung heavily on one hip with one of his legs clutching at my protruding belly, dragging the pedal-less ride-on toy he called his sports car, I'd crept us along excruciatingly, each step a victory. Homeless people had used the bridge for shelter even then. I imagined Hunter, tiny, not tiny, squatting beneath the perilously high bridge, watching cold rain fall.

A week after Hunter left, he texted me just after midnight. "Mom, can you meet me? I'm at the all-night Starbucks at U Village." Grappling with the tiny buttons on my flip phone, I promised to be there soon. I pulled my clothes back on and rushed into the rainy night. Ten minutes later, I saw Hunter near the back of the coffee shop. Most of the people bent over their laptops looked like college students, and he blended in. Clutching a plastic bag of dirty clothes, he rose to hug me. I held him close, kissing the side of his head. He smelled unwashed.

Hunter was wary of answering my questions about how he was getting by but seemed eager for news of Sawyer and Lillie, my parents, my sister's twins. I fetched him coffee and a blueberry muffin and ordered a double short decaf latte for myself. Our visit lasted fifteen minutes. "Thanks, Mom," Hunter said, rising. "Um. You wouldn't be willing to wash some clothes for me, would you?"

I met his eyes and screwed one corner of my mouth tight but reached for the bag. A pattern was established. Hunter would summon. I'd drive to meet him, buying him food or coffee, sleep deprived but grateful to see him. I barely slept anyway. Meeting Hunter in the middle of the night was infinitely better than lying in bed imagining his demise. I jumped at every chance to connect. I bought him meals, coffee, toiletries, trying to do what I felt I could, and Barry did the same.

Maybe three times, I brought those bags of Hunter's filthy clothes home, washed them, and returned them to him. I hoped the drugs could be parsed out from all the rest of it, that carrying off his dank socks and muddy T-shirts was a neutral way to help. It's just . . . I was his mother, so recently his mommy, taking care, taking such care.

Barry and I welcomed the calls, the texts, because they flooded us with relief that he was still alive. They bolstered our morale. They kept us sane. The messages themselves hardly mattered. We tethered Hunter to us by phone for our sakes as much as his. This was new territory for Barry and me. Hunter's not living in the house was one thing. But we still wanted desperately to help him.

In between the midnight meetings, we had sporadic email contact with Hunter. He used the Seattle Public Library's computers, sometimes emailing daily. "As long as Barry or I are here, you can come by and shower or eat," I emailed. "We love you, no matter what. We have had several thoughts about how we might be able to work toward your being able to live here again, if you want to. Obviously, these all involve your being willing to get back into NA and be drug free. Those doors are never closed, Hunter. If you're able to be clean and sober, we will gladly give you a home."

"I really, really want to make a plan to stay clean and sober and live at home again, and I have been trying to think of some good strategies with which to do so," Hunter responded. "I love you and Dad, so so so much, and I am so so sorry for deceiving you and being an asshole. You don't deserve it, and I wish with all of me that I had tried harder to control myself."

Barry and I met Hunter for breakfast at 14 Carrot Café, a favorite spot in the Eastlake neighborhood near Lake Union, and talked about what it would take for him to be able to live with us again: total abstinence from drugs and alcohol, agreeing to submit to regular drug testing at a lab where a technician would observe him producing the urine sample, regular attendance at NA, including finding a sponsor, and getting a job.

"I don't know," Hunter said. "I'll think about it."

Thanksgiving

Nearly three months went by. We saw Hunter rarely, and the emails stopped. I found I needed something to hold on to, something to bind me to the earth, keep me from flying into a million pieces, atomizing. A touchstone. I found a chunk of Tibetan turquoise marked with flaws and veins and drilled as a bead. Small chunks of crimson coral were fitted into the blue-green rock, held fast with tiny silver-colored pins, the whole thing polished. It fit into my palm like a skipping stone, like slingshot ammunition. I threaded the bead on a thick red cord, knotting both ends. I wrapped the crimson cord around and around my hand, tucking the end under, tethering myself to this chunk of the physical world. Driving, I clutched the smooth facets, and for whatever reason this held me together. I cannot say why doing this consoled me. It was a private ceremony, a tiny ritual that was within my power.

Magical thinking had always comforted me. My first childhood religion was Presbyterianism, and while the weekly Sunday sermons schooled me in boredom, I found the notion of guardian angels intriguing. At five, I'd fall asleep on my back listening to the swamp cooler's thrum, my arms stretched out, palms open, feeling my personal angels cradling my hands. Although I'd questioned, weighed, and set aside most of the early aspects of my received religion, I still felt guardian angels. I willed them now toward Hunter.

to sleep, i picture you engulfed by
angels:
you in the center, angels
all around.
is it an army of angels?
is it a robe of angels?
is it a jacket of angels?
is it a blanket
of angels?
is it a
prison
of angels?
is it a
shroud of angels?

i see their wings, gigantic,
protecting
or inhibiting,
obscuring you.
their wings, mostly, their strong
angelic wings.

I was brimful of sorrow at Hunter's situation, and the smallest
nudge could send my grief cascading over. Any moment of physical
release—stretching at the end of an exercise session, for example, or
sitting in the melting heat of the gym's sauna—became a vent for the
pain I was barely repressing every other minute of my daily life. My
fear for Hunter's present, for his future, for his very life saturated me,
subsuming everything. All this seemed endless, eternal—a place I'd
lived forever.

Only the distraction of work briefly displaced this terror, and then
only when I pushed into the process with my whole being and all my
faculties. Getting the Seattle World's Fair book ready for publication
was my chief occupation. My coauthor and I had turned in the manu-
script to our editor right before Hunter returned from rehab. We were
now incorporating the edits, digitally lobbing completed chapters
back and forth to one another. We were also sourcing imagery for the
book, which was to be lavishly illustrated. We combed archival photo-

graphs at UW Special Collections, Washington State Archives, and the Museum of History and Industry, and met with memorabilia collectors to photograph artifacts. Captioning even a single photograph—identifying the six almost identical-looking crew-cut astronauts posed with NASA Pavilion administrator James Webb atop the Space Needle, for example—could take hours of research.

The weather grew colder. Lillie's class collected jackets for "The Homeless," as the xeroxed letter in her backpack put it. The class with the most jackets won. I drove from thrift shop to thrift shop—Goodwill, Value Village, Salvation Army—buying the thickest, warmest hooded coats on offer. They filled my trunk. I bought jackets imagining Hunter wearing them, all of them, hoping he did indeed have a jacket.

Lillie carried the bags and bags of Homeless Coats to St. Lucy's the week before Thanksgiving. The school invited families to help distribute them and to "Feed the Homeless." Lillie and Barry did this, rising early, passing steaming cups of Starbucks to men and women gathered in a downtown park. "You might see Hunter there," I had warned Lillie, and she'd looked away.

"I've thought of that," she murmured. But they never saw him.

I had no idea where Hunter was sleeping or how he was living. I saved two coats and carried them in my car in case I saw him. He called me, and we briefly met. I bought him sandwiches, coffee, nail clippers, a toothbrush. He took a coat, thankful. A few weeks later, he called again. The coat was gone. He took the second. The next time I saw him, the second coat was gone. Lost, stolen, bartered, sold, forgotten?

We were estranged, but tiny ties still normalized our situation, infinitesimally. Hunter wore contact lenses, cleaning them somehow, showing up on the porch gruff and unwashed when he needed a new pair. We'd let him shower, watching the bathroom door, meditating on his presence, appreciating the moment that was all we had. He'd put on new contacts, take another bottle of solution, exchange the stiff reeking socks he'd worn for weeks for a clean pair of Barry's, accept a fresh hot meal. Then he was gone again.

We knew that helping Hunter in this way was "enabling" behavior, but we did not care. It was also compassionate, a mercy we had the power, the privilege, to provide. Our choice, as we saw it, was stark.

If Hunter died, would we prefer our last encounter to have been barring the door and toeing the don't-enable line? To have told him, "No, Hunter, you cannot come in and take a shower, and this is a direct consequence of your continuing drug use." Or would we rather the encounter involve helping him meet basic human needs? Serving Hunter, clean from the shower, momentarily warm and dry, oatmeal and coffee? Oatmeal and coffee were insufficient incentives for renouncing heroin, we saw that. But they provided a few minutes of solid, humane connection, and we were willing to settle for that.

Barry and I talked all the time about our choices with Hunter, trying together to negotiate the messy line between enabling and compassion. We did not attempt to teach him a lesson by freezing him out of our lives. We understood that addiction is impervious to that strategy. We held Hunter at arm's length to shield Sawyer and Lillie from his continued drug use. We still felt capable of maintaining some relationship, battered as that was becoming. We saw his basic human dignity. He was exactly as much our beloved son as he had been at two months old, two years, twelve.

He still had a cell phone, on our plan. He called us, sometimes nightly, when things were worst. After the first month, we did not rise to meet him in the night. We called or texted him, not very often, trying our best to teach ourselves to disengage from a problem we were learning, excruciatingly slowly, that we could not solve.

Every time I saw him, my heart knew it was the last time. I let this knowledge—this collection of Last Times—sit in my consciousness, fragile sparrows on a thin wire.

It was Thanksgiving week. My father had been ill, so ill we thought that he would die. His kidneys failing, paralyzed by gout, he lay on the sofa in agony. We thought it might be his last Thanksgiving, and my mother had rented a beautiful old house on Vashon Island, a short ferry ride from Seattle. My sister and her husband and their twins—born so early but thriving now—arrived. My brother flew in from Dubai, where his architecture work was based. They all settled on Vashon, with the plan that Barry, Sawyer, Lillie, and I would come and go during the holiday weekend.

The night before Thanksgiving, as I crumbled cornbread to let it get stale for stuffing, I heard knocking on the door. Lifting the curtain,

I peeked out, noted that the blizzard that had been predicted had arrived. Hunter was huddled, nearly lying down, on the doorstep. Even through the glass, I saw him shaking. I opened the door, and he tumbled in.

"Barry," I called upstairs, "Barry, Hunter's here, come quick."

Hunter's temperature was 104. His throat was raw. "He has tonsillitis. I'm going to call in a prescription," Barry said.

"I need a hot bath," Hunter moaned, his teeth chattering.

Staring at the closed bathroom door, listening to the water run and then to silence, I felt paralyzed. My relief that Hunter was living mixed with shock and fear at his condition and uneasy anxiety about his presence. He was very sick—he would stay, of course. One of us would stay with him. Someone would help him, feed him, watch him. Be sure he got better. Make sure that when he recovered from this illness, he did not steal from us.

I settled Hunter in his old bed in the basement, pulled the covers over, patted him in. I left him ginger ale, smoothing his shoulder. "I love you, Hunter. You will get better soon." He moaned in reply.

Over the next four days, Hunter slept in the basement, cocooned in darkness. I took him soup, juice, crackers. Washed the filthy clothes he'd arrived in. Threw out the socks. Encrusted and foul, Hunter's socks broke my heart repeatedly. His feet, his feet, his road, his pathway. Hunter hated that I saw these things as metaphors, but doing that was one of my survival skills.

Barry, Sawyer, and Lillie spent most of this time on Vashon. I had baked the pies and made salad, cornbread stuffing, fresh cranberry sauce. Keeping a small portion for myself and Hunter, I'd packed the rest, sent it to my extended family. The house was still: me in the living room, Hunter asleep below. I balanced softly on this strange but peaceful ledge, soaking up his presence. I let myself fully appreciate his being alive, safe and warm, for this moment anyway.

After the first two days, I noticed that Hunter's symptoms had shifted. While he seemed stronger in some ways, he seemed worse in others. His hands and feet began to spasm. He looked as if he were crying, his nose ran. Still feverish, he tossed in his bed, agitated.

"Hunter, what's wrong, do you feel worse? Should I call Barry?" I asked him.

"Mom, go away, I don't want you to see me like this. Please, I'm okay, just—go away," he begged.

I realized then that what was happening was opioid withdrawal. Something that, when Hunter was born, I never dreamed I'd see. I climbed the stairs but kept my vigil. When Barry came back, he talked with Hunter, assessed the situation. "He seems to be getting through the worst of the withdrawal," Barry said evenly, "and his fever is gone."

My mind began to process the impact of this progress. Would Hunter stay clean, was he now done with drugs? Could this illness, the pain, his fear, have been what 12-Steppers called hitting bottom? If so, what then? Would he agree to the terms we'd laid down at the breakfast meeting and stay here with us?

On the fourth day, I heard him moving in the basement. "Hunter, how are you feeling?" I called down.

"I'm feeling better, thanks," he said. "I'm going out now. I have to meet a friend."

"And do what, Hunter, score drugs?" I snapped. "Your dad said he thought you were through the worst of the withdrawal symptoms. Isn't it better? This is a chance to start recovery again. Are you sure you should go out right now?"

Hunter refused to meet my eyes. He grabbed his jacket. "Where's my backpack?" he said.

I'd kept the bag upstairs with me after I'd washed the filthy clothes and repacked them. I hadn't dug deeply into the pockets, knowing what I'd find there, wanting not to find those things. His illness, I had told myself, made his presence in the house a humanitarian effort. For these few days, Hunter had been too weak to actively break rules or cause us harm. It had been such a relief just to take care of him, to comfort him.

"Thank you for letting me stay while I was sick, Mom. I love you," Hunter said, hugging me. "Tell Dad and Sawyer and Lillie I said goodbye. I'm sorry I didn't get to see Suz and Kevin and the twins and Uncle Matty. Tell them for me, will you?"

"Will you be back?" I asked him, knowing he knew that being back in our house meant abstaining from drugs.

"Mom, I don't think I can," Hunter replied.

Harm Reduction

Being home—or maybe being back on the street after having been home during his illness—gave Hunter the impetus to try abstaining from heroin. A week after Thanksgiving, Hunter asked Barry to help him get placed on the harm-reduction drug Suboxone.

Suboxone is the brand name for the oral formulation of the drug combination buprenorphine/naloxone, which is used to treat opioid dependence. This drug can simultaneously prevent heroin withdrawal and block heroin's euphoric high—in other words, Suboxone can stunt both the urge to use opioids and the fear of not using them.[7]

As soon as he hung up the phone, Barry found a doctor with prescribing privileges and arranged the visit. He met Hunter in the U District early on the cold morning of the following day, and they drove to Swedish Hospital's Cherry Hill campus in the First Hill neighborhood near downtown. Barry had trained resident physicians at this hospital during our first five years in Seattle, when he worked at the Seattle Indian Health Board, and Dr. Shaw, the addiction specialist Hunter was about to see, had been one of those residents. Nurses and medical assistants greeted Barry curiously as Hunter sat, morose, beside him in Dr. Shaw's waiting room.

Hunter declined Barry's offer to sit in on the visit. "I want to do this alone, Dad," he said. "I'm eighteen, I'm not a little kid."

The appointment was lengthy. When Hunter finally emerged, he looked relieved. "He started me on it. He wants to see me again in a few days to be sure the dose is okay."

I drove Hunter to his next appointment and took my turn in the drab reception room. My wait was brief. "I'm supposed to see him every ten days now," Hunter explained.

Once we'd agreed to help Hunter get Suboxone, we didn't feel as if we had much choice about letting him move back in with us. He seemed penitent and motivated to correct his past behavior. We wanted to give him the best chance to succeed on this medicine. We were relieved not to have him on the street but also guarded. Hunter agreed to start looking for work immediately.

Barry and I stepped back from trying to control Hunter's recovery. We did not demand that he attend NA meetings, nor did we insist that he submit to drug testing as a condition of living with us, although Dr. Shaw would test him before issuing each prescription renewal. We also allowed him to self-administer the Suboxone. We could have kept the medication in our possession, doled it out, but we chose not to. We felt that Hunter had to be responsible for his recovery, including managing this harm reduction drug.

"Hunter has started taking a prescribed drug called Suboxone that will hopefully help him stay off heroin," I'd told Sawyer and Lillie at breakfast the day Hunter was to return. "Barry and I are going to let him live here again, at least for a while." Both kids were silent. Lillie stirred her Cream of Wheat. "How do you guys feel about that?" I asked.

"I don't really know," Sawyer muttered. "I mean . . ." His words trailed off. Lillie raised her eyebrows but said nothing.

And so, house key once again in his pocket, Hunter settled back into his basement bedroom.

I feared theft. I tried to keep my purse with me everywhere, all the time, bringing it into the bathroom when I showered and sleeping with it under a heap of pillows right beside my bed. I tried to keep minimal cash on hand, to keep track. I felt again the familiar queasy sensation of opening the small black leather coin purse where I'd stowed, I thought, four ones and three fives, and finding three ones and two fives. Had I miscounted? Forgotten a small purchase?

December days passed. For a week or two, Hunter seemed calmer and more focused. He typed up a resume, struggling to do so because he had little to include—a few weeks scanning high-resolution images of historic photographs of Pike Place Market for a *HistoryLink* book project his freshman year, volunteer work at Shoreline Historical Museum to fulfill a community service requirement during his second diversion, the GED. He scanned job postings online and left the house most days, resume in his backpack.

"Do you need a ride to Dr. Shaw's?" I asked Hunter the morning of his next appointment.

"Thanks, Mom," he said, "but I can bus there."

By Christmas, Hunter's mood had taken a sharp downturn. He was surly and difficult to be around, and because Sawyer and Lillie were on winter break, they bore the brunt of his peevishness and sarcasm. Wanting to give them breathing room, I took Sawyer and Lillie to Portland for a quick two-night trip. We wandered around downtown, ducking into shops to escape the relentless rain, and spent hours browsing at Powell's Book Store.

While we were gone, Barry found Hunter sifting through our bedroom closet. "Is it okay if I borrow a pair of your socks?" Hunter asked, his hand drifting from the little bowl into which Barry routinely tossed his change each night to a nearby stack of neatly paired socks.

Barry handed him socks. "I don't want you to come upstairs unless your mom or I are up here, Hunter," he said. "Starting right now."

But Barry worked twelve-hour shifts at least three days each week. If I was not actively guarding the upstairs, Hunter routinely roamed. "What are you doing upstairs, Hunter," I would shout, hearing his footsteps from the kitchen. "You're not supposed to be there."

"I'm looking for a plain undershirt," he'd call, and then bang down the stairs and out the front door before I'd had a good look at him.

About a week after the trip to Portland, days before Hunter's scheduled appointment with Dr. Shaw, Barry walked into Hunter's basement bedroom unannounced and found him, his raised arm tied off with a leather belt, lighter and spoon beside him, shooting up.

"Hunter, what the fuck are you doing?" Barry shouted. Hunter sprang from the little couch and pushed roughly past Barry, belt still dangling, syringe in hand, and pounded up the basement stairs, Barry on his heels. Reaching the front door, Hunter threw it open. Shoeless, coatless, he ran into the cold.

I had been at the grocery store. "Can someone help me carry?" I started to call as I walked into the living room, but then saw Barry sitting rigidly at the pine table, his palms flat on the wood as if trying to summon strength from the trees the table once had been. I quickly took the scene in. Barry wasn't crying. Surely that ruled out overdose. My lips involuntarily tightened. "What happened?"

As Barry finished telling me what he'd witnessed, we heard a key turn in the door. Hunter stepped into the living room's warm yellow light. "I need shoes and my coat," he said. We followed him to his bedroom, where he grabbed jacket, sneakers, backpack. There was little conversation. Hunter allowed me to hug him, briefly, before striding out the front door and down the stairs into the four p.m. early January dusk.[8]

It was Sawyer's sixteenth birthday. We had all planned to celebrate at Volterra, a cozy Italian restaurant in the Ballard neighborhood. When Sawyer came home from school a few minutes after Hunter's exit, we told him that Hunter had relapsed. The weight and sorrow of the news flooded his face. I hugged him, thinking he might cry, and felt his arms envelop me tightly, then soften. He pulled away and shook his head. "No words," he said.

Barry methodically changed the locks. Lillie's ballet carpool dropped her back home at seven, and we repeated the news. She sighed. "That's so sad," she said, wrapping her arms around Barry and me together. "But we can't let this spoil Sawyer's birthday. I just need a minute to change out of my leotards. I hope we're still going to Volterra."

We drove to Ballard. I thought of Hunter on the street, felt the familiar fear for him. But this latest go-round of Hunter's lies and relapse left me numb instead of raw. Lillie has it exactly right, I thought to myself, as Barry eased into a parking space on Ballard Avenue. It's sad, but our job now is to honor Sawyer's special day, not veer off kilter, not let this spin us off our own axis.

We were a four-top, neatly spaced around the square table, one person to a side, but Hunter's presence swirled through the candlelit dining room, haunting us all. It was the first time a birthday celebration had not included all five. Broken, no longer whole, we were determined not to disintegrate, no matter how fragile we had become.

We stayed upright, all of us scarred, continuing, even somewhat relieved, if we were truly honest. The strain of having Hunter living with us, stealing from us, drugging himself, left us exhausted, angered, frightened, and exasperated. Despite his prescription for Suboxone, Hunter had valued heroin over his home and family.

Lights in the Night

The House on Stilts was Hunter's idea. Our small backyard was sweet and adequate and matched our modest cottage, but to nine-year-old Hunter, it lacked adventure. "Why can't we build a tree house," he asked, eyeing the slender apple tree whose fruit no one would eat, even in apple cobbler. "It's much too small," we told him, "it could never hold the weight." "How about a tree house with no tree on stilts?" he wondered. And so he drew the plan, and he and Barry built it.

The House on Stilts was high enough that it took clambering up a knotted rope to enter. There was a screen door with glass panels that could be slid across the screens to winterize, and windows made of salvaged ship portholes. Other windows were old stained glass, raised by tugging ropes through cleats. The largest window was double-hung, its wavy panes salvaged from a house long gone. All these materials Hunter and Barry collected diligently, combing through windows at a salvage yard, driving to the marine hardware supply in Anacortes, where they'd once seen ships' portholes for sale.

The rain drummed heavily on the sheet metal roof of the House on Stilts. One wall was pierced with threaded holes into which rock-climbing holds could be fitted, their pattern of reach and pull adjusted from time to time to keep things interesting. These holds covered the wall's exterior. Grasped by eager little hands, stretching arms and legs extended fiercely, the climbing holds were once a mighty challenge. Hunter, Sawyer, and little Lillie worked their way slowly up the wall, clinging by tips of fingers and toes, as near the top as they could get. As they grew older and the climb less of a challenge, the holds became a nimble pathway to the nearby garage roof, where Lillie liked to take a book on sunny afternoons.

Hunter loved the House on Stilts: playing in it, climbing on it, braving the night inside its ample shelter. At 8 x 12, it seemed cavernous when newly built, well suited for sleepovers where ghost stories (always told by Hunter) frightened his best friend, Alex. Sleeping bags, chapter books, flashlights, board games: it was the children's space, their hideaway.

As he grew, Hunter used the House on Stilts less frequently. One night during middle school, sleeping out there with his friends Jeremy and Pete, the three snuck out and roamed the streets, their dark shapes flitting past my window as they went. Crossing the tiny yard to investigate, I found them missing. For the first time, I felt the fright mixed with irritation that would later become so devastatingly familiar. Hunter's slipping out poked a tiny but troubling hole in what I'd thought of as his understanding of my expectations.

Barry was out of town, working a twenty-four-hour rural emergency room shift. I phoned my father, asked him to come and stay with sleeping Lillie and Sawyer, and drove up and down the neighborhood, peering into the late-night Starbucks, shining my lights at bushes. The boys came back eventually, tried to sneak in, were apprehended. Hunter was scolded, his friends sent home.

The world might say, this is what kids do, but I came to see Hunter's first dash that night away from home's protection into a wilder, darker world as a small seed that in time grew into the poisonous thorn-studded briar forest of opioid addiction. Now he was drug addicted, barely of legal age, and on the street again.

I thought of Hunter constantly. He hovered on my shoulder, in my heart, dead, alive, tiny, his current age. He occupied my brain as I pushed through research, as I wrote. Some days, once I'd sent Sawyer and Lillie off to school, I could not leave my bed but dragged my laptop in with me as I huddled in the blankets. I struggled to wrestle my brain free of the pounding fear for Hunter's safety. I measured my success in sentences, not in pages.

One evening as I climbed the stairs to bed, I thought I saw a light flicker in the House on Stilts. The tiny threaded holes drilled to allow various placements of climbing holds meant that a flashlight or a lantern or a match inside cast light that shone through the wall. I pressed my forehead to the window, strained, saw the flicker again, and I knew in my bones that it was Hunter. A wild, animal happiness bubbled inside me, a sort of giddy relief at knowing where Hunter was, exactly, on this frigid night.

The next night, the flicker moved again. I looked into the House on Stilts early the next morning and saw Hunter sleeping there, bundled in a coat and wrapped in an unfamiliar blanket. Even in the morning cold the room smelled rank, thick with cigarette smoke and soured socks and unwashed human. I watched him sleep—I hoped it was sleep, held my breath until I saw his chest move. I backed away, not ready to do more with this discovery than treasure it. A few nights later, I pointed out the flickering light to Barry.

We sat with the knowledge of Hunter's presence for a week or more, relieved to see him there, feeling that he was safer in our backyard than he would be in a doorway, a park, or a homeless shelter. I concentrated better than I had in months. I wrote hard and fast in the mornings, looked in at him, saw him breathe, verified that he was living. He came and went stealthily, though I sometimes saw him scurry by. To my immense relief, he was always alone. The House on Stilts was now his squat, but not a shared one.

One afternoon, I was disturbed to see Hunter's friend Jonah stride into the backyard, hoist himself up the swinging rope, peer in the window. Hunter was evidently not there, and Jonah quickly left. The next time Hunter called me on his cell phone, I said, "Hey, we've seen you climbing into the House on Stilts, are you staying there?"

"Yeah," he said, "is that okay?"

"I saw Jonah look for you. Who else knows you're staying there?" I asked.

"Nobody, just Jonah, I wouldn't tell anyone else, I don't want anyone finding me here."

"You can stay, Hunter, but please don't smoke in there, it scares me with those blankets. And you cannot, cannot bring drugs there, you have to promise me you'll never do that—it is our property, just like the house, and we don't want anything illegal anywhere near."

"Oh, yeah, I promise, Mom," he said, "I won't do any of that."

And then, of course, he did do all of that.

He asked for a Thermarest and a warm sleeping bag, and those requests seemed reasonable. How could giving him blankets to keep warm be anything but compassionate? The nights were cold. The wooden floor was hard. We tucked a Polarguard sleeping bag into the House on Stilts, along with an inflatable pad.

I tried to shield Sawyer and Lillie from the brutality of Hunter's drug addiction, to insulate them from the loss of their brother, but I could not. "Hunter is staying in the House on Stilts," I warned them. Lillie's face hardened at Hunter's name. She wanted no part of his schemes, his thefts, his drugs, his slipshod life.

"Hunter comes to Cloud City sometimes," Sawyer said. He worked at the café on weekend mornings. "He's actually there a lot, drinking coffee from the honor bar." I took to stopping by and stuffing a five- or ten-dollar bill into the little box meant to receive a dollar a cup.

Lillie and Sawyer kept their distance from Hunter now, to my relief, but I clutched precious memories of the years before, trying to hold them. Three siblings, close, brothers loving and celebrating their younger sister, letting her grab a plastic light saber and join their Star Wars battle, patiently playing Candyland again and again. These memories affirmed the existence of that time: we were a loving unit. Hunter, Sawyer, and Lillie rowed as one. Now Hunter's addiction and the life it brought felt like splashes of bleach distorting and discoloring the pattern of the life we'd had, erasing it. I battled to retain those pictures, mentally begging, please, don't take this too.

We kept the house doors locked, barricading ourselves physically and emotionally. Hunter couldn't steal from us, he wasn't in our constant presence, we didn't have to interact all day long. The House on Stilts became our satellite, Hunter's safe house from the streets, but also, if we were honest with ourselves, a protected place to use his drugs. This was the kind of complex grey space I hated, lacking moral clarity when you peeled back the obvious top layer of what was right and what was wrong.

I loved Hunter, and he was a threat. These facts coexisted. Sawyer and Lillie needed stability. Hunter was destabilizing. He was dysfunctional, as were our interactions, but the family, the ship, Sawyer and Lillie and Barry and I, remained upright, afloat. Hunter had jumped overboard repeatedly, and we had tried to haul him out of the shark-infested waters, yet there he was, fins all around. We could not envision abandoning him to his fate, sailing away. So we extended oars that were compassionate and enabling, both: food, shelter, clothing.

Hunter came and went from the House on Stilts, like some elusive boarder. The situation was unreal, but I couldn't stop the urge to normalize it. "What are you eating, Hunter?" I asked a few times. Sometimes the answer was food from street feedings—a sandwich, apple, juice box, cookies—nestled in brown paper bags like the ones Lillie and her Girl Scout troop occasionally prepared to feed those in need.

One day at Safeway, I found myself shopping for Hunter. What was small, relatively nutritious, easy to open, required no refrigeration and no dishes? Pop-top single serving cans of tuna fish with mayonnaise and seasoning already mixed in. Pull-tab cans of pineapple chunks, peaches, or pears. Apples and bananas. Shelled nuts. Granola bars. Peanut butter, jelly, a bag of bread. It was like planning for a camping trip without a cooler. A simple, familiar task: nurture my child. I savored feeding him again in this back-assed way that made me a shade of happy.

A few weeks later Hunter asked whether I could take him shopping for food. He chose similar items, augmenting them with two giant bottles of drinking water, and then with potato chips, Pepsi Throwback, Chips Ahoy, a pack of cigarettes. I bought these things without remarking on their nutritional content. All his life, Hunter had listened to me make each grocery store trip a teachable moment about healthy eating, and even my indefatigable nature grasped the irony of our current situation.

I left Hunter other offerings. It felt strange and wrong and simultaneously right. If Lillie baked, I'd leave a plate of cookies just inside the door of the House on Stilts. I did the same when I made breakfast muffins. "Thank you so much," he'd say when he saw me later. "Those were delicious, thank you."

On his nineteenth birthday, I bought a slice of coconut cake from a neighborhood fixture, the Queen Mary Teahouse—the only cake

Hunter liked as much as mine. I left the boxed slice atop his crumpled sleeping bag. Happy birthday, Hunter, I scribbled, I love you, xxxooooxoxo.

Before long, we were offering Hunter a plate at dinnertime, carried out the back door and through the yard. In the morning, the empty plate would appear on our back steps. It was a kind of twisted room service. This practice was clearly crazy but humane. On this and every point, Barry and I constantly weighed the question, could I live with this? If Hunter died tomorrow, could I live with this decision made today?

I also think some deep maternal instinct recognized that Hunter's drugs and life on the street had rendered him feral. The plates of food, the cookies, were my attempt to gentle him, to lure him back into craving our comfortable middle-class life more than he wanted heroin. The urge was deep and beggared rational thinking. I was casting spells, weaving nets. Hunter was Persephone, captured by addiction/Hades while picking poppies. I was Demeter, desperate to welcome him back above ground.

Sometimes Hunter phoned us at bedtime, asking for a hot-water bottle. We filled these for him. Like suppers, like cookies, they normalized our bizarre situation. Hot-water bottles may seem quaint, but in our house they were talismans of comfort, warmth, and security, fighting the chill in wet Seattle winters. Within the crazy logic of our situation, the thought that Hunter wanted a childhood consolation and the knowledge that I could provide it soothed the raw corners of my soul.

When Hunter left the House on Stilts, I sometimes climbed the rope and stood or knelt amid the heaped foul-smelling clothes and sleeping bag, lighters, cigarette butts and ashes. Hidden just slightly, a bent spoon and ribbon of blue rubber. Scattered beneath the piles, bright orange syringe caps. We had voluntarily relinquished the moral high ground. But I was balancing fear of what would happen to him if we forced him out with terror of him setting himself on fire while cooking heroin in a sleeping bag or smoking there or of finding him some morning, dead of an overdose.

Hunter craved not only heroin but Harry Potter. After he asked, I took the hardback books out to the House on Stilts one by one. Was it a last good thing, an unbroken connection with his childhood? Was it escape into a wholly crafted, deeply familiar world? That he wanted these books gave me hope. Let Hunter be, I begged the future, like Harry Potter: The Boy Who Lived.

In my longing to comfort that boy, I ended up enabling the opioid-addicted man. During Hunter's weeks in the House on Stilts, we averted our eyes from the glaring reason he was living there instead of in his basement bedroom or in his own apartment or in a college dorm. We were again a cracked but complete family. It felt nearly ordinary if I squeezed my eyes shut tight enough. I wanted that so terribly: to paste all five of us down like some collage of stick figures, a happy line, hands glued back together.

If Hunter had been following the more traditional path we'd envisioned for him—teenage jobs, high school graduation, helping to pay for college with work-study—Barry and I would still have had to learn to let him go. We would have known, though, that doing so was in his best interest. We'd have negotiated the shift from actively parenting to enjoying our grown child as a functional adult. Hunter's opioid addiction meant that instead of helping him launch, we lashed ourselves to him, trying to arrest his fall.

We felt lucky to have this quiet yard and this small hut that had been charming as a place to play, even if now a sad and sorry shelter. Hunter was in terrible condition, but we at least knew where he was. There was a cost: Hunter's presence brought the grim details of his situation closer to our other children. And what did letting Hunter, in active addiction, live in the House on Stilts teach Sawyer and Lillie? That nothing breaks family? Or that there was nothing Hunter could ever do that would finally be too much?

I carried Hunter's mail to him, left it inside the winterized screen door: collection letters about the phone he'd bought when he'd been roped into a phone scam operation and the occasional offer from the Johns Hopkins Center for Talented Youth—he'd qualified for the program in middle school. His ballot came—I'd made sure Hunter registered to vote, along with registering for the draft. He had been interested in politics since childhood. I hoped he would focus and ink in the bubbles. I put the ballot and a pen and stamps inside the House on Stilts.

Though we were now fully in touch with Hunter, his comings and goings remained his own, mysterious. Sometimes he was gone for days, other times he stayed put and didn't leave the House on Stilts except to find a bathroom someplace—a coffee shop or the nearby playground, I wasn't sure. He told me he sometimes showered at a city pool, but judging from his smell, this wasn't often.

At night, I watched the pinholes in the House on Stilts glinting like fireflies. I decided that they flickered when Hunter shifted positions in his sleeping bag, the battery powered camping lantern we'd provided casting shadows that his movements pierced. I feared the kind of flicker that looked like flame, sometimes straining against the window glass for five minutes, ten, hoping for no eruption. These moments frightened me. But the nights when the pinholes were dark scared me more.

One night, when the flickers seemed more intense than usual, I rushed downstairs, barefoot, out into the cold wet grass, my nightgown trailing. "Hunter?" I called, hoisting myself high enough to look into the door. The House on Stilts was empty. Inside it, the lantern shone steadily, false comfort on so many nights, I quickly understood. Did he forget to turn it off? Was it a nightlight Hunter left for me, a kind deception?

Hunter seemed to realize he was heading for some kind of bottom. He had been living in the House on Stilts for nearly two months when he asked me to give him a ride to King County Detox. "I've called them for days waiting for a bed," he told me, "and they'll have one this evening. I need to be there by seven."

I felt a surge of hope. Hunter wanted to detox, and he had taken the action required to arrange it himself. "Of course," I said. "Of course I'll drive you."

It was the pitch-black early evening of Seattle in March. Heading to detox, Hunter looked unsurprisingly terrible. He smelled of cigarettes and stale sweat. I'd Mapquested King County Detox, and the route was familiar: the same road we'd taken every Thursday for five years en route to our weekly Lunch with Daddy Day at Barry's old community clinic. I remembered reaching back to hold Hunter's small hand as he traveled in his car seat listening to Guy Clark cassettes.

King County Detox was housed in an old facility, shabbily utilitarian, with picture windows in every room. These windows shone a cold fluorescent light as we pulled up, framing the stultified patients inside. Some curtains were drawn. Some people perched on beds, others curled into themselves, others paced. Reception was beyond a locked entryway. If hotel reception areas strive to be inviting and hospital receptions attempt to calm, King County Detox shouts, You are lucky that you're not in jail. This is a bench in hell, but at least you haven't yet burst into flames. Get the fuck in, or don't—we don't much care.

"Should I go in with you?" I asked, steeling myself for the judging eyes of whoever kept the gate.

"I'll do it," Hunter said quickly, "but if you could wait awhile, just to be sure they let me in . . ." We hugged. I told him he was doing a good thing for himself, and he shut the car door. Standing outside the detox under thin light, he waited to be buzzed inside, then was gone.

The neighborhood felt dangerous. I pulled my car to the parking lot's edge, then thought better of it when I noticed someone crouched there, smoking or doing something else. Closer to the building, I tried to see what was happening in the reception room. Hunter was there, then wasn't, then he was again. He seemed to have been taken deeper into the facility, and I tried his cell phone, but, of course, they'd taken it from him. Eventually, I drove back home.

For a few days I pictured Hunter safe in detox. I held the thought of him experiencing some kind of peace. After a week, it seemed strange that he had not yet called. I phoned the detox: Is he still a patient? "Hunter," the woman said. "We don't have a Hunter . . . oh, Hunter—he left last week. Wasn't here forty-eight hours."

I hung up the phone and climbed into the House on Stilts, feeling its desolation. My hope for Hunter over the past days had been tentative, fragile. But it had been hope. I couldn't know where Hunter was, couldn't undo his drug addiction, couldn't make him do anything that matched my choices. I saw that a little more fully now.

I could, however, set the House on Stilts in order. I grabbed a laundry basket from the basement and piled Hunter's filthy, stinking clothes into it. Later, I would sort them—the colors dulled by grime, the darks soiled invisibly, the whites so far beyond bleaching I threw them in the trash. I washed what clothes I could. When they were dry, I folded them neatly and stacked them in Hunter's old wardrobe, in the basement area formerly known as Hunter's room.

I tossed the sleeping bag, the pillows, the homeless-person blanket onto the grass outside the House on Stilts. Some would be washed, some thrown away, some donated. Filled a trash bag with the debris of Hunter's residency: old food, some of it moldy; scraps of newspaper; the untouched ballot; discarded drug tools—sky-blue rubber strips, cigarette lighters, burned spoons, blaze-orange needle caps, syringe wrappers. He'd been using, we had known that, although we'd turned a blind eye. I put the camping lantern in the basement and the Harry Potter volumes back in the living room bookshelf. I swept the floor, and then I scrubbed it on my hands and knees.

When I was done, the space was cleansed and empty. The next day, Barry would fit the door with a lock. I sat on the floor and breathed, thinking of Hunter, knowing he'd been alive in this place and loved, knowing that his time here had not changed his situation, even as it damaged and compromised and reassured and comforted and de-based the rest of us. I cried. And then I climbed down the rope and reached back up to shut the door.

The Visit

The day was dark and cold, as usual. Lillie and Sawyer were both off at school, and my pressing goal was to drive to the specialty photo lab that was processing high-resolution images for the Seattle World's Fair book. I had to pick up a disc of finished images—Elvis Presley's visit to film *It Happened at the World's Fair*, a Kodachrome taken in the World of Tomorrow, the Monorail being christened with a bottle of champagne—then get those to the book's designer before noon. I hurried through the breakfast dishes, intent on getting out of the house.

Above the water's flow, I thought I heard knocking, hesitant but repeated. Peeling back the long red dish gloves, I hurried to the front door and lifted the curtain.

Hunter looked back at me, bedraggled, shivering. I had not seen Hunter in the two weeks that had gone by since we had locked the House on Stilts. I hesitated just a moment, then opened the door, hugged him, allowed him in.

"I really need a shower," Hunter said, "Can I please just take a shower, and can I see if there are any more of my contact lenses in the basement? You look busy. What are you doing today?"

"I have a super busy day," I said, trying to think fast. "Okay. Okay, you can shower, but please try to be quick, I've got to go down to Panda Lab and I'm in a huge hurry. But are you hungry? I can cook you something fast while you shower if you want."

Hunter agreed to eggs and toast. I heard the bathroom door click shut, the shower water start. This is enabling, I muttered to myself, cooking him food, letting him shower when I really need to leave the house. I couldn't say no, couldn't quite, although it threw my plans off kilter. I ground the coffee beans, melted butter, sliced sourdough bread. I thought about his bulging dirty backpack, which he'd carried into the bathroom with him.

"Your food is on the table, Hunter," I called, thinking that his shower had gone on so long the hot water would be running out, if it hadn't already. I gathered my things, made sure my purse was safely on my shoulder.

"That felt amazing," Hunter said, emerging slowly from the bathroom wrapped in Barry's robe. "The food smells great! My clothes are really dirty, and I didn't want to put them on again. Do you think you would let me take a few of the clothes I left here? Could you maybe wash these if I leave them?"

He sat at the table, started in on eggs, sipped the creamy coffee, breathing the fragrances in deeply. I saw him shut his eyes to taste more fully, that beautiful thing he always did, savoring the moment. I had an instant of sheer gratitude to once again witness this particular Hunterism, to see him here, alive, being nourished by food I'd prepared. I watched him finish everything on the plate.

"Okay, Hunter," I said, "I'm sorry to have to kick you out, but I'm in a huge hurry. You can go down to your room and look through the wardrobe—all the clothes you left are there."

I put my shoes on, brushed my teeth, checked email. Hunter lingered in the basement. Time ticked by. "Hunter," I finally called, "what's going on?" I made my way down the basement stairs, entered his old room.

"I'm just so comfortable," Hunter said, "can't I just sit here for a little bit?"

He held up a William S. Burroughs book he'd read before, a finger pressed between the pages to mark his stopping point. "It's the first time I've been really warm for so long. Can't I just sit here and rest for a little while longer?"

I felt frustration, simmering, rising up hard. "Hunter, I've GOT to go pick up the disc of images. Our deadline is really tight right now."

"Can't I just stay?" he pled. "I promise I'll just sit here and read, I won't go anywhere else, please."

I knew it was completely stupid, knew it was a huge mistake, but I felt desperate. I could not physically get Hunter up the stairs, out of the house, and he was clearly not planning to go easily. Seattle Center Foundation had commissioned the World's Fair book and timed its launch date to the fair's anniversary celebrations. The book's lavish color illustrations meant that, to be made affordable, it would be printed and bound in China, then sent back to Seattle on a container ship. It was imperative that books arrived in time for the launch, to which hundreds of fair-related VIPs were being invited. Delivery under those conditions had necessitated rigid deadlines. The images were finally ready, and I had promised to deliver them to Nancy, the designer, today. I now had only thirty minutes to get to Panda, park, and pick up the disc. My brain felt fuzzy, achy, with the stress of the decision.

"Okay," I said suddenly, "Hunter, okay. I will let you stay here, but you must not leave until I get back. You have to promise to just stay here and read, not go anywhere else in the house, not leave, and I will be back as fast as I possibly can."

"Thank you! Thank you so much, Mom, I'll stay right here," Hunter said gratefully.

I dashed to the car, roared down our street toward the freeway. What the hell am I doing, I thought, imagining him wandering the house, sifting through closets, scouring the drawers for quarters, for who knew what. I slammed into a parking place—mercifully open right in front of the tiny photo lab abutting Seattle Center, ran in, signed the invoice, grabbed the disc.

On the freeway again, heading north, I resisted speeding, but only just. My task was accomplished—the designer was on her way to my house to get the disc—but I felt rising panic. "Hunter," I said sharply as I entered the house, not sure on any level what I might find.

"Oh, hi," he called, "I'm ready to go now, thanks so much for letting me stay."

I heard his rapid footsteps on the basement stairs and hurried toward the kitchen, where the stairs emerge onto the ground floor. Hunter was already at the back door, hand on the knob, and he was carrying—dragging—a giant bag, the huge Nike duffel Barry had used since college.

"Wait! Hunter, what is in that bag?" I demanded.

"Oh, it's just some books I'm going to sell, they're my books, don't worry," he said.

"You didn't say anything about gathering books to sell, you said you wanted to read and rest and stay warm," I countered, trying to control the wail I felt building in my chest. "And that bag is your father's, he would absolutely not want you to take it, you've got to leave that bag."

"I'll bring it back," he muttered, twisting the doorknob.

I sprang forward, grabbing the bag's handles with both hands. "Hunter, you cannot take this bag. And you've got to open it. I want to see what you are taking."

"Don't, Mom," he said dangerously, "don't do this." He tried to wrench the bag away, but it was heavy and I was holding on hard. I stepped on either side of the end nearest me, clamped my feet around the blue nylon. "Open it," I said. "I will let you take out any books that are yours, but you can't take the bag."

The duffel, four feet long, seemed far too heavy for just books. I felt something large, bulky, maybe made of metal, weighing down my clutching feet. What does he have in here, I wondered frantically? Tools? Maybe an electric saw? "Hunter," I repeated, "open this bag."

"No," he said angrily.

"Open it."

"No!" He wrenched again, and I fell to my knees, clutching the bag with my whole body.

Hunter was enraged. He pulled the bag angrily, yanking me with it. "Mom, let go!" he shouted.

"I will not let go! And you will either leave the whole thing or you can open it and take your own books!!" I gritted out.

I kept my iron grip on the duffle bag because of my certainty, my conviction, that the sweet person I knew was still deep within this angry Hunter would not let him hurt me.

Hunter pulled even harder, felt me tumble with his pull, seemed to hesitate just for a second.

"Okay!" he said, clearly furious at being thwarted, stronger than I but still unwilling, in the final pinch, to physically harm me to get his way. "Okay! I'll open it!"

He pulled the zipper slowly, trying to control my view. I saw a flash of a familiar cover, another. "Those are MY books!" I shouted. "Hunter, those are some of my very favorites, and you KNOW it." I gathered Jack Finney's *Time and Again*, an illustrated history of Vanessa Bell and Duncan Grant's Charleston Farmhouse, William Carlos Williams's *Collected Poems*. "These are my books. These are NOT your books!"

"Oh," Hunter muttered, "I didn't know those were in there. Mine are further down . . ."

"Hunter, there's something else in here, something heavy, what is it?" I asked, still making sure not to slacken my feet's hold on the duffel.

"Nothing," he said, "it's nothing."

"Hunter?"

"It's nothing!"

I knew I had every right to demand that he show me what was in the bag, but I decided not to force this point. Let him save face a little, I thought, knowing I cared more that whatever was in there stayed in the house than that I knew exactly what it was.

"Okay. You don't have to tell me what this is, but you cannot take it and you cannot take this bag. You can carry it downstairs, and you can put back whatever this is and my books, and you can take out just your books and show them to me. Then you can leave," I said, seeing a way to dodge the impasse. I suddenly felt deadly calm, no longer frightened.

And so he did it, dragging the bag back down the stairs. I heard him shuffle through the basement, replacing the something heavy wherever he had found it. I heard some books flung down, heard him sifting through, gathering others. He quickly climbed the stairs, books in his arms.

"See! These are mine, my books!" He fanned them out, still angry. They were books I remembered buying for him, books he'd loved, treasured, read repeatedly. I felt tears spring to my eyes. "Hunter, those books are special to you, are you sure you want to sell them?" I said softly. To me, the books were physical manifestations of emotional touchstones, not just things.

"They're mine, and I'm taking them," he said. The back door had come open during our struggle, and cold seeped into the warm shadowy kitchen. Cramming the books into his bulging backpack, Hunter turned sharply from me, strode out the door.

As soon as he was gone, I started shaking. I locked the door he'd gone through, dove down the basement stairs. The duffel bag, splayed open, disgorged books, mine and Barry's. I looked around, trying to fathom what the heavy object had been. The Cuisinart ice-cream maker, maybe, remembering how heavy its compressor made it. Hunter had lived with us when I bought it, knew how long I'd waited for the sale. He would have figured it had value in a pawnshop. I checked that the basement door was bolted. At least he hadn't left planning to sneak back and retrieve what I'd forbidden him to take.

Upstairs, rain streaked the window. Hunter was somewhere, clean from his shower, angry, recently fed and warmed, hurrying toward Half Price Books, where he could sell his volumes, treasured now not for their stories or emotional connections but for the ease with which they could be transfigured into heroin. I thought of him reading, ten years old, curled beneath the yellow light under a blanket.

Shut it out. Shut the door. Hunter is not that boy, I told myself. He is a desperate soul, a desperate man. This Hunter, always, again, was killing that one, scribbling over my memory of the reading boy like a black marker disfiguring a freshly painted wall.

The Climb

Hunter was on the street about a month after his disturbing visit. One evening in late spring, he showed up filthy at the door and asked Barry to help him get into medical detox. Only Hunter's coverage under Barry's health insurance made this possible, because medical detox (in which the detox process is managed by physicians and its symptoms eased with medication) happens in the hospital.

Hunter spent a week in Swedish Ballard Hospital, detoxing from opioids under medical supervision, between clean sheets, served three hot meals a day, cocooned from his own harshest symptoms. Just before discharge, he was given an injection of Vivitrol. One dose of Vivitrol blocks the effects of heroin and other opioids for a full month at a time. The FDA approved Vivitrol for opioid dependence in October 2010, less than a year before it was prescribed for Hunter.

"This feels like something really new," Barry said as he hung up the phone with Hunter's doctor. "Hunter agreed to Vivitrol. He chose it of his own free will. This seems like the most solid commitment to sobriety we've seen him make so far."[9]

Vivitrol was a powerful hedge against the risk that Hunter would relapse on opioids. The doctor put Vivitrol directly into Hunter's system with an intramuscular injection. There was no way he could sell the drug or share it with a friend. Each dose of Vivitrol prevented him from getting high for a full month, even if he wanted to. Hunter had failed abstinence and then failed Suboxone. Vivitrol offered Hunter a chance, at the age of nineteen, to begin rebuilding his life. Even college seemed possible.

In spite of Vivitrol's curtailing the risk of Hunter's relapse, the thought of his living at home again worried us gravely. We saw little other choice. We let him in, although we braced against his stealing. Barry and I slept with wallets under our pillows. Sawyer stashed his allowance in a secret compartment in his bedroom, and Lillie hid her piggy bank. I vowed never to let my purse leave my sight.

Sawyer and Lillie absorbed their brother's presence silently. Lillie, purposely busy, kept herself apart, rarely interacted. Sawyer let Hunter hang out with him, playing X-box, watching movies. After a few weeks, we gave Hunter a house key. Having him in the actual house again seemed unreal.

Hunter also asked to see a counselor, and together we located a woman within walking distance of our home. Hunter saw her weekly, and while he didn't tell Barry and me what they talked about, we took his initiating therapy and then getting himself there as good signs.

I quickly learned that even with insurance coverage, obtaining Vivitrol was far from simple. Hunter's April shot, administered in the hospital, had been straightforward. For subsequent months, an insurance representative explained, we would need prior authorization. Monthly, Hunter's addiction medicine physician was required to justify the prescription, then fax this paperwork to our insurance company. They assessed the doctor's reasons and decided Hunter met their coverage criteria (opioid use disorder diagnosis and having failed Suboxone), and then communicated this to the pharmacy. We paid our $200 copay, and the pharmacy dispensed the syringe. Hunter took this to his appointment, where the Vivitrol was administered.

I was extremely grateful Hunter had access to the drug, but coordinating and jumping through the hoops was exhausting. The first time, I arrived at our pharmacy to pick up the syringe. "Oh gosh, I'm so sorry, but we're out of stock of Vivitrol. Come back next Tuesday," the nice pharmacist who'd filled the kids' antibiotic prescriptions for the past fifteen years suggested.

"But Hunter sees his doctor TOMORROW," I wailed, completely losing my composure and bursting into tears. The sales clerk standing beside the pharmacist reached over the counter and handed me a tissue. "Okay, don't worry," the pharmacist soothed. "I'll call around. I heard they might have some at the store over in Ballard."

In May and again in June, Hunter got Vivitrol. Each time he took the shot, he became angry and morose for days. He snapped at all of us, especially Sawyer. He holed up in the family room, lights off, stretched on the couch under a blanket, unable even to distract himself by reading. The drug made him feel suicidal. Hunter had never mentioned suicide before, and he was not threatening it now, but hearing how Vivitrol made him feel alarmed us.

"I'm worried what's making him angry isn't Vivitrol's actual physical effect," Barry told me when Hunter was out of earshot. "I think he's mad that having it in his system means he can't get high for a full month, even if he decides he wants to. I think he's resentful. He has to keep choosing to take it, you know. He can refuse any month. We can't force him."

I really hoped Barry was wrong. The way I saw it, once the first hard days after the shot had passed, Hunter seemed miraculously better— mature, a loving son, communicative, on course for the first time in years. I leaned into the feeling, afraid it would give way, but that didn't happen. This change, the chance to know Hunter as a grown person, a dear young man, was heady. We spent real time together just talking. It was bliss.

One afternoon, as Hunter ground coffee and waited for the kettle to boil, I asked him hesitantly how he'd gotten by when he was living on the street. He shrugged slightly, as if he'd like to push the thought aside, then sighed. "Oh, Mom. Different things. I slept on friends' couches when I could find someone who'd let me. I stayed at a few shelters, but my bag was stolen at one of them, and I didn't like the way it felt to be in that room with all those other guys." He fell silent, then added, "I slept in the park a couple of times."

"In Maple Leaf Park?" I asked, thinking about the little covered area on the park's service building and the dank concrete bathroom building by the play equipment. There were many places at this familiar park half a block from our house where someone might sleep, I realized.

"Once. And at Wallingford Park, you know, by the Good Shepherd Center," he said, naming the capacious building the Catholic church had operated as a home for wayward girls decades ago, which now housed dozens of small nonprofit organizations and a preschool. Remnants of an old apple orchard surrounded the sprawling three-story facility and its cheerful playground designed around the theme of children's books.

"Wow. Did you think about all the times we played there when you were little? Do you remember all that—that fun we had all those years?" I wondered, feeling the start of tears.

"Of course, Mom," Hunter said, putting his arm around my shoulder. "Of course. I remember everything."

I found him bent over the Japanese box I used to store some of my makeup. He looked embarrassed. "What's up?" I asked.

"Do you think anything in here would work to cover up the marks?" Hunter wondered sheepishly.

"Marks? What do you mean?" I was confused.

"The track marks, Mom. The scars on my arms. I hate how they look. Dad told me they'll fade eventually, but I want something to cover them 'til then."

Hunter had almost no clothes when he returned to us. We shopped, not extravagantly, but enough to meet his immediate needs. He started applying for jobs online and picking up applications when he left the house. He wanted to look nice for interviews, he said.

"Can we get me some Doc Martens?" he asked. "Those are good walking shoes and they last forever." He was so changed, so mature sounding, so grounded. The shoes were expensive, but I bought them.

"Take care of these, Hunter," I told him.

"Oh, I will. Thank you, Mom."

In early June, Hunter surprised Barry by suggesting that he, Barry, and Sawyer climb Mt. Rainier. Doing so would require training sessions outdoors, something Hunter hadn't been willing to do for years. Barry loved little more than sharing nature with our children, and Hunter's childhood had been filled with outings like this. Barry now jumped at the chance to get Hunter and Sawyer out into the natural world again. The three of them began squeezing as many training sessions as they could fit into Barry's days off work.

In mid-June, as I was lining up the authorization for the July shot, Hunter complained again of the side effects. "I know you can take naltrexone as a pill, right?" Hunter asked Barry. "I hate the shot. It makes me feel like crap, way worse than like crap, actually. I want to go on the oral version instead of getting the shot." Hunter's doctor allowed that this would be acceptable as long as Hunter actually took the daily dose. Concerned about the suicidal feelings the injections had caused Hunter and happy with his continued improved behavior, but with misgivings, Barry and I agreed to the plan.

Hunter's job had not materialized. Catalogs for community college—a stepping-stone to a four-year school, we hoped—languished beside the sofa. I initiated discussions with Hunter on both issues, and when those went nowhere, I nagged. "Do you talk about this in therapy?" I asked him, feeling hopeless. "Because you should."

"Yeah, Mom, I do," he said. "I'm working on it."

Hunter started oral naltrexone. And one week later, Hunter's money requests slowly began again. There was always a reason: bus fare, getting his hair cut, a book, taking a girl to the movies. This last worked best on me. I wanted so much for Hunter to have a happy life, knew how he'd longed for a girlfriend in the past. Hunter knew this.

"He's asking me for money," I told Barry. "I don't want this to be what I worry it might be."

Barry shook his head. "Damn it," he said. He and the boys had trained for the climb twice that week, outings that had included breakfast on the road, a favorite tradition. "He's doing great with everything we're working on for the climb."

I knew this meant increasingly long hikes and practicing rope work. They were enjoying each other's company.

"This week, though, now that you mention it, Hunter had reasons he wanted to borrow twenty bucks after both of our training sessions," Barry said.

Nevertheless, the first weekend of July, Barry, Hunter, and Sawyer headed out for Mt. Rainier. Hunter was being pleasant but seeming insincere. Barry was extra cautious, keenly aware that he could lead the boys into a situation that would put all of them at risk. He tried to read the tea leaves: was Hunter in good shape? Could he be part of a dependable team, as he would have to be if the climb were to proceed safely?

At the campsite, Hunter offered to shave strips off a piece of firewood for kindling, something he'd done many times before. He borrowed Barry's Leatherman, and then he jammed the blade deeply into a piece of wood, twisting it sideways until the blade snapped at its hilt. Hunter was well aware that this was not how to get a knife out. He'd taken several years of wilderness awareness classes in our home-schooling days, and the long Outward Bound trip had required a daily use of camping knives. He understood good knife skills. Snapping the blade was a warning sign that his attention had wandered.

Barry was irritated. This was about much more than the loss of the Leatherman. Barry had taught all the kids outdoor skills on our long family trips and on wilderness outings he'd made with each kid individually. Hunter had always shown competence with tools and the outdoors, and Barry had valued that and felt it was part of Hunter becoming a man. Seeing that Hunter seemed to have lost this competence deeply concerned Barry, but he held his frustration back, not wanting to turn the climb into a fight.

The boys were drinking water nonstop, consuming much more than Barry had planned for. He melted so much snow for extra water that their stove fuel was nearly used up. Barry drank less than he usually did, less than he needed. They dug a platform for a tent at 11,000 feet, on the Cowlitz Glacier.

That night the boys relaxed and reveled in each other's company. Sawyer was as happy and animated as Barry had seen him in years. Sawyer—who of the four of us was in many ways most connected to Hunter—was finally relaxing, trusting that the real Hunter, the brother he knew, was back.

Barry awoke dehydrated and glum. In light of the knife incident, he felt unsure of Hunter's judgment. He worried that the boys still lacked the skills to tackle the climb—they'd had only one day of practicing how to self-arrest any possible fall using the ice axes they carried. To climb by their chosen route—Gibraltar Ledges—the three of them would need to be roped together and to either place anchoring devices in the snow as they went (a painfully slow process) or else plan to arrest any fall by quickly planting their ice axes into the steep snowy slope. A failed self-arrest could mean that all three of them plunged toward serious injury or death. Barry had known a man who'd died on that route several years before. Climbing is inherently dangerous, but the key to keeping the danger at a reasonable level is to know when to continue and when to turn back. Barry knew too much. He told the boys that it just wasn't safe to go up in this situation, and they came back down.

Lillie and I had spent the time Barry and the boys were gone washing our clothes and packing. The signs Hunter was giving off were ominous, and I was relieved that the special trip I'd planned for Lillie and me would give me ten days before I would have to directly deal with whatever happened next. We were spending half the trip in New York and the rest in DC.

"Good luck this week," I said, hugging Barry when he dropped Lillie and me at SeaTac Airport. "Let me know what goes on."

Jonah

The night was warmish cool, Seattle late July, and cloudless. Jonah and his friend Joseph and Joseph's girlfriend, Caitlyn, walked away from King County Detox in the Rainier Valley, gleefully crossing the bleak parking lot of that particular circle of hell. The boys were leaving against medical advice: in other words, before the evil hours of puking and shaking and detoxifying were upon them. Worse luck for both, they'd landed there together, more or less, acquaintances ripe to convince each other that this place was fucked, the whole idea of detox shitty anyway, and no one could keep them there, so they were fucking done.

Carried by Metro bus across Seattle, they hopped off on the Ave. Did they score there? Or had Caitlyn managed that beforehand? They split the drugs and, alone, Jonah headed west, toward Tamlin's house, rather than north toward home—where his parents and sister slept, thinking he was safe for the moment in detox, hoping that this respite would wean their boy off heroin and give him back to them.

(Hunter told me all of this. This is his version of that night's events—which he said he heard from Tamlin—colored, shaded, by my horror, repulsion, and antipathy.)

Tamlin's house was large, unlit, beautiful in its decrepitude if you appreciated decay. Tamlin's mother, Lana, was asleep but Tamlin had a new girlfriend and was entertaining her. She was so new, in fact, that when he heard Jonah's insistent tapping on the old oak door, Tamlin let him in without accepting Jonah's offer to split the bag Jonah carried in his pocket. The new girl knew nothing of Tamlin's heroin habit, and he was not prepared to raise the curtain on this aspect of himself, at least not yet.

There were no rules and few expectations in Lana's house. The kids came and went, hung out, got high, slept, woke, did it again. Lana and Tamlin's was the place these kids ended up when they'd sneaked out of their own houses, when they didn't want or weren't allowed to go home. Sometimes Lana would keep the kids from leaving the house when they were drunk or high—safer, she maybe thought. It was a lax house in many ways, but Lana, who had herself been raised by a heroin-addicted mother, was doing what she thought best, mothering in her own through-the-looking-glass fashion. The cops, called to the house from time to time by neighbors or for domestic disputes, knew Lana and Tamlin well.

When Jonah showed up, Tamlin shuttled him into one of the unused bedrooms, returned to the new girlfriend, settled in. At dawn, Jonah's room was still. Tamlin looked in, then he looked more closely. He must have known.

Tamlin went for Lana, woke her. "You have to look at Jonah," he begged. "Jonah got here late last night but now—you have to look at him." They called 911.

The ambulance arrived, sirens wailing, the fire trucks too, rescue workers crowding between overgrown fir trees, up the old front stairs, filling the dusty hallway and the unused room. Jonah was dead. Tamlin phoned Hunter, waking him here at home. "You've got to tell Kara, man," Tamlin said grimly. Kara, Jonah's girlfriend, a world of heartache and hope in her own sad story, away at summer school.

Why wasn't Hunter at Tamlin's that night? He easily could have been. This was a week after the Mt. Rainier climbing attempt, but for whatever reason Hunter had stayed at home.

"Lana and Tamlin told me they wished I had seen Jonah's body," Hunter told Barry tearfully. Lana, who did not use drugs herself but tolerated their use in everyone around her. Tamlin, who had used with Hunter many times. That these two felt Hunter's drug use so extreme that only seeing a friend's dead body might have stemmed it set a deeply troubling benchmark. Months later, Lana called Barry and me to describe a recent interaction she'd had with Hunter. Reminiscing, Lana said she and Tamlin always described Hunter as a "garbage-head," meaning completely opportunist in his drug consumption: he would take anything.

Lillie and I were in DC the night Jonah died and had seen *Wicked* at the Kennedy Center. Returning to the hotel, happy, I phoned Barry to touch base on how his day had gone. "Poor Hunter," Barry said, "got some hard news."

"Oh, no." I guessed. "Did someone die?"

"It's Jonah," Barry told me, "he overdosed and died at Tamlin's house sometime between late last night and this morning."

I pictured Jonah as I'd last seen him, waiting on the front porch of our house for Hunter to come home. That kid, the most relaxed and the least threatening of any friend of Hunter's in recent years, was dead.

It is not difficult to buy heroin in Seattle. A 2018 report on Seattle's KIRO television about the city's skyrocketing opioid crisis included an interviewee who said that if you walked along Third Avenue between Pike and Pine Streets downtown saying "black, black, black," someone would offer to sell you black tar heroin before you had gone more than a few feet. That one could easily score drugs on Broadway in the Capitol Hill neighborhood, and on the Ave in the U District, was general knowledge even when we moved to Seattle in 1993. Drugs are even more widely available here now.[10]

Barry put Hunter on the phone. "Oh, Hunter," I told him, "I am so sorry. I love you so much. This is just tragic." He sounded broken, caught up in something monumental. "It's not fair, Mom. He was such a good guy—funny and smart. It isn't fair."

"I'll never shoot heroin again," he promised Barry tearfully, but it didn't last. Barry told me that Hunter's shock wore off in forty-eight hours, and the surly edge crept back, hardened. "The cops are trying to pin the blame on someone," Hunter told me when Lillie and I got home, "but it was no one's fault."

I turned that over in my brain.

The week between Lillie's and my return from Washington and Jonah's memorial service is a blur to me. Something was wrong, maybe food poisoning, maybe a virus, washing over me, purging me, leaving me weak. My eyes hurt when I opened them, so I lay in bed wearing a sleep mask, half-listening to commentary on *Mad Men* DVDs, sleeping, cocooned, suspended. Hunter came and went, grieving.

Jonah's parents were mindful of how his death impacted his friends and tried to find some solace in the thought that lessons learned from this loss might save someone else. In the midst of planning Jonah's memorial, they gathered the tribe for an outdoor session with grief counselors and spray paint and a videographer who captured Jonah's friends' memories of him. They went public with the story of how he died, were interviewed with his girlfriend, Kara, on local television, talked to the newspapers.

I watched them mourn. I was excruciatingly aware that our positions were completely interchangeable. The difference between Hunter alive and Jonah dead was a whim of fate. The horror of Jonah's family's loss was searing. I sat with it, haunted and stunned.

I tried to see the physical implements of Jonah's death in their most abstract form, but it wasn't easy. I started research, learning, for the first time, these basic facts: Scottish physician Alexander Wood developed the hypodermic syringe in 1853. Syringe barrels were initially made of metal, but by 1866 they were made of glass, allowing the person preparing the injection to see the level of liquid remaining in the barrel. The opium poppy plant's Latin name is *Papaver somniferum*. To harvest opium, incisions are cut into the plant's seedpod. Milky white sap—the opium—oozes through the incisions. The sap dries in the sun, turning dark brown, and is then scraped off and in modern times transported to a laboratory, where it is refined into morphine. One hundred pounds of opium yields ten pounds of morphine. In 1874, British chemist C. R. Alder Wright discovered that when he boiled morphine with acetic anhydride, the process produced diacetylmorphine: heroin.

This time, research rendered things worse. Thinking about the invention of hypodermic needles and heroin made me feel desperate, powerless, as if a giant wave were just about to crash down, inundating everything I cared for. I felt as if that nineteenth-century medical breakthrough had swollen into an ocean of opioids, a flood of death and sorrow. Jonah's tragic demise, enormous as it was to those who loved him, was just one drop of this insidious rising tide.

"Jonah and Hunter are middle-class kids from caring families," I railed, as Barry did the dishes. "I've never used any drug, not even pot as a teenager in the 70s, not coke in college, and you know how many people were into that. You don't use drugs. Jonah's parents probably don't, because Hunter says they're active in their church. And yet these boys stick needles in their arms?"

Barry explained that the upsurge in middle-class heroin use seemed to have started when OxyContin was recently reformulated to make it harder to abuse by ensuring that it can't easily be pulverized and snorted. Many people who were addicted to OxyContin were apparently switching to heroin. Heroin was easy to come by and inexpensive.

"What happens when someone overdoses on heroin and dies?" I asked him the next morning. I was still trying to come to terms with what had happened, to calm my imagination by forming a true picture.

Barry explained that opioid overdose kills by repressing the respiratory drive. Breathing doesn't usually stop completely, but it slows to three or four breaths a minute instead of the minimum of twelve for someone at rest or asleep, so that oxygen levels in the blood fall to a very low level. This causes anaerobic metabolism in the tissues, which increases lactic acid. Reduced respirations also cause buildup of carbon dioxide, which in the blood acts as a weak acid. High carbon dioxide is what drives respiration in a normal person.

"When you hold your breath and your lungs feel like they're bursting, that's not because of lack of oxygen," Barry concluded. "It's because of high carbon dioxide. The overdosed person's carbon dioxide rises, but he feels no distress. His breathing stays really slow. Eventually, the acid buildup starts to interfere with the function of the diaphragm muscle. The slow respirations become weak. Breathing stops first, then the heart."

Jonah's parents asked Hunter and Jess to help them pack his things and clean out his room. Hunter was not sure why. Maybe they thought the chaos there would send some message to the living boys. Maybe they wanted the chance to talk to Hunter and Jess about their risky paths. Maybe they just needed the moral support from Jonah's close friends to face dismantling their son's most personal environment.

Take what you want, they told the boys, and Hunter brought home a bag of Jonah's flannel shirts and a denim jacket.

At our urging, Hunter wore a suit on the bright Saturday a few days later, when Jonah's friends and family gathered to memorialize his brief life in the auditorium of one of the several high schools he'd attended. Barry and I found seats halfway back from the stage, looked around to see whether any of Hunter's friends' parents had shown up. "We aren't the only parents here who know their kid's on thin ice," I whispered to Barry.

Teenagers comprised the largest group of mourners, along with puzzled families who'd known Jonah as a little boy, before he went astray. No one who knew the young Jonah could match up the carpool buddy, the jokester elementary school classmate they remembered, with the trajectory of the dead young man.

"I haven't seen him in a long time—since junior high," one childhood friend recalled. "But I remember him as being so great, so funny, such a great, great guy." There was an open microphone, and kids streamed past it, fighting for self-control or giving way to tears. Neither Hunter nor Jess joined the memorializing. I couldn't see their faces but watched the back of their heads a few rows in front of where Barry and I sat, paralyzed, clutching each other's hands. Jonah's little sister eulogized him beautifully, heartbreakingly, held up by two friends.

Jonah's family screened a public service announcement reiterating the state's 911 Good Samaritan law, which promises protection from prosecution to anyone calling in a suspected overdose, and no prosecution of the victim if he or she survives. Mourners then watched the slow extended video that had been shot in Jonah's bedroom and at the outdoor wake.

Tamlin was long gone by the time of Jonah's memorial. Lana, justly panicked in the hours following their discovery of Jonah's body, had spirited him into a neighboring county's detox unit, and then, mortgaging her house to raise the funds, into a six-month rehab program out of state. He was the last person who'd seen Jonah alive.

"Won't the police want to question Tamlin?" I asked Hunter. "Is he even allowed to leave? How can they investigate if Tamlin is out of state?"

"I don't think they want to ask him anything more than they've already asked," Hunter said. "The 911 cops pretty much blamed Lana. They told her that if she hadn't run such a loose house, if she'd had better discipline, this never would have happened."

We three drove home after the memorial service, spent. As our car neared the house, Hunter grew tense. As soon as we were inside, he descended to his basement room, changed clothes, and then strode to the open front door.

"Don't you think you should stay here?" Barry said.

"Hunter, please rest—please stay. Haven't you been clean since Jonah died, isn't this better?" I begged.

"I'm going," Hunter said.

"We will drug test you when you come back," Barry told him.

"Then I won't come back," Hunter replied.

I had the chance to hug him, to reach on tiptoe and kiss his head. I'd kissed him on his head since babyhood, though seldom lately. I had always told him that a mother's kisses were magical, that they sank into the just-kissed child, becoming part of that child forever. I hoped there were enough of my kisses in Hunter to comfort him, that I had imbued him on some level with something beautiful and pure and freely given.

I don't remember more about this leave-taking—part of the coping strategy that I was slowly learning was to let the pain of the moment flow through me and out, not to dwell there. This sometimes worked, but at the cost of memory. Enough to know he left, taking the ever-present backpack, long sleeves hiding his track marks, fading into the summer sunlight.

We realized later that while he was living with us, most likely just before and after the Mt. Rainier climb, Hunter had sold his bass guitar and amp, as well as many of our possessions. At the time, though, we had not perceived that things were disappearing. He took CDs from drawers we rarely opened. A battered violin no one had learned to play and that had been stored in a basement cupboard. Tools that were only missed when they were needed, months, maybe years, after they disappeared. And Barry's climbing gear, used on the Mt. Rainier attempt with Hunter and Sawyer. Gone.

The Passport

"Mom, this is Hunter," he said when I answered, his voice tightly cheerful. "I haven't seen you for a while and I miss you and I was wondering if you'd be willing to meet up and buy me a cup of coffee?"

It was early November. My day had been jam-packed: a phone interview with a Portland radio station about the book, a noon presentation about the fair at the Broadview Public Library. It had been nearly a month since we had seen each other. I'd bought him a burger that time, and then a toothbrush and nail clippers. "Okay, Hunter," I said, "I'll be there in a few minutes."

I drove rather than walked the few blocks to Cloud City Coffee, feeling lazy about it. Sawyer had gotten a job busing tables there when he was fifteen. I don't think he's working today, I thought to myself as I pulled in. I could see Hunter, jumpy-looking, sitting outside the restaurant, clutching the bike he'd usually had with him during recent encounters. I wondered, again, whether it was stolen, or whether this transportation meant he was a courier for some dealer.

We filled our cups at the honor bar, added cream, went back outside. Hunter made small talk, seeming scattered: how was I, how was my work going, how were Barry, Sawyer, Lillie. He barely drank his coffee, refused my offer of something to eat. I noticed a spray of tiny specks of dried blood on his dirty khakis. Held my tongue.

"Hey, ah, I actually just remembered that I need to be somewhere really soon, could you maybe drive me to the U District?" Hunter asked.

"What about your bike?"

"Oh, yeah, ah, um, let's put it in your car, it will fit, I think it will fit," he answered, rolling the bicycle toward my old Saab. As soon as I unlocked the doors, he began pushing—shoving—the bike into the small back seat. I flinched as a grease streak stained the already dodgy tan cloth upholstery.

"Hunter, please be careful!"

One last push, door slammed, and we climbed into the front seats. "Oh, ah, I meant to tell you, I really need my passport, Mom. I lost my ID card, I have no ID, I can't buy cigarettes or anything. I've got to have it."

Many thoughts flashed through my mind: No ID means no one will be able to identify his body if he overdoses. He is an adult and the passport is legally his. If he loses it (when he loses it), someone will sell it, steal his identity. Or maybe he knows how valuable United States passports are and wants to sell it himself? Having that passport in the strongbox means I know he cannot leave the country, cross a border. If I stop at the house to get the passport, he will ask to come in, and he will follow me and see where I hide the strongbox. Or I will have to leave him unwatched, and who knows what he could steal in the time it takes me.

I paused. "Okay, Hunter, I guess I can do that. You know you need to take really good care of it, right?"

"Of course," Hunter replied.

I pulled onto our street, parked in front of the house. Thinking quickly, I suggested he stay in the car. "It will be faster that way."

"Okay," he said.

I grabbed my purse, my keys, let myself in, unearthed the strongbox. A green rubber band held our five passports together, Hunter's in the middle. I should at least copy this, I thought, and splayed it quickly on the printer-copier, taking an image of the picture page. I noticed that the emergency contact line was blank, so added my name and phone number. There, I thought. If someone uses this to identify him, they will call me, we will know. I locked the front door, took the stairs quickly, and was back behind the wheel. I'd been gone five minutes, no more.

Hunter had opened the glove compartment and was trimming his fingernails with the clippers he knew I kept there. "Thanks, Mom," he said as I handed him the passport.

We drove toward the U District, mostly silent, me thinking about the passport. Our family trip to London had prompted Hunter's first passport. He had been nine years old. We'd spent two weeks in a flat near Tower Bridge, eaten British chocolate bars in tube stations, explored Hamleys toy store, tramped through unfamiliar neighborhoods looking for a fencing gear outlet. The three kids played fierce puppy in the grass across from Buckingham Palace. It was so long ago, another lifetime.

"This is fine," Hunter said quickly, suddenly, "pull over, this is fine."

"Okay, hang on," I answered, looking for a clear spot at the curb.

"Thanks, Mom, thanks for the coffee. I'll talk to you later," Hunter said, wrestling his bike out of the small back seat.

"Okay," I offered, "bye, I love you." He jumped onto the bike, pedaled away rapidly.

I took a moment to gather myself, turning to see what further damage the bike had done to my poor upholstery. As I glanced back, my eyes locked on the small well between the front seats, the place I kept my ten or twelve favorite CDs, the ones that had helped me through the awful months when driving was the best time to listen, cry, scream. *The Essential Leonard Cohen*, the *Garden State* soundtrack, *Spring Awakening*. *Cobblestone Runway* by Ron Sexsmith. Jacqueline du Pré's haunting rendition of Bach's Cello Suite no. 1 in G. *I'm Alive* by Jackson Browne, Townes Van Zandt's *A Far Cry from Dead*. Jakob Dylan's *Women and Country*, Cowboy Junkies' *Lay It Down*. The well gaped back at me, empty. The compact discs were gone.

"Goddamn it," I screamed aloud. "Damn you, Hunter!" I threw the car in gear, roared off in the direction Hunter had just ridden. My gaze whipped back and forth, scanning each face. He might have sold them at that horrible place he'd pointed out to me, the place you could always get used music and electronics. I parked, purchased a parking sticker, my hands shaking as I keyed in the information. Rushing into the dark cavelike shop, I pushed quickly to the counter. Two thin, bored kids lounged behind the register, both chill, neither much interested in me.

"Excuse me, but did you just a few minutes ago buy about ten CDs from a guy with brown hair, about six feet, wearing an orange T-shirt? Just a minute ago?"

"Um, no," one of them answered.

"Well, when you buy do you take ID?"

"Yeah," the other said.

"Did you just buy from someone who used a passport as ID?" I plunged on intensely.

"No, we didn't. We haven't bought all day, we aren't buying today because we don't have cash for that right now."

I turned, rushed from the store, stood on the Ave completely flustered, looking up and down the street.

And then I saw him. He was coming out of a door in a nondescript building, one of those doors that leads to stairs for the upper floors above the retail area. I saw him lean to unlock his bike, and I sprinted across traffic and down the sidewalk. Before he'd looked up from the lock, I was there. I grabbed the handlebars, held on hard.

"Hunter, what did you do with them?" I said loudly.

"I don't know what you mean," he said, the bike unlocked. He straightened.

"My CDs, you took my CDs from the car, what did you do with them?"

"I did not take your CDs from your car," he said coolly.

"Hunter, you did. They were there when I drove to the coffee place, and I think they were there when I drove you down here. Did you grab them as you were taking your bike out? Or did you take them when I was in the house?"

"Mom, I didn't take your CDs, and I have to go now," he said firmly, trying to make a stand. He began pulling the bike away from me, steadily. I gripped the handlebars more tightly. "Let go," he said. "Let go!"

I raised my voice. "I won't until you tell me what you did with the CDs you stole from my car."

A woman passing us looked at me briefly, at Hunter, walked on. I noticed a police officer about a block away. "Hunter, should I call for that cop? Should I get him involved?"

"I didn't take anything," Hunter repeated stubbornly but softly.

"Do you think I'm an idiot?" I asked him. "A total idiot, because obviously I am some kind of idiot, I trusted you enough to put you in my car! I never guessed you'd steal from right under my nose. They were in the fucking car, Hunter, where are they? I just want them back! What did you do with the CDs you stole? I already checked the place across the street, and they aren't buying. Are they in your backpack? Are they in your pockets?"

More people were noticing. The sidewalk was crowded, the Ave was always busy. Hunter tried to wrench the bike away, but I held on. "WHERE DID YOU SELL THEM?" I shouted.

"Okay! Okay. I took them to that place right under the Neptune Theater, in the basement."

The Neptune was half a block from where he'd had me drop him off. He'd sold those CDs almost before I realized they were gone.

I grasped the bike for a few more seconds, coursing with adrenalin, furious. Hunter looked aside, refusing to meet my glare. "We are done," I shouted. "Hunter, we are done. I'm finished. I don't want you in my life anymore."

I released the handlebars, turned my back, walked quickly to the car. Shaking, I drove the few blocks to the Neptune and found the dark stairwell leading to the basement. Used Records and CDs, the small sign read.

The man behind the counter was my age, maybe a few years older. Holding back tears, I said, "Excuse me, but did you just buy about ten CDs from a guy who was about six feet tall, brown hair, orange T-shirt, who used a passport for identification?"

"Yes, I did," the man replied.

"That was my son. He is addicted to heroin. I was giving him a ride, and he stole those CDs right out from under me. I just want them back. I'll pay whatever you are charging. Do you still have them together?"

"I thought there was something fishy about that kid, but he didn't look quite the type I watch for, the people who try to sell stolen goods. I'm sorry about your son," he added. "I do have them still together."

Reaching into a box behind the counter, the man retrieved the handful of familiar discs.

"You can just pay me what I gave him for them," he said, "and that's fifteen bucks."

"That's so, so kind," I said. "This whole thing has been horrible, but it makes me feel a tiny bit better, getting them back." I paid him, gathered my music, and moved toward the door.

"I'm sorry about your son," he said again. "These things . . . are hard."

"They are," I agreed. "Thank you. Thank you for knowing that."

I was exhausted, demoralized, but also somehow elated. I had them back. Hunter had taken something, he had taken everything: my trust, my understanding of what it meant to be a parent, my faith in what love could stretch and rip and pull to include, to cover. He had taken so much of my happiness over the past years, he had taken my innocence, taken my peace of mind, taken my joy. Taken my hope for his future.

But he had also taken this small handful of my compact discs. He had taken them from me. And I had gotten them back.

Flying East

By late November 2011, Hunter had been living on the street for more than four months. We didn't know how Hunter supported his addiction, and we didn't ask. Barry met with him sometimes when he called, buying him a meal, unwilling to forgo these brief chances to see him.

I sometimes saw Hunter from the car—sitting at bus stops, walking down the Ave. Something had broken in me after he'd stolen the CDs from my car, but something else had started growing: a core of self-preservation, the strength I needed to finally climb toward some sort of inner peace and grace, regardless of anything to do with Hunter. Still, I was always aware that I should memorize each glimpse, in case it proved to be the last time I saw him.

The 1962 Seattle World's Fair book had launched, as scheduled, on October 21, the forty-ninth anniversary of the fair's closing day. Because the Seattle Center Foundation, which had commissioned the project, wanted to maximize the book's impact, my coauthor, Alan, and I agreed to promote the fair's history throughout the anniversary celebration, which spanned an entire year.

And so, as autumn lengthened, Alan and I began to speak at bookstores throughout King, Pierce, and Snohomish counties and to give the visual presentation we'd developed at libraries, historical societies, and private venues across the state. We had at least one presentation every week but usually three or four, including television and radio interviews. Barry and I juggled his work shifts, all my events, but especially those requiring travel, Sawyer's and Lillie's school happenings, Sawyer's counseling appointments, and Lillie's lessons and *Nutcracker* rehearsals. Hunter weighed heavily on my mind through all of this.

Barry met Hunter at Starbucks one rainy night. Hunter was huddled in a chair, his phone charger plugged in nearby. Barry bought him coffee and food, talked briefly—there was little to say once he'd reported family matters. The conversation was one way—Hunter could share nothing. It was painful to see him filthy, as well as clearly miserable and almost certainly high.

Heroin users describe the drug's effect as being akin to pulling up a warm blanket. The opioid, for a little while, renders them numb to the world. Their pain is still present, but they do not feel it. Each user has his or her own story—of course they do—but there is something larger, I think now, that is driving people of all ages and backgrounds to sacrifice all other aspects of their lives to be that kind of numb. What is the pain, the wound, in the larger sense?

I wondered, sometimes, whether one of the wounds festering in Hunter's generation was 9/11, an event that Hunter experienced at the age of nine. Those horrific images, the planes plunging so purposefully, so remorselessly into their targets, played on America's television sets in endless loops. We did not have television, sparing Hunter, for a little while, from having that brutality thrust upon him. I recalled unrolling the *New York Times* on September 12, the front-page picture of people falling and jumping off the Twin Towers, and instinctively hiding the photograph from Hunter, who was working on math nearby. Over the next months, I read victims' obituaries in the paper's "Portraits of Grief," tears rolling silently down my cheeks. The children understood in a broad sense, and we discussed sometimes, why I cried this way, daily. Maybe, exposed to so much death suddenly at such an age, Hunter's generation feels that reality more than most?

Heroin use among Hunter's peers was on my mind, but I was beginning to understand that opioids respected no boundaries. Seattle, famously liberal, leans toward harm-reduction strategies for people with addiction rather than punitive measures. The overriding sentiment is that our opioid problem is so extensive that arresting our way out of it is impossible. Police here carry the mandate to help users and arrest dealers. Users are offered treatment, although the need for beds overwhelms the county's capacity.

Because I spotted Hunter several times sitting on a particular corner in the U District with the bike beside him, I thought he might be delivering drugs. I knew that if this were true, he might end up in jail. I started scanning the King County Jail Inmate Lookup website nearly daily, hoping to find his name. In jail, Hunter might be safer than on the street, I reasoned. I worried most of all that he would overdose.

As the Seattle weather worsened, Hunter grew despondent. Some nights, he would appear on our doorstep late at night, always so late that Lillie and Sawyer were asleep. Wet, cold, unwashed, still on drugs, he'd beg to be let in, but we'd refuse. We could not open ourselves or Sawyer or Lillie to living inside the world that came with his addiction.

One night, Barry met Hunter at a pizza parlor, driving through forty-degree temperatures and heavy rain. They ate silently, and after dinner, in the car, Hunter began sobbing uncontrollably. A few minutes later, he fell asleep.

Barry drove home, parking the van in front of the house. He folded down the rear seat and removed the middle ones, clearing a space large enough to sleep in, barely. Hunter slept on as Barry brought out sleeping bags, Thermarests, and pillows. Stretching the gear in the cramped space, Barry rolled Hunter into the down bag. The two slept side by side until dawn.

Hunter asked to go through medical detox again, but there were no beds. We waited for a bed to open, Hunter spending two more nights in the van. The following afternoon, Hunter went back to Swedish Ballard Hospital's detox unit.

It was the Monday of Thanksgiving week. We knew Hunter would probably be released on Saturday. We knew going through detox would be useless unless Hunter had more time in a rehabilitation facility —more time to remain drug free in a supportive environment without the streets' temptations, more time to think about his life. Hunter agreed to this. "But no 12-Step," he told Barry. "Please. I hate the Higher Power stuff. It really doesn't help."

We were back in the confusing swirl of trying to figure out where to send him, how to afford it, playing catch-as-catch-can, aware that Hunter's life might hang on this decision. "Remind me how much we now have in savings," Barry asked me as he sifted through rehab websites. I paid the bills and had been trying to skim something from household expenses every month to replenish the emergency fund we'd drained to send Hunter to Pacific Recovery the year before.

"Maybe $3,500?" I said, knowing there was not likely to be much more.

On Wednesday morning, my mother called. "I hope you don't mind, but I've been looking at rehab places on the web, and I think I've found one. Wouldn't that be a miracle? It's near Des Moines, Iowa, and they don't use 12-Step."

"I cannot believe this place exists," Barry said after reading through everything. "It sounds like exactly what we're looking for." It did feel like divine intervention.

Instead of 12-Step, the Iowa program relied on a mix of behavior modification training, cognitive behavior and cognitive skills training, and life skills exercises. More amazing still, they promised to take clients back for no additional fee if, after finishing the six-week program, they stayed in touch with a counselor but still relapsed. We hoped we wouldn't have to use this guarantee.

An intake coordinator took insurance details over the phone, promising to check our benefits and call back within the hour, which he did. Barry found me in the kitchen mixing pumpkin pie filling when the return call ended. "This is really incredible," he said. "There's a nonrefundable $3,000 bed reservation fee due up front, but they say our insurance will cover everything else." He shook his head. "Can you believe that?"

We picked Hunter up from the medical detox unit at Swedish on a cold Saturday morning. He looked horrible, sick to his stomach, with greenish skin. He looked like what he wanted—other than his drug of choice—was to crawl deep inside the warmest bed in the darkest room imaginable. Instead, he signed release papers and climbed—surly—into the van.

He had a backpack but only a light jacket. He wore black Converse high-top sneakers, more rips than canvas, the Doc Martens apparently long gone.

"You need a coat, Hunter, Iowa is cold. And you need boots," Barry told him.

Hunter said nothing.

We drove to the used sports equipment store where Barry had found climbing and ski gear in the past.

Hunter flinched a little when the car pulled up but went inside with Barry. They came out quickly—there was nothing suitable. Barry later told me the salesperson had recognized Hunter and looked surprised. It wasn't until months later, when Barry was packing for a climbing trip and discovered his own gear was missing, that he understood the salesperson's confusion: in the brief period between the Mt. Rainier climb and Jonah's memorial service, this store was where Hunter had sold the stolen gear.

Time was running out before the flight was due to leave, so we drove to REI. The three of us pawed through expensive jackets, looking for bargains that would keep Hunter warm. I held up an overstuffed down coat.

"No," Hunter said, "that's like the coat I wore and slept in when I was on the street. I don't want a big-assed homeless coat."

As much as I resented Hunter's pickiness, I had to give a mental nod to his word choice: "big-assed homeless coat" might indeed describe what I had bought at the thrift stores, what I'd seen him and many other apparently homeless people wrapped in. Could the disdain Hunter now expressed toward these coats be a sign of progress? I wondered.

Eventually, we found a warm black Thinsulate number that begged to have a lift ticket dangling from the zipper. To see Hunter looking as if he should be heading down a black diamond run was bittersweet.

We drove to SeaTac Airport, and I hugged them both goodbye. The prospect of Seattle without the pervasive stress of Hunter's drug use, of his homelessness, was comforting. How can I love someone so much but feel such great relief when they are distant, I asked myself. My heart felt safer, somehow.

Barry and Hunter flew to Des Moines, spent the night in a hotel, found boots at Wal-Mart, then drove to a tiny town where Hunter entered the detox portion of treatment. After those first days, Hunter was moved to the residential unit to start the program.

Unlike Pacific Recovery, there were no weekly phone reports. This was just as well. We were so weary that we needed rest more than re-assurance. And we knew better now that this was Hunter's work. That unless he was working harder at his sobriety than all of us who loved him, no program anywhere would help.

Market Street

With Hunter far from Seattle, I tried to leave survival mode behind, to focus on the present, and to process the reality of what we'd been through. Hunter's drama unfolded across neighborhoods I navigated constantly, every place layered with happy recollections that our recent past had steadily defaced. Hunter's absence halted this toxic leaching of my memories. Distance also meant that he could not materialize at the front door. The question, then, of where he'd live after his time in Iowa was pressing.

On January 13, 2012, a Friday, Hunter was discharged. Barry flew to Iowa, interrupting a new leadership position at work that he'd only had for a week, with the goal of helping Hunter settle. We understood that sustained behavior changes take longer than the six weeks he had spent in rehab, and we felt adamant that he should be, now, someplace new. Living with us during his attempts on Suboxone and naltrexone had not helped Hunter and had destabilized the rest of us. We knew his presence in our house put us at risk and that our house offered him too many temptations. So did Seattle, for that matter. We doubted Hunter would stay clean in a place that was so saturated with unhealthy associates and associations.

Hunter had told us on the phone that he wanted to live in St. Louis, where someone he'd met in rehab lived; the two thought they could room together, eventually, at least. Meanwhile he would try to find an Oxford House recovery home in St. Louis.

Oxford House is a well-reputed network of chartered, democratically run, self-supporting, drug-free homes in the United States and Canada. Each house is single gender.[11] Oxford Houses have strict admittance and maintenance criteria. Demand for Oxford Houses generally far outstrips supply. When vacancies do open up, Oxford House residents interview and vote on which applicant to accept. Houses typically choose the applicant they deem to have the best hope of success: someone with a job and good social support.

When Barry arrived in Iowa, Hunter had done no research. Passiveness toward self-care and even basic planning had been part of Hunter's problem since he had fallen into the drug scene. Was he so passive because of some damage drugs had done to his brain? We knew that substance abuse changes the reward center of the abuser's brain and alters their ability to process information and to make positive choices, but we did not know to what extent, if any, this had happened to Hunter.

We also acknowledged the possibility that, while Hunter had chosen to go through medical detox and agreed to follow that with rehab, he might not yet be able to exert the effort continued recovery would demand, or even want to live without heroin. Hitting bottom, in theory, can push a person with addiction past the point of tolerating the brutal life that often accompanies the high they crave. Had Hunter reached this point? Barry and I couldn't know.

We felt that both rehab programs had confronted Hunter with the reality that maintaining sobriety required him to take responsibility for his actions. The dialogue in which Pacific Recovery had engaged Hunter had not sunk in. After six weeks in the Iowa program, Hunter's lack of research on the Oxford House situation was a chilling sign. Barry and I grimly considered this probable evidence that Iowa's lessons had been no better absorbed.

Temperatures in Iowa hovered in the single digits. Barry phoned me as he warmed the car while Hunter was saying his goodbyes. "Hunter has made no advance connections at all with Oxford Houses in St. Louis," he said, beleaguered.

"Shit." My natural impulse was to jump in with both feet, try and fix this, start to direct the situation, but I held back. Barry was boots on the ground with Hunter. How to proceed would have to be his call.

Having no better plan and having already purchased his own return ticket from St. Louis, Barry decided to press on. He and Hunter made it as far as Hannibal, Missouri, where they huddled in a cheap motel that lacked a working heater. They reached St. Louis before noon the next day. Using Barry's laptop and a coffee shop's Wi-Fi, they looked up phone numbers of Oxford Houses with vacancies. There were few. Almost no one answered Hunter's calls, but he left several messages. One of the houses set an interview with him for seven-thirty the following morning.

That night, Barry and Hunter watched *The Girl with the Dragon Tattoo* at a mall theater. Barry later told me he was happy that they could still watch a movie together and discuss it afterward.

In the morning, Barry found Hunter almost impossible to awaken. They arrived at the Oxford House appointment just in time, driving through the downtrodden neighborhood, searching for the correct address. Hunter entered the run-down house but came out again immediately. He'd misheard the interview time, he told Barry. The real time had been seven a.m., and two other men had shown up then. One of them would get the available room.

Barry and Hunter spent the rest of the day driving through St. Louis locating all the Oxford Houses where Hunter had left messages. No one had yet returned the calls, and Barry's plane back to Seattle was to depart at four p.m.

"Why don't you pay for a hotel room for me for a week? I could keep looking for an Oxford House, and maybe someone will call back," Hunter suggested.

"I don't think that would be a good idea," Barry said. "Maybe St. Louis isn't the best place for you to be—what about Oxford Houses in the West, closer to areas you're at least familiar with?"

Barry was desperate. He had no choice but to fly home or risk his job. Leaving Hunter in a hotel in St. Louis, where he knew no one but the kid he'd met in rehab, who was now incommunicado, would have been madness. Crazier even than the situation they were in.

They looked online for Oxford Houses in New Mexico, where we'd spent some time during Hunter's childhood, but found few. There were youth hostels in Santa Fe and Albuquerque. Barry called the Santa Fe hostel, which had an open-ended plan, and explained the situation. The hostel owner said Hunter could stay. It was a temporary solution to a problem that had no good answers, no clear escape route, but it was a tiny immediate plan, a compromise, that allowed Barry to feel he could fly back to Seattle: Hunter would end up in a facility that had agreed to take him, in a town that was at least familiar to him and to us.

Barry drove Hunter to the St. Louis train station and bought him a ticket to Santa Fe. They ate lunch. Barry had almost no time to make it to the airport but couldn't bring himself to cut the meal short. "I felt strongly that it might be the last meal Hunter and I ever shared," Barry told me at home that night. "It was this horrible sensation of dread, a sort of premonition. We finished eating. Hunter walked out of the station and we hugged goodbye, and I just totally lost composure—I started crying and I couldn't stop. Hunter told me not to worry, and I turned away and walked three or four long blocks along the empty sidewalk under the interstate, back to the car, just sobbing uncontrollably. I felt sure that I would never see Hunter alive again."

I understood that sensation well—I felt that way each time Hunter and I said goodbye. Over the years, I'd learned to live with this feeling. I felt even a little grateful for it, in a twisted way. I knew it made me notice that moment with Hunter, deeply take in even the terrible partings, honor all those last connections. Someday, I knew, a parting would indeed be the last one, either because of his death or my own.

The Amtrak train took twenty-four hours to travel between St. Louis and Santa Fe. We waited for confirmation of his arrival, braced, as always, for bad news.

I thought of Hunter on the train, remembering how he'd loved trains as a little boy. We'd visited train museums, ridden on vintage trains, studied old locomotives. Camping in New Mexico when Hunter was five and Sawyer two, we'd happened upon the tiny town of Madrid, halfway between Albuquerque and Santa Fe on the Turquoise Trail. An Atchison, Topeka & Santa Fe locomotive near the Madrid Old Coal Town Museum fascinated Hunter. He'd spent an hour in the locomotive's cab in the blazing heat, passionately imagining himself as the engineer, his agile little mind propelling him on to further adventures.

Now, at two weeks shy of twenty, Hunter seemed dispassionate and far from engineering anything. He was passive, a passenger, his train something Barry had put him on in desperation.

He called from Santa Fe. The trip had been uneventful. He'd walked from the station. He had a private room at the hostel. He planned to get some sleep.

"I walked around Santa Fe," Hunter reported the next day. "It feels familiar, for sure, but I don't recognize anything specific. I sat by that streambed that goes through downtown. Do you know what I'm talking about?"

"Sure, that's the Santa Fe River channel," I said. "It flows out of the Rio Grande, the one we swam in on that trip when you were eight."

"Santa Fe River," Hunter snorted, "that is hilarious. It's barely a trickle."

Two days later, he said, "This place is okay, but I don't feel at home here." He didn't want to look for work or even stay at the youth hostel.

Barry and I scrambled for some other place to park him, somewhere safe and settled and well away from Seattle, where the eventual failure of his recovery seemed a given. We searched the internet for solutions in New Mexico—volunteer farm work? Helping at a monastery? Hunter seemed clueless, paralyzed. Once again, we were doing the work.

Should we have left Hunter to his own devices? Let him really and truly succeed in recovery—or fail—without our support of any kind? That was parental cold turkey, and we were not ready for that. Hunter had been through rehab, and, as far as we knew, he was not now using drugs. He sounded anxious and unsettled but clear, not jittery or evasive.

We were trying to be a bridge Hunter could traverse into a post-addiction life, not be his crutch. We understood intellectually that he needed to make choices, do things for himself, but he *wasn't*. This living paradox was unsustainable, but we felt locked into it, balanced on a knife edge with this beloved, maddening, no-longer-child we wanted desperately to help but had no way to understand. Addiction had rendered him our personal Zen koan. Our responses could be no more linear than his questions.

"I think I'd like to check out Albuquerque," Hunter offered. Okay, Barry and I thought, glad he'd come up with any next move at all. A short bus ride took him there, and he checked into a cheap motel, calling us from the front desk so that we could give the bored young clerk a credit card number. Hunter had spent the forty dollars Barry had given him in St. Louis to cover food and asked for more money. Uncomfortable at doing so, again we compromised.

"Okay, Hunter," Barry told him. "There's a Walgreens down the road from your hotel on Central Avenue that handles wire transfers. I'm going to send you fifty bucks for food. Make it last."

Albuquerque was a place Hunter had been many times when we visited our friend Lauren. Lauren had known Barry and me since college and remained one of my best friends. She had absorbed my agony through many phone conversations as Hunter's life went wrong. She was generous of spirit but extremely savvy. Unplayable. Lauren's work with troubled kids gave her deep connections to social services agencies. She might be able to help Hunter settle and gain traction in Albuquerque—if he stayed.

When Lauren picked him up at the motel, she was surprised at how calm Hunter seemed, how easily he settled into conversation with her. "He's really smart," she told me on the phone that night. "We talked a lot about what he might want to do, and, as you know, he has no clue what that might be. That makes it hard. I could help him try and get services, maybe get a job. I could even imagine him using my house as a sort of base. But he says he isn't sure he wants to stay here. I asked him where he wants to go, but . . . well, you know, he doesn't know."

Into this impasse, to our immense relief, Barry's brother, Colin, an attorney and near professional surfer, and Colin's wife, Susan, an obstetrician-gynecologist, suddenly offered that Hunter could live with them as a paying guest. Hunter agreed to this plan.

Hunter had never held a job, but Colin was eager to help him find one. Until he did, Barry and I would foot the bill for Hunter's keep. On the assumption that regular exercise would help build healthy habits, organize Hunter's thoughts, and occupy some of his time each day, Colin wanted Hunter to have a gym membership. Barry told Colin we'd cover this cost.

"That gym membership is pricy," I complained to Barry after he'd gotten off the phone with Colin. "And he really wants us to pay rent for Hunter?" I tried to picture our family situations reversed. It was hard to imagine Barry charging one of his siblings for food expenses and Seattle's going housing rate if we ever took in one of their kids. Charging the niece or nephew some sort of rent directly, perhaps.

"You know, Paula, there's no one else volunteering here," Barry reminded me. "If we want Hunter under their roof, we pretty much have to go with their terms."

Colin had been Barry's and my fiercest critic during Hunter's tumble into addiction. He was relentless, opinionated about what we were doing wrong. His voice blistered us through the phone line. We were not doing nearly enough, not nearly, he made us know. Hunter was sneaking out of his basement bedroom—we couldn't sleep in front of the door every night? "Move Sawyer down there," he shouted. Find the biggest key and lock Hunter in. "You let him get away," he told me once, harshly, and I dropped the phone, screaming back, anguished. After that, I hung up whenever Colin called. Barry talked to him but often ended conversations by slamming down the phone.

Colin seemed sure that he could guide Hunter better. He loved Hunter, and he'd generously involved himself in several pieces of the story, surfing with Hunter when we'd sent him to visit Barry's father and be out of Seattle during the Folklife Festival weekend in 2008, checking Hunter out of Pacific Recovery on a day pass and driving him to San Diego to see Grandma Joan. Taking Hunter in now was Colin's chance to act on his conviction that he could bring Hunter around. And although Barry and I had both been seared by past interactions, Colin's offer was generous. It was our best option. We booked a Greyhound bus ticket from Albuquerque to Santa Cruz. Lauren drove Hunter to the station.

Colin and Susan and their twin daughters, Hallie and Mollie, who were Lillie's age, were living in the rented basement of the house next door to their own home while their house underwent an extensive remodeling project.[12] It was tight quarters with scant kitchen facilities, and they ate out a lot. The girls, Hunter's cousins, were kind and accommodating, although it soon grew clear that Hunter wasn't willing to take on household responsibilities that they, six years his junior, took in stride.

Hunter turned twenty on February first. Colin and Susan helped him find a psychotherapist, and he began weekly appointments. Colin spent hours after work biking with Hunter, surfing, going with him to the gym, trying to help Hunter feel healthy and relaxed, to motivate him to take control of his life, with little visible success. Hunter hung out during the day, went to the gym if prodded, attended NA meetings when Colin insisted.

"Colin says Hunter's a pain sometimes," Barry reported after a phone call. I rolled my eyes. "He says Hunter reads a lot of books all day and watches television. He never helps out around the house. I feel as if Colin is finally starting to understand a tiny bit of what you and I have been dealing with. I mean, good luck *making* Hunter do anything."

"What books are you reading?" I asked Hunter when we spoke later that week.

"I just finished this great book called *The Thief*, by a Japanese author, Fuminori Nakamura. I think the translated version just came out—it's hardback, from the library."

"Interesting," I said. "Anything else?"

"I have three Paul Auster books—*Sunset Park*, *Invisible*, and *Moon Palace*. I read his *New York Trilogy* when I was in Iowa, and I really liked it. I just read Ken Kesey's *Sometimes a Great Notion*. I know you liked *Electric Kool-Aid Acid Test*, and that's about Kesey, so you might like *Notion*, although now that I think about it, probably not. I'm also reading a lot of Charles Bukowski," Hunter explained.

In late February, Barry flew down for a brief visit. "I surfed with Hunter," he told me when he got back, "and that was fun."

"How did he seem?" I asked, tentatively hopeful.

"The same. Just the same. I mean, he looks healthier physically, he has a tan, but . . ." His words trailed off. "You know," he sighed. "Otherwise unchanged."

Hunter flew home just for the day on March 26 to make a court appearance concerning an incident that had occurred the previous fall. Hunter had hidden on a loading dock at the University of Washington to try and sleep and been discovered and cited for vagrancy. Colin found Hunter a Seattle attorney, who met Barry and Hunter outside the courthouse an hour before Hunter was due in court.

"This is a misdemeanor, and since committing the offence, you've been to rehab, you're doing well, and living with your uncle out of state," the lawyer, Kris, said. "I think the judge will look favorably on all of that."

"What about the heroin?" Hunter casually inquired. Barry's jaw dropped. Kris looked confused. "The cops searched my backpack and they took it from me."

Kris called his assistant, who called the court to double-check the charges. "Just the vagrancy," she reported several minutes later.

The heroin in Hunter's possession could have resulted in a felony charge, but it had not. "My God, there's always some surprise plot twist, isn't there?" Barry told me that afternoon. "But Hunter looked good in court. The judge dismissed the charges." We met my parents, who missed Hunter terribly, for a quick meal, and then Hunter flew back to Colin and Susan.

Meanwhile, at home, the six-month celebration marking the fiftieth anniversary of the Seattle World's Fair began on April 21. My days were crammed with public appearances to support the book, which had been used as the bible for a documentary about the fair. My co-author and I had been interviewed and then helped pitch the book on air during public television pledge drives. The exhibit we'd curated for the Museum of History and Industry opened in a former fair building at Seattle Center, whose campus had been the site of the fair. I was relieved during this hectic time that Hunter was safely elsewhere.

Colin tried to help Hunter get a job several times, but nothing panned out. Colin and Susan both had long conversations with Hunter. They introduced him to their friends, including him in every aspect of their lives. Hunter remained passive, unwilling to take action for himself. After no-showing several appointments, he was no longer in counseling.

As Hunter's presence in their home wore on, Colin's patience frayed. He had tried all his ideas, but Hunter was unmoved. By June, Hunter had lived with Colin and Susan for six months and things were tense. One afternoon, a massive rainstorm swept through Santa Cruz, and the family rushed to move their furniture—which was outside, unprotected, because of the renovation project—out of the deluge. Hunter helped to move one chair, then went back inside and lay down. Colin followed him and confronted him about his behavior. They argued. Hunter fled the house and hitchhiked to San Francisco.

Colin was frantic. He got in touch with Hunter by phone and drove to San Francisco to retrieve him. Hunter returned with him and spent that night. The next day, while Colin was at work and the girls at school—Susan was in Wisconsin at a medical conference that Barry was also attending—Hunter took a large amount of cash from the house, hitchhiked to San Francisco once again, and got high.

Unlike past relapses, this time Hunter seemed to express immediate regret. He was on Market Street, he texted Barry, and he planned to kill himself. "Don't worry, you've been a good dad," he wrote. Barry called Hunter's cell repeatedly, but he didn't answer. I opened my cell to find Hunter's text: "I'm sorry, Mom."

Frantic, sure that this was a goodbye message, I called him back immediately, got no answer. "Hunter, Hunter, please, please call me back, I am so worried about you. Please be okay, please, please, don't hurt yourself. You know my life would be over if you killed yourself, I could not go on. Please be careful, I love you. We can help, please call us, please."

A few minutes later, Hunter called. "I'm sorry," he said sheepishly. "I'm okay. I'm just so fucked up, I've fucked everything up again. I can't do this."

We talked, he talked to Barry, Barry and I talked to each other. Eventually, Hunter agreed to go back to rehab. The Iowa facility, as they had promised, agreed to admit him for six more weeks at no charge beyond what insurance covered.

Colin drove to San Francisco, picked Hunter up, and drove to the airport in San Jose, where the ticket we'd purchased was waiting. Hunter boarded the plane and headed back east.

Runaway Bunny

I kept *The Runaway Bunny* in the wicker filing basket under my desk, tucked in the back of the overstuffed manila folder marked "Hunter." I had a love-hate relationship with this particular copy, valuing the momentary catharsis the slim cornflower blue paperback had once given me, traumatized by the events that had demanded that release. Now, filing away the Iowa rehab paperwork, I found the book and turned the pages slowly, thinking about how it had come to be.

One afternoon, during the months leading up to Hunter's first trip to rehab, I was walking toward the University of Washington to use the library. Overwhelmed with grief and anger, making my way down the memory-scarred Ave, an image from Margaret Wise Brown's beautiful picture book came to my mind: two white rabbits, mother and child, nestled within a glowing red cave secreted in the roots of a towering tree. The book had been one of Hunter's many favorites, and we had read it together countless times, Hunter's small finger tracing the mommy and baby bunny in Clement Hurd's soothing illustrations.

The Runaway Bunny tells the simple story of a mother's boundless love for her son, as demonstrated through the inexhaustible patience she shows him as he tests his boundaries. "Once there was a little bunny who wanted to run away," the story begins. "So he said to his mother, 'I am running away.' 'If you run away,' said his mother, 'I will run after you. For you are my little bunny.'"

I was possessed, entranced, with the analogies between the bunnies' story and my own. The bunny son's relentless compulsion to break away from his mother felt devastatingly familiar.

I veered into the University Book Store, climbed the broad stairway to the children's department, bought a copy, then crossed the UW campus to Suzzallo Library. Settling at one of the long shared oak tables in the placid reading room, I turned the book's familiar pages. Tears streamed down my face, but the students who sat nearby politely ignored them. I took out my pencil and started annotating Margaret Wise Brown's text.

"If you run after me," said the little bunny,
"I will stop going to high school and stand on the corner smoking cigarettes and not even look chagrined when you drive past me."

"If you stand on the corner smoking cigarettes," said his mother,
"I will sniff your hair and jacket as you walk into the house and fish crumpled tobacco from your pants pockets before I put them into the washer."

"If you sniff my hair," said the little bunny,
"I will begin smelling of more dangerous substances you may not even recognize."

"If you begin smelling of things I do not recognize," said his mother,
"I will begin sifting through the heaps in your bedroom, looking for clues."

"If you begin looking for clues in my bedroom," said the little bunny,
"I will leave what I want for you to find and hide the rest."

"If you hide the rest," said his mother,
"I will imagine the worst and blame myself and mourn for the thousands of hours I spent kissing your head when you were small."

"If you blame yourself and mourn those kisses," said the little bunny,
"I will unlock the door and walk away into the night."

"If you unlock the door and walk away into the night," said his mother,
"I will bake cakes and cookies and make sandwiches and long to nourish you."

"If you long to nourish me," said the little bunny,
"I will turn my back on you and my face to the wild world and I will upend the streams and rivers and lakes and oceans and drink them all."

"If you drink all the streams and rivers and lakes and oceans," said his mother,
"I will lie down and become the sand that sifts around you as the black wind howls."

"If you lie down and become the sand," said the little bunny,
"I will put on leather boots and walk through the dunes of you and listen to the crunch under my soles."

"If you put on leather boots and crunch me beneath your soles," said his mother,
"I will deepen my every hollow and be a grave for whatever you have found to bury."

"If you become a grave for what I have to bury," said the bunny,
"I will become a man and I will bury in you the boy you loved."

"If you become a man and bury in me the little boy I loved," said his mother,
"I will bear witness to that boy, as a kitchen door on which the yearly crepe myrtle bloom has been recorded, or the doorframe that was yearly marked with pencil to track the progress of the children's growth, still sing their story silently under the sandpaper, under fresh paint."

I never made it to my research. When I got home, I transformed the book's last pages into a scrapbook, gluing in pictures from our family's happier days.

I wrote on the title page, *The Runaway Bunny: A Don't-Read-Aloud Book*, adding to myself, "Burn this."

Drugstore Cowboy

The constant hovering threat of Hunter's death was like a coming plague. Barry and I were trying to mount his—and our own—immune response. Trying to help Hunter battle opioid addiction meant wrestling an abstraction. Each time we strained and tried to help him fling away this unseen foe, addiction rushed back, harder, fiercer, more relentless.

The blows kept coming. Any disaster might have pierced the hope that we held power to save him. Any attack awakened us to the reality that opioid use had altered his brain. Any assault crumbled conviction that this time—each This Time—would be the turning point.

Rehab guaranteed a roof over his head. The prospect of Hunter's being homeless again was horrific and absolutely a real possibility. Only Hunter could stay clean, we knew that. But if we could help ensure him shelter, someplace, anyplace but where we were, we knew that we would make that choice. Enabling, compromising ourselves, showing compassion. These labels, once again, were vastly insufficient for the reality of feeling our way through addiction's labyrinth.

When Hunter's six weeks in Iowa were over, he told us that he thought Portland, Oregon, would be a good place for him to be, someplace to try and stay clean and sober and to start to rebuild his life.

He'd used the rehab facility's computers to research Oxford Houses and other sober housing options and had found a place in Beaverton, near Portland. Taking that initiative seemed like a good sign. The house Hunter located was not an Oxford House, but one of several sober homes owned by two men who ran them for profit. Living in sober housing would mean that Hunter would have to find a job and that he'd have to submit to and pass random drug tests. Failing a urine test would get him kicked out.[13]

Barry and I bought Hunter a plane ticket from Des Moines to Portland. Barry drove four hours south to meet him at the Portland airport on a Saturday—the Beaverton group home could not process Hunter in until Monday. Barry and Hunter spent a pleasant if surreal weekend at the Ace Hotel in downtown Portland, passing the time.

The Portland Ace is a hipster hangout. Housed in a former flophouse/single room occupancy hotel in the heart of Portland's recently gentrified Pearl District, its lobby is funkily furnished with a massive couch and table around which laptop/tablet/smart-phone users settle, engaging in parallel play while they suck down Stumptown coffee. We'd stayed at the Ace as a family when the place first opened, marveling at the long stark hallways, unchanged since Gus Van Sant filmed wizened, ancient self-described junky William S. Burroughs there in *Drugstore Cowboy*, back when the Ace was still a grimy SRO called the Clyde Hotel. Across the street from the Ace, out of step with its now tony neighbors, lingered the shady, saggy Joyce Hotel, its transient population mirroring the kind of guests the Clyde once attracted.

Barry and Hunter met with the Beaverton sober house managers on Monday morning. Barry later said he got bad vibes from the men—strange nonverbal signals that made it difficult to gauge their sincerity. He felt, though, that he had little option but to trust them.

Hunter's life had confronted Barry and me repeatedly with choices for which there were no good answers, only solutions that seemed, at the particular moment of any given decision, to be less bad. We were glad Hunter was not using drugs, and we wanted to support his sobriety. But we knew, now, that taking Hunter in after his first rehab, then while he took Suboxone, then naltrexone, had ultimately not helped him and had exhausted the rest of us while we put ourselves at risk for his sake.

We were beginning, finally, to lose our stupendous naïveté, to realize that our continued certainty that things would get better with Hunter was a form of magical thinking. We saw more clearly now that opioid addiction is a foul toxic stew, understood more fully that each dose Hunter had taken had carried him further from our original shared values. We were far from willing to turn our backs on Hunter, and we had drawn many lines in the past that we had, quickly or eventually, let him cross. We drew a line now, though, that was bright and firm and that we would not violate: Hunter was never living in our house again.

Hunter signed paperwork agreeing to the sober house rules: look for and find a job, do assigned chores promptly, submit to random drug tests, know that if you fail a urine test, you will be asked to vacate within twenty-four hours. In that case, you will forfeit all prepaid rent. Bank of America issued a cashier's check for $2,000, one-third of the six months' rent that particular sober house required for a new resident to join them. It would take us a few weeks to come up with the balance, and the managers reluctantly agreed to wait for it. They promised to help Hunter get an Oregon ID card and apply for honored citizen status, a Portland euphemism meaning he was either elderly or disabled or recently through a rehab program and so could ride the bus and light rail at reduced rates. With their help, Hunter was also able to sign up for food stamps—$120 each month, reloaded on a plastic card.

Barry took Hunter to the Beaverton Target to stock up on underwear, socks, toiletries, bedclothes. They stuffed these in the van, along with a futon donated by our college friend Byron, who was active in Portland's recovery community and wanted to support Hunter's recovery. Barry helped Hunter settle into his room and left, hopeful that this was the beginning, finally, of Hunter's path to independent living.

Two weeks later, we sent the sober housing manager the $4,000 balance. We'd now prepaid six months' rent, $6,000.

Barry drove down to Portland to visit Hunter briefly soon after. "He acted guilty and evasive," Barry told me when he got back. "I have a bad feeling something's going on. You know how hard it is to tell when Hunter's high—I mean, we've been through that so many times. But that guilty look he gets is always a bad sign."

I'd asked Barry in the past why it was hard for us to see heroin's immediate effect on Hunter, and he'd pointed out that heroin in the bloodstream has no odor. Users build tolerance very quickly. The high is briefer and less intense and even less obvious to the outside observer. This was true, in Barry's experience, even when the observer was a health care professional.

I knew the guilty look Barry was describing. It was, for Hunter, the kind of revealing behavior poker players call a "tell": some change in demeanor that gives an astute observer a clue to the cards in the player's hand. The guilty look was one of Hunter's tells. So too was sudden solicitous behavior on his part—how were we doing? how was our day going?—questions he didn't usually ask.

The next week, a resident who had befriended Hunter failed a drug test and was asked to leave. Hunter called, distraught. "He was a good guy," Hunter said. "Now what will happen to him?" The day after, the sober house manager called Barry. They'd tested Hunter since his friend had relapsed. His test was positive. He had twenty-four hours to get out.

The sober house let Hunter leave his baggage and his bed in their garage. "A lot of people who get kicked out leave stuff there," Hunter said nonchalantly. "They said they'd keep it safe." The six months' rent was gone, including the balance sent so recently that it had barely cleared the bank when he was booted out.

Hunter spent—or said he spent—a few days in the Portland detox center. He called when he was out, saying the sober house managers had given him the number of some friends of theirs who didn't exactly have a sober house but who were part of the sobriety community and sometimes rented a room to people in recovery. Hunter had talked to them, and they would take him in. It was a lot to ask, he said, but he was sure this time he'd make it. Could we, would we, pay the $800 rent?

I see it, now, as progress that although we gritted our teeth and wrote another fat check, further eviscerating our emergency savings, Barry and I did not rush down to Portland and physically help Hunter make the move. It was, for us, a baby step back from enabling. We were fully aware that we were rescuing Hunter from multiple failures, that our deep fear of having him on the street again was our primary motivator. Barry remembered the train station in St. Louis and his intense premonition Hunter would die.

So we rescued Hunter, again, from homelessness. We faced this decision slightly more starkly, however, and with better acknowledgment of our complicity than we'd brought to the previous moments of choice. Our vision was clearing. Slowly but certainly, we were learning not to cloak the young man before us with our emotional connections to the boy he'd been. To see Hunter the eighteen-year-old without seeing him at eight had been nearly impossible. Seeing Hunter at twenty without imagining him at two was gradually becomingly less difficult.

Sawyer and Lillie felt the yank and jolt of Hunter's yo-yoing even when he was not physically present in our lives. "Hunter is living in Portland, in sober housing," I told them, knowing that if they wanted to know more, they would ask. I didn't want either of them to have to wade through Hunter's problems constantly, didn't want his life to be the focal point of theirs. Lillie was just about to graduate from St. Lucy's. She had a host of friends from school and a tight cluster of girls with whom she'd studied ballet since second grade in the Cornish College of the Arts Preparatory Dance Program. Sawyer had quit the job busing at Cloud City weeks before and had quickly been hired at Flying Squirrel Pizza, a nearby neighborhood favorite, where he was learning the ins and outs of working in a restaurant kitchen. His girlfriend, Carney, was often at our house, baking cookies with him while describing the latest antics of the kittens she fostered for an animal shelter.

Sawyer had vivid memories of his brother before Hunter went astray. Hunter had been the beloved older brother, played with, looked up to. Together, they had negotiated childhood, had adventures, shared a bedroom and friends. Sawyer could contrast drug-addicted Hunter with the preaddiction version, could love that dearly remembered person, even while the current Hunter wreaked emotional havoc. Like Barry and me, Sawyer was forced to bear this pain.

Lillie was seven, eight, when Hunter started down his bad path, and much of her subsequent Hunter-related energy was spent keeping out of his way. She seemed to me to see the world—and Hunter—in terms of black and white. She held herself apart. She claimed to have little memory of their earliest years together. But Hunter was still her brother, and his actions took a toll.

We realized that even though Lillie really didn't want to know the details of Hunter's life, there was a part of her that needed to reach out to him, that needed—not closure—but a sort of touchstone moment. Because of this, around the time she started high school, Barry took Lillie down to visit Hunter. She'd said, "Where *is* he, even?" She needed to know.

Hunter was living in the second sober house when Barry and Lillie visited. They stayed in a small hotel nearby, meeting Hunter for meals and taking him into Portland to Powell's City of Books. Pictures snapped that weekend show a happy Lillie, Hunter's arm slung around her shoulder. Barry thought Hunter seemed well and settled.

A few weeks after Barry and Lillie's visit, Hunter called me and asked if I could come down for the weekend. "I miss you, Mom," he said. I booked a ticket on the Bolt Bus—the low-priced line that runs continually between Seattle and Portland—and one night at the Mark Spencer Hotel. Close to Powell's, the Mark Spencer was our family's second-choice place to stay when the popular Ace was booked up.

On Friday, as I packed my bag, Hunter called my cell phone.

"Uhm, I have to tell you something. I still want you to come, but, ah, I had a little relapse and I got kicked out of my housing. I can still hang out with you, actually it is easier because I can be in Portland all the time, we won't have to go back and forth to Hillsboro, but I know you might not want to come now."

I was stunned—I was always stunned—but not very surprised. I felt disappointed in Hunter but not angry with him. Anger was too taxing. He had been honest with me this time, that was good, warning me of his relapse while I still had the chance to change my plans. I weighed my words and spoke evenly. "Hunter, you say a little relapse. What does that mean?" I asked him.

"I used once, with a friend, and they tested me right after, but that's all. I haven't used again. It really sucks that I got kicked out, but the guys say that if I go to detox for a while, they'll let me back in. I'm going to try and get into detox, but I really don't think I need it. I'll go, though, so I can move back into the house after. If you come down, I might only get to see you once—if the detox has a bed on Sunday morning, I'll have to take it."

The many times in the past that I had been with Hunter when I'd later realized he was high or desperate to be high had used up my capacity to be with him in either of those states. If he was using drugs, I was not going. "Hunter, can you promise me that you aren't using?" I asked him. "I don't want to be around you if you're using."

"I promise, Mom. I'll understand if you don't want to come, but I only used that once. I'm not using."

Standing on the edge of Seattle's International District the next morning, waiting for the Bolt Bus, I hoped that Hunter—who'd lied to me so very often—had told the truth.

I saw Hunter before he could see me. He was leaning against a building as the bus pulled in, cigarette balanced casually between his fingers. I saw him scan the windows, looking for me, as I made my slow way down the aisle. The windows were coated, allowing me to study Hunter without his knowing it, and I looked deeply, trying to guess if I'd been right to come.

He broke into a grin as I climbed down the steps, hugged me tightly. "Mom, I'm so glad you could come," he said.

What did we do that weekend, where did we go? We walked—it sounds so ordinary, but each step was sacred to me, moving through the city in Hunter's company. He seemed secure but hesitant, street-wise but wary. "I didn't get into detox this morning, obviously," he said. "We have this afternoon, but I might get a place tomorrow. I've got to be at the shelter by seven to get a bed for the night. Is that okay?"

"Sure, Hunter, sure, and we can do whatever you want—what would you like to do?"

He did not ask to stay with me in the hotel, and I did not offer. Barry had stayed with him in hotels, sleeping with his wallet deep inside the pillowcase, but I knew that would be too much for me. I loved Hunter, but I could not trust him. Learning not to trust him had taken me so many years, and it was where I was now, where I lived, permanently.

We dropped my small bag at the Mark Spencer and hit the streets, Hunter matching my pace. We wandered Portland, talking sometimes, balanced in each other's company but without too much to say. The conversation we'd had, so to speak, over the last five years lay heavy between us: the drug use, the lies, the many thefts. I knew myself to be an easy mark and found it was safer to listen to him than to talk. I wanted to form a picture of who Hunter was at that moment and to be fully present. To appreciate Hunter without rehashing the past or quizzing him on the future.

We ended up in the Hawthorne district, a laid-back neighborhood near downtown that centered on a spine of retail shops—used clothes and record stores, funky cafes, an aging movie theater. Hunter wanted coffee, so I bought a cup and watched him breathe the steam, close his eyes, taste it like nectar. We wandered the residential streets, past 1920s bungalows with wide porches. "I'd love to live here," Hunter said, "I really like this neighborhood and I bet I could get a job around here someplace."

"That would be great," I offered evenly. "Maybe someone in Hawthorne is looking for a roommate. You could check Craigslist . . ." The thought of his jumping somehow into a satisfying life, becoming a healthy young man on a chosen path, shimmered before me. "You could take college classes, maybe, once you got on your feet."

We bused downtown. Out of the corner of my eye, I watched for drug-related signs. What did drug-free behavior look like for him, I wondered. I'd first known he was using heroin by finding syringes, blue elastic bands. Not from behavior changes. Was I stupid? Sitting beside me on the Portland TriMet bus, Hunter seemed—normal. Whatever that was, for him, now.

"I need to get my hair cut," he said suddenly. "You wouldn't be willing to pay for that, would you?" The old twisted question, asked so that to agree to his request, I must deny the assertion. Why does he ask that way, I wondered.

"I would, I guess," I said. "Where can you get your hair cut around here?"

All action, Hunter strode off past former warehouses now transformed into artisanal bakeries, chic clothing shops. "There's a place this way," he said. He ducked his head into a small stylish barber shop. "They can take me now, and the cut will take twenty minutes. It costs thirty-five bucks, is that all right?" I felt the queasy foreshadowing of a scam, hoped I was wrong about it. My choice was either to walk in and debit for his haircut—Mommy pays—or hand him forty dollars to pay himself. Should I be sure, risk his humiliation, and perhaps unseat the delicate truce that had been carrying our togetherness along during the visit by using my debit card? If I gave him the cash, would he use it to pay and tip? Was the price really thirty-five, even? Could the hip barber, clippers in hand, sell dope on the side? Was this a trap, another way to milk me?

"Thirty-five?" I asked the barber, looking straight into his eyes. He nodded, not too interested in the transaction. I pressed two twenties into Hunter's hand. "The extra is for the tip," I told him a bit too loudly. "I'll sit outside on the bench. It's such a pretty day."

It was managed as well as it could have been, I told myself. When Hunter emerged half an hour later, his head shorn, he thanked me for paying. "How do I look?" he asked.

We went to Powell's, bought books. "If I lived here," I told Hunter, "I'd come to the Powell's events every night. Look at the authors who are giving readings!"

"Maybe I'll do that," he said idly.

The evening ended early, as Hunter had explained it would. Retreating to my calm hotel room, I decompressed, read books in bed. I'd loved being with Hunter so far this trip, soaked in the gift of his company. But it was also draining, certainly to me, maybe to him.

My phone rang early the next morning. "They close the shelter first thing in the morning," Hunter said. "You have to be awake and out. I've been walking around for a while. Can we get breakfast?"

We walked together to an old-fashioned diner, ate our eggs and hash browns.

"What happened with the detox?" I asked. Hunter shook his head, gulped coffee.

"No room again," he said.

We walked through downtown Portland toward the river, past Voodoo Donuts, past the Sunday Market underneath the bridge. I was not certain where we were exactly, but Hunter knew. We crossed the river, walked more, crossed back over another bridge.

"Do you want to see a movie?" Hunter asked, hopeful.

"Okay," I quietly replied.

In one of twelve box theaters in a downtown metroplex, we watched *Looper*, a movie Hunter correctly predicted I would like. I marveled at the way he knew my taste still, knew that the film's time-travel construct would suck me in, that its particular kinds of violence wouldn't disturb me, although many violent movies do. I watched the screen, but I watched Hunter, too. Sitting side by side, we were together, still, suspended. I tried to recognize the moment's holiness, to hold it, memorize it.

The film was done, and then the visit. Thai noodles from a food truck, collect my luggage, a hug goodbye. "I love you so much, Hunter, thank you for inviting me down," I told him as we parted. All the way back to Seattle as I perched on the hard back seat of the Bolt Bus, Hunter's face swam before me. For all the parts of the visit that had been tricky, I felt I had experienced something tangible, something pure, something that was mine and Hunter's in an old good way.

Detox never had a bed, or so he told us. Over the next few weeks, staying in homeless shelters, Hunter called many times, insisted he was clean. "If you could just help me stay in a hotel, just for a little while, I'll find a room to rent, I promise, I'll find a job, I just . . . I just can't stay in shelters anymore. Please."

We were trying to be helpful but not enabling. There is no such path.

Hunter rented—we rented for him—a room at the Joyce Hotel. The room was rented by the almost week, six days, because only people who had jobs could get the discounted weekly rate. Weeks stretched into months as Hunter ostensibly looked for work, ostensibly looked for more permanent and less expensive housing.

We let ourselves believe, willed ourselves to hope, that he was honest with us when he said he wasn't using. We knew the rule: Trust, but verify. The logistics of verification were so daunting, the relief of being able to assist him from four hours' distance so great, that we ignored our inner voices and past experience and all logic.

Hunter told us he pursued housing leads on Craigslist, looking for shared houses or people who wanted to rent out a room. Most times, he washed out during the phone interview. No one, it seemed, wanted to rent to someone with no job, no student status. His parents would pay? Potential landlords smelled a rat.

Get a job, then try for housing, we urged. Or find a place to volunteer, where you can be reliable and earn a reference. Sign up for a community college class, anything, something you'll like, film studies or creative writing or political science. We'll pay, of course. Then you can tell the landlords you're a student.

Sawyer and Lillie and Barry and I drove down to Portland the night before Thanksgiving, stayed at the Ace. Hunter's flophouse, the Joyce, across the street, was a grim contrast to the vibe at our hotel. The next day, we shared Thanksgiving dinner in a restaurant catering to families like ours, people who loved each other but circled warily around some wound, some crack, some damaged broken place. The food was bad. Our fellow diners looked as displaced as we felt.

We made the trip again on Christmas morning, flying along the empty freeway. Sawyer and Lillie tolerated my urge, and Barry's, to be with Hunter on holidays—or rather, not to let him be without us.

Both trips were brief, both a relief, but stressful. Hunter seemed okay to us, if cagey, but was he cagier than usual? With all of us together, he was thrust awkwardly into the oldest sibling role he'd left behind years ago. We danced the familiar useless dance of encouragement, talked about job, room, college. Even to us, the lines were tiresome, futile.

Six weeks later, Hunter turned twenty-one. Barry and I drove down to Portland, met him near the Joyce. He seemed okay, but then I'd lost capacity to judge his layers of behavior. Partly to save myself, I kept my heart from reaching out toward him, held back from the old maternal pull, loved him at arm's length. It was my main defense.

We bought him books at Powell's, saw *Argo*, went out for sushi. Lillie had baked a birthday cake, which he took gratefully. We spent perhaps six hours together, the three of us. He was a man, no little boy, but we were, for an afternoon, a kind of restored although battered unit: Barry and I, and Hunter—this soul we'd called into being so long ago, this now familiar stranger.

We hugged goodbye outside the Joyce. His arms were strong, his jacket stiff and fumed with cigarette smoke. He thanked us for coming, sent love to his siblings, turned to go. Eager, it seemed, to be quickly somewhere.

A week later, he phoned, so excited that his words tumbled over themselves. He'd found a place to live, a room in the home of a nice couple who rented out their basement. One of the two rooms, which shared a kitchen, was rented to a Salvadoran man who worked long hours and sent money home to his family. The other room would be Hunter's. He planned to look for work as soon as he was settled, and the homeowners—the husband worked from home—might have some odd jobs for him, things he could begin immediately.

Rent was $600, steeper than we'd hoped, but the set-up sounded good. The husband, Charlie, called to confirm that we'd be paying. "Hunter seems like a good kid," he said to me. "He . . . he is," I hesitantly agreed.

An email Barry sent to Hunter (subject: Plan for monthly financial support) detailed the kind of help we were trying to offer and our instructive guarded hopefulness. We would send Hunter the monthly rent check, and he could deliver it to Charlie's wife, Glenda. Hunter's food stamp card reloaded with $120 on the fifth of every month. Barry advised him to use this on groceries. We planned to send Hunter $120 on the nineteenth of each month, and Barry strategized that he should use this on basic food supplies, especially items with longer shelf lives. Additionally, we'd send what worked out to ten dollars per day, which Barry advised should cover a pack of cigarettes every two days and three coffees a week "Set aside money for emergencies," Barry wrote. "Obviously, the less you smoke, the more money you will have available for other purchases."

Hunter moved and settled in. A few days later, he called, happy to report he'd cooked a steak, his first in many months. It had been fun, and it had tasted wonderful.

Two weeks later, the shrill phone cut through my concentration as I wrote.

"Ah, I'm looking for Barry? This is, ah, Charlie Jones," the man's voice said.

"Barry's at work, but this is Paula. Is this about Hunter? Is he okay?" My heart began to pound, imagining an overdose, Hunter dead in the basement bedroom.

"Ah, okay, yes, ah, Hunter is okay, well, we had some trouble. He, ah, well, he stole some jewelry from us . . ."

My pulse grew faster still as Charlie explained. Hunter had called them and confessed that he had helped himself to jewelry in their bedroom several times over the days he'd lived there. He'd wandered through the house when they were elsewhere, taking what he found: Glenda's heirloom emerald ring, some gold bracelets. "He took my wedding ring," Charlie said. "It hasn't fit well in a while, so I wasn't wearing it, but . . ."

"Oh, no," I stammered, "I was afraid of this."

"Hunter isn't a bad kid," Charlie said, "but he's confused. I went through something like that and I'd like to help him. I guess he's had some trouble with drugs? He says a friend came down to Portland from Seattle, and he relapsed. He might need someone just to show him a better path."

This left me nearly speechless. "That's very generous of you," I finally mumbled, "but this has been going on for quite a while—about six years."

"Six years," I heard him mutter to Glenda, and her gasp.

I was completely horrified. I felt dizzy and realized I was hyperventilating. There were details to cover with Charlie, reparation to arrange, but I felt too emotionally overwhelmed to wade in. "I am so sorry," I told Charlie, "but I can't be the one to handle this, I can't take being the one. I will call Barry, and he will call you back immediately, is that okay?"

Barry, his work interrupted by a Hunter crisis for perhaps the hundredth time, was just as horrified but better able to compose himself than I had been. He called the Joneses back, heard what I'd heard, and more.

"Hunter told Charlie he was ashamed and sorry but that he had relapsed. He is downtown and still has the pawn tickets, but he's spent the money. I told Charlie and Glenda that we would pay to get their jewelry back. Charlie's meeting Hunter to get the pawn tickets. He doesn't want to involve the police. He told me he was even willing for Hunter to move back in if he went to detox. Can you believe that? I told him that was very generous, but for us this was Hunter's last straw. We were not prepared to pay his rent or offer any other financial support."

Barry and I knew that we had helped this happen. We had paid for it to happen, paid Hunter's rent there, willed ourselves to believe that he had turned a corner. We would not have him in our own house unwatched, but we had helped him enter someone else's. Revulsion, remorse, and shock rose up in me.

I felt not only these emotions but also closure, strangely, and something that was almost relief. I knew suddenly, certainly, finally, that something was over permanently. Loving our child, wanting him to be the person we believed he had been, thinking that was possible in spite of all external indications, Barry and I had deluded ourselves completely, fooled ourselves again. I saw it thoroughly for the first time.

I'd felt attached to Hunter from the moment of his birth. Now, for the first time, I felt the click of Hunter and myself detaching from one another. Separated. Really. Finally. I understood in my head, but also in my deepest soul, that Hunter was in no way an extension of me. He never had been, and he never would be.

The Joneses got their jewelry back, all but one ring. They called to thank us for paying the pawn fee, still kind, still generous. "What can we do to get Hunter's things?" Barry asked them. "You shouldn't feel you have to store them. Should we drive down and pick them up?"

"What things?" Charlie asked. "He only had a paper bag with a few clothes in it when he moved in. We wondered about that . . ."

I thought of all the housekeeping supplies Barry had bought, the futon, the chair, clothes, bedding, when Hunter first moved into the sober house in Hillsboro. I thought of the clothes we'd bought him at Red Light and other resale stores on our visits, the books from Powell's and other books I'd mailed him. All, I imagined, monetized, sold at a loss, put in his veins. Charlie and Glenda must have thought us very odd, willing to pay our grown son's rent but giving him not even a change of clothes, a second pair of shoes.

The knowledge that he'd come to the Joneses' house with nothing gave the lie to Hunter's claim that his relapse was something new. The truth was clear enough—it had been for months, if we'd been honest with ourselves. Other than the room fee at the Joyce, which Barry had paid every six days on his credit card, most or all of the money we'd been dripping into Hunter's pockets had gone for drugs. We had not wanted to know that. We loved him and wanted him off the street, and we had ignored the glaring reality of his drug use because that would have meant withdrawing our financial support and leaving him to whatever came next. What happened with Glenda and Charlie forced us to stop deluding ourselves and made us ready to stop trying to protect Hunter from himself—or almost. Fearing the reality of being completely out of touch, we hesitated to take Hunter off our phone plan.

Hunter texted me once: Mom, I'm sorry.

I texted back: Hunter, I will always love you, but I cannot help you anymore.

A month later, Hunter's old friend Tamlin's mother, Lana, left a message on our answering line. "Hunter called me from a pay phone," Lana said, "and asked me to let you know that he's lost his phone, or it was stolen. We talked a little, but I called him on his addict bullshit, and he hung up on me. I thought you'd want to know about the phone."

Love Is

I've read that when an airplane is about to crash, a prerecorded voice barks, "Brace! Brace! Brace!" I had been braced for Hunter's death for six years now. He was still living, despite my terror, despite all odds.

After the failure of our last attempt to help Hunter, I knew, on an almost cellular level, that Hunter would die. Or Hunter would not die. But that utterly nothing I might do—or not do—would tip the balance. I understood that Hunter's addiction was something I could not change. Gratitude for the wisdom to finally accept this truth bloomed in me, seeping through everything.

After a few months, I felt compelled one day to take a yoga class. The next day, I went back to yoga, the next day to modern dance. Moving so mindfully, I took the first steps toward letting go of the years of bracing. I needed teachers, classmates, insight from others. I needed healing and release, and I began to find those through moving, listening, and breathing. "The breath is central to the practice," one of my yoga teachers says. I am breathing now.

Maybe all children recede as their adult selves emerge. Maybe parents whose children stay the path can see the progress, watch the growth, like time-lapse photography. For Barry and me, the dissonance between who we felt Hunter was as a little boy and the actions he took as a teenager and young adult nearly destroyed us. They broke the childhood moments, burned the bright pictures one by one. I knew rationally that Hunter's childhood was warm and loving and full of goodness. But what came after did its best to rob me of that certainty.

My work, I now saw, my Hunter work, was to see those moments without clutching or judging them. I hoped they could again be something I knew I owned rather than something I felt was stolen from me. A friend once told me, after her house was burgled and irreplaceable heirloom jewelry taken: "Those things are out there, still, and they still belong to me, wherever they are." This brought her peace about the loss. I tried to let the millions of bright moments that were my memories of Hunter's childhood be like that: still out there, and still mine.

People with drug addiction cannot help but see their families as prey. It does not mean they love us less. The need to fund the addiction is completely opportunistic, and families—open, vulnerable, loving, trusting, wanting desperately to normalize the person with addiction and see him once again as part of their whole—are nature's perfect victim, a ready source of cash, given or taken, to the same end.

I had made the journey from denial and revulsion in response to this fact to an understanding that people with addiction did not—my beloved son did not—mean this personally. I now fully comprehended the reality that Hunter loved me, loved his father and sister and brother, even as we separated ourselves from him, accepted distance that brought protection, reinforced our boundary walls. Addiction destroys relationships, including the addicted person's relationship with himself. Craving and terror of experiencing the agony of withdrawal impel a person with addiction to prioritize the substance they crave over everything else.

I finally clearly saw that we could not heal Hunter, however mightily we would have if we could. We could not get clean for him or maintain his abstinence. We could love him fiercely, but we could not repair addiction's damage for him. Unless the person with addiction is striving even harder for wholeness than everyone who loves him, he will remain fragmented, broken from himself and from others. Trapped by the physical toll the abused substance takes and by the chaos into which craving that substance and struggling to obtain it have the power to cast him. Society, friends, and family can support recovery. Harm-reduction drugs—Suboxone, naltrexone, methadone—

can help. But only the person battling addiction can do the work of recovering.

For families, the struggle to decide and decide and decide what choice to make in each separate instance—the struggle to support without enabling—is never over. There is no inoculation against addiction. Opioid addiction has no boundaries—whether class, income, race, or gender. It sinks its fangs with equal fervor into beloved children and neglected ones, into the ones society predicts will fail and those who appear most destined for success. It happens in all kinds of families. Parents, siblings, spouses, and other family members are collateral damage.

I write this knowing that there are people who will judge our actions, question every choice, find us deluded, lacking. Those to whom this shattering of the idealized child has not happened or has not happened yet. But there are others—good parents to whom this bad thing is now happening—who may feel less alone for knowing my story. This is for them: You do not love a person with addiction any less when you stop allowing him or her to prey upon you, but you do value yourself more.

I still love Hunter. The difference now: my love for Hunter *is*. It cannot any longer *do*.

Requiem

the light is still

At the still point of the turning world.

—T. S. Eliot, *The Four Quartets*

I wrote Hunter's story for the same reason I wrote poetry about him: to focus my own suffering, to stop myself from howling through the streets. The poems allowed me to experience the pain of Hunter's opioid addiction as laser-like rather than as a tsunami, at least briefly. I had to pare away the mother I'd been and the child I'd had from the mother I was now and the young man he had become. To gnaw myself out of the trap, at least a little.

There was a moment when this story ended with Hunter in recovery. I'd sat—as if in meditation—with the reality of his addiction. Sat with it, letting it be.

Hunter lived on the street in Portland and the surrounding communities. He was arrested for vagrancy several times, each time serving about a month in jail. During one of these terms, a fellow inmate talked to him about turning his life around. For the first time, Hunter was able to hear this message. "I'm so young," Hunter told me during a phone call from jail. "I am so young, and my life doesn't have to keep going in this direction."

Hunter came back to Seattle when he was nearly twenty-two and began to find his way. He accessed social services aimed at young people between the ages of eighteen and twenty-five, becoming a client at the University District YouthCare, housed in a cheerful rundown cottage near the Ave. He showed up, I learned much later, three times a week, sharing meals and meeting with a counselor named Jesse. Jesse helped Hunter brainstorm what his future might look like and plan the steps to make that future happen. First on the list was affordable housing, and with Jesse's help, Hunter moved from a friend's couch into transitional housing in Seattle's downtown YMCA.

He lived alone—one of the program's rules was that no one but the resident could ever enter any room, with the exception of a regular inspection to make sure things were relatively tidy. The housing program offered counseling and emotional support, helped with job searches, and required residents to maintain employment. Hunter worked awhile as a sidewalk canvasser trying to convince passersby to donate to a children's charity, then got a job stocking shelves at a dollar store. He learned to care for himself, even had houseplants.

Hunter also learned to live without the drugs he'd lived with for so long. Much as he'd given himself to drugs, he gave himself to abstaining from them. He alone had decided to do it, this thing that only he could do, one of the many things Barry and I had finally accepted that we as his parents were powerless to do for him, however desperately we had tried.

We saw him—at first not often—in coffee shops, at restaurants, eventually even inviting him into our home sometimes. Slowly, my long-schooled wariness gave way to something perhaps less wary. He found a centering, grounding girlfriend. He got a new job washing dishes at Essential Bakery, a warm café in the Madison Valley neighborhood near downtown. After nearly two years at the Y, Hunter rented a room in a house nearer the café.

Hunter's recovery was like a ship on the horizon, far from my place on shore. I shielded my eyes, squinted, tried to surmise whether the vessel drew closer. Did it grow larger? Seem real, stop feeling like mirage? I couldn't tell. The ship was steady, locked in my sightline, appearing seaworthy. Like my unending love for Hunter, that had to be enough.

I wondered if those past years could ever recede so thoroughly that they ceased to define me. I felt pretty sure that my fear of returning to that black hole would never ebb. I knew in my bones how high we dangled, and what a long way down the plunge could be.

A year, a little more, went by.

The job went first, although we didn't know it at the time, and then the girlfriend. Hunter asked us to help him meet his rent. We did, swallowing our suspicions about relapse. Feeling it, fingers in our ears, hands across our eyes.

Hunter told me later that he'd relapsed after taking a single pill prescribed for his girlfriend following her wisdom teeth surgery. "I thought I could take one of her pain pills. Just one," he said. So started the unraveling.

He was soon evicted, facing the street. It was January, snowing that year. Barry took Hunter to motels each night, paid for his room. "Please, please help me get another place to live," Hunter begged. "I'll get another job, I will pay my own rent," and Barry and I lay awake, three a.m. (yet another night, again another) and said to each other, "We can't do this again. We cannot live with Hunter on the street."

We were well aware that rescuing Hunter in this way could be considered enabling him. We chose to do it anyway. We had learned during his previous periods of homelessness—more than nine months total in Seattle and about seven, including several months serving sentences for vagrancy, in Portland, how brutally we also suffered when Hunter was on the street. The thought of his sleeping rough in snow or beating rain was heartbreaking, and so was the knowledge of how dangerous living on the street inevitably would be. Hunter rarely hung onto identification cards, and I was haunted by the thought that he could die and remain unidentified, that he could disappear and we would never know.

Another factor influenced our decision: we no longer believed that the discomfort and indignity of becoming homeless as a direct result of his action or inaction would teach Hunter a lesson. That kind of cause-and-effect reasoning, our years with him had taught us, was inordinately simplistic. We chose to house Hunter out of compassion for him as a human being and to spare ourselves the anguish of his homelessness. It was the merciful decision for all of us.

Hunter found what must have been among Seattle's most modest apartments, a former storage room updated with bathroom and kitchen in the basement of a 1950s building on Capitol Hill, overlooking the freeway. Barry cosigned the lease. Hunter moved in. Eighteen months passed. There was no job, but Hunter took some community college classes for a while, or said he did. There were family dinners at which he seemed okay, sometimes.

This did not last. By spring 2017, the downward plunge was obvious to everyone, including Hunter's landlord. Lost keys, damaged smoke alarms. The night he broke down his own front door. Hunter's unsavory houseguests, the landlord reported in increasing desperation, made the other tenants nervous. When Hunter complained of a clogged kitchen sink, the landlord's plumber found a crack pipe. Hunter's behavior was erratic. Heroin again, we thought? Then later, meth? Denial, still. Hunter's. Our own.

The landlord finally gave Hunter one month to vacate the apartment. During the weeks of his eviction, Hunter admitted his relapse, his relapses. Tried to get into detox, didn't. At twenty-five, he still had Barry's health insurance coverage. "If Hunter isn't working harder than anyone else at being clean, it will not work," Barry and I told each other. That mantra, a groove worn smooth.

One tranquil dusk, Hunter stopped by the house looking for Barry, who was still at work. I invited him in and heated up some dinner for him. Hunter told me he'd taken someone's prescription Suboxone. On Suboxone, he seemed calmer and more mature, something we'd observed when he'd lived with us briefly in late 2010 and had been prescribed the drug.

We sat side by side in the quiet dining room. Hunter ate, then we drank tea. He talked for almost an hour. Most of that time, Hunter and I held hands, something we hadn't done since he was a little boy. It was then he told me about relapsing with his girlfriend's wisdom teeth pain medication.

Barry and I cautioned Hunter that his landlord's eviction proceedings were nearing a close and that we could not rent him another place. The afternoon of his final night in the apartment, Hunter asked if we would buy him a cheap phone and a bus ticket to San Francisco. A fresh start, different detox options, rehab maybe. And so we did.

Our final moments with Hunter were on the sidewalk outside his apartment. We hugged him: Barry, me, Barry again, told him how much we loved him. "I love you guys so much," he told us. "I know so many people whose families have given up on them."

The next day, Barry texted him at the bus's departure time: "Hi, Hunter. Have a safe trip. Let us know when you get there."

"I will," Hunter texted back. "I love you. Boarding now."

The rest stop was in a place called Central Point, a tiny town in southern Oregon. The bus, witnesses later said, pulled out early. Hunter, his just-bought food in his hand, raced after it, caught up, banging on the door. "My stuff's in there!" they said he shouted. And suddenly, instantly, unspeakably, his life was over.

His death was random. No fault of his. It could have been any passenger, but it was Hunter. Our Hunter, crushed beneath the wheel. That light-filled effervescent little boy. The handsome man—so young —who'd battled through ten years of darkness and who, despite all that, retained a core of love for us and a tenacious primal determination. Plucked by fate or karma or destiny, and by the unforgiving bus, from any future, bright or terrible. Full-stopped.

Hunter carried no identification. He had lost dozens of ID cards over the years. Lack of ID was one reason he was traveling by bus, not by train. The much-folded plastic grocery bag he'd left on the bus— "My stuff's in there!"—not even full, held all he owned: five shirts, swimming trunks, two pairs of well-worn shoes, fifty-seven cents, a Buddhist singing bowl, a cardboard sign for begging. And three treasured books, limp from repeated readings: Michael Chabon's *The Amazing Adventures of Kavalier and Clay*, Stieg Larsson's *The Girl Who Kicked the Hornet's Nest*, and Yann Martel's *The Life of Pi*.

His name was on the bus manifest. Detectives found what they believed to be his Facebook page. The damage to his body meant they could not match a photograph. It took nearly thirty-six hours for them to contact my sister, who was a Facebook friend. She phoned Barry at work to break the news, left a distraught message on my cell phone telling me through sobs that she loved me and that I should leave the meeting I was in and go straight home. Barry and Lillie met me at the door. We summoned Sawyer. And so we five were four.

One warm May night twenty-six years before, Barry and I had wooed Hunter Brown's essence from the cosmos. Birthed him and nurtured and guided and encouraged and shaped and tried to limit him. Then learned to let that go. To accept the illimitable risk over which all of our love was powerless. When Hunter died, we knew with excruciatingly hard-learned certainty that his path was his own. And since addiction had abducted him, that path felt finite. Hunter's death had always, in its insistent insidious way, been hurtling toward us. Not this way perhaps. But somehow.

We flew to Medford on the earliest flight, drove through the brilliant morning sun past arcs of sprinklers watering a golf course, around the freeway exit's lazy curl, to the mortuary, where we claimed Hunter's body. They draped him carefully—we could not, did not want, to see it all. We heaped him with roses and lavender from our front yard. Held his hands and each other's to form one more circle. Told him we loved him. Stayed until each of us, in our own agonized moment, had said goodbye.

Barry and I flew home two days later, carrying Hunter's newly burned, freshly cooled ashes, silent, solid, Hunter transmuted, retrieved but not rescued. A rigid plastic box contained all that was left of him, touch-near. I cocooned this anointed receptacle within my softest leather bag, sometimes heavy on my shoulder, sometimes clutched to my chest. That drift of dust, that life, caught up.

Burned and boxed, Hunter weighed what he had weighed at three or four years old. I pulled the bag close, lifted Hunter to my left hip, holding his ashes in the exact spot where I had endlessly nestled him when he was small, swaying slowly left, right, left, right, that soothing arc of baby calming, still innate. TSA agents took him from me, waved their wand over him, handed him back.

Barry and I passed the nights suspended sleeplessly above the simmering cauldron of our loss, like bedmates in a burn unit. During the days we functioned, barely, until a wave of grief at some poignant fragment of the precious ordinary—the bagel shop where tiny Hunter had perched in a highchair, the precise spot on the living room's golden plank floor where boy-Hunter once read comic pages—ripped out our sutures. Some days were better, the nights less often.

This was the closing of a story I could never have imagined, starting with the midwife's joyful "head's out!" and ending with my hands,

Barry's, Sawyer's, Lillie's, six weeks after his death, covering the burial vault that holds Hunter's ashes, shoveling on the dirt. That beginning. And this end.

At dusk a few days after Hunter was killed, I sat on the back steps listening to bagpipe music floating over from Maple Leaf Park. I heard Hunter's voice in my head. His voice was clear, mature, and deeply loving. He sounded whole. He sounded healed.

"Here's what I taught you, Mom," I heard Hunter say. "You control nothing. That's why I came."

"But did you have to die, and in this way, to convince me?" I asked him in my head.

Hunter said, "I guess I did. My whole life I was trying so hard, and I know it looked like I was always failing. But my mission was to change you, Mom, and that was a really hard job, and I did it, Mom. I did it."

The love in Hunter's words and tone comforted me—and broke me open. I felt their truth. I felt that he was leading me toward the deepest kind of wisdom. I remembered that young mother I'd been, so sure my efforts at perfection would balance life's equations. I thought of my excruciating struggle to help Hunter during his battle with addiction, to somehow will him into wholeness. I thought of all Barry's and my choices, our compromises made through and because of our boundless love for Hunter. The bigger, harder, and more compassionate lesson was eternal, karmic maybe, a larger all-encompassing truth that had been present all along. Hunter, my beloved teacher, had made me see it: I control nothing. This is a freeing and a place of hope. This is a steady and a fragile holding rather than fierce attachment. This is a bright enlivening still point, the still point at the center of the turning world.

Hunter's death thrust us into mourning, a deeper mourning than addiction's slow erosion of our hopes for his future had wrought. The loss was real now, not imagined, more nuanced because, for the first time in a decade, we did not have to brace for more.

I'd thought that little boy Hunter was dead already, that I had let him go because holding those memories during Hunter's years of struggle hurt too much. In the aftermath of Hunter's death, I realized I'd been wrong to think that. I'd built a massive dam, a wall of granite, between myself and that beloved child, just to survive. With Hunter's death, the granite cracked, then crumbled. I found that I could gather all the precious, poignant, hilarious memories of that little boy into my arms again. I held my little boy as I wept for my grown son, and felt him hug me back. Heart to heart, we mourned the loss of Hunter's future.

I found comfort in places I'd not been able to go in years, places we'd claimed when Hunter was young: the old ravine near our first house, Pike Place Market, parks all across Seattle. Even the University District, even the Ave. Places I'd felt were stained by Hunter's hard times instead felt blessed.

Through all of Hunter's struggles, Barry and I were fortunate to have family members who acknowledged this central hub of our life: Hunter's complex relationship with us and his addiction issues. While some of them judged us, they did not judge Hunter. Our families shared our quashed hopes and guarded despair about Hunter, and all continued to love Hunter in their various ways, even up until the very end.

One of the strange shell tides of Hunter's death has been that old friends from the days of his childhood have washed up, dear as ever, comforting us. Many of them hold impressions of Hunter that essentially reflect his inner being, reveal who he was without the thick coat of addiction obscuring his true nature. They return Hunter to me, fresh and new and perfect.

I struggle with the knowledge that I can never talk with Hunter again, even about just casual things—politics, movies, what books he's reading. He understood me on an essential level. Even in the midst of the dark years we shared, our living thread of deep recognition tied us together, under everything, despite it all. I saw this bond shimmer through our agonizing interactions, and it gave me strength. It strengthened Hunter too, I think. That deep connection is who Hunter and I essentially were and remain. I am grateful.

As I reclaim my good memories of Hunter, I must also hold memories of the searing decade we endured. Part of living in balance is claiming the truth that Hunter squandered all we gave him: our love, our hope, our optimism. That brutal shard remains. Mourning does not alter it. Grief smooths it not at all.

It is disorienting to know that my work as Hunter's mother is over now. I will spend the rest of my life processing that quarter-century relationship, living into the hard-won lessons he taught me. And I will miss him so much, always. I do not believe that I will ever be done grieving this loss, but I will honor everything we shared, both good and terrible. I hope this will release us both.

ACKNOWLEDGMENTS

My husband, Barry Brown, lived through these experiences with me and then repeatedly relived them, reading and commenting on countless drafts during the five years in which I wrestled with this project. He has been this work's great champion. As Guy Clark would say, too much (in this case, thanks) just ain't enough. My precious son, Sawyer Brown, and precious daughter, Lillie Brown: I love you so much and I am proud to be your mom.

Thanks to my generous first readers: Barry, Sawyer, and Lillie Brown, Laurie Amster-Burton, Peter Andersen, Elinor Appel, Lauren Baldwin, William Davies King, Priscilla Long, Marie McCaffrey, Jennifer Ott, Patrick Shanahan, Dana Standish, Melissa Walsh, and Kate Willink. To Meaghan Dowling, whose thoughtful comments greatly enhanced this effort. To Julie Myerson: empathizer, cheerleader, steadfast supporter.

Heartfelt thanks to everyone at University of Iowa Press, especially to my editor, James McCoy, for recognizing this story's value and for holding my feet to the fire. Thanks to my copyeditor Carolyn Brown for helping me through the final lap.

Deepest thanks to everyone who listened during the years this book recounts, especially Peter Andersen, Lauren Baldwin, David and Shirleen Becker, Matthew Becker, Susan Becker and Kevin Hamilton, Donna James, Sally James, Donna Morton, Elizabeth McKinley Moore, Melissa Shaffer, Dana Standish, and Kate Willink. Thank you to the "St. Lucy's" moms who told me they prayed for Hunter, especially Amy Caldwell, Gayle Graham, Christina Hammond, and Karen Hoffman. To David Buerge. To my HistoryLink.org colleagues, especially Priscilla Long, Marie McCaffrey, Jennifer Ott, Alan J. Stein, Cassandra Tate, and the late Walt Crowley. To teachers Linda Hilliard and Nayantra Nand, whose kindness comforted me during the dark months of Hunter's tenth grade year. To Tom Franzen and his steadfastly compassionate Franzen Renovations crew. To Detective Eleanor Broggi, Catherine Hendricks, and Dr. James Walsh. To Karen Maeda Allman, Abigail Carter, Rene Kirkpatrick, Sonya Lea, Rachael Levay, Nicole Mitchell, Peter Mountford, and Andrew Solomon. To Alex, Sam, Hannah, Melissa, and Brad Shaffer, for many years of love, support, and acceptance. To Glynn Russell, who gave us the best year in Hunter's adult life. To all of my yoga teachers at Community Fitness and ShefaYoga, especially Puja Telikicherla. To Lee Cook, Jennifer Racioppi, and Reese SanAgustin. To Elizabeth Chaison, Lisa Hensell, and Broehe Karpenko. Finally, to the late Terry Derouin, a fierce and awesome "St. Lucy's" mom. Thank you all. May light perpetual shine on Hunter, and may he know that we remember him.

NOTES

1. In July 2018, I tried again to get a copy of this police report, filing a Free-dom of Information Act request with the University of Washington Police. After repeated delays, in January 2019 University of Washington Public Records compliance analyst Kathleen Burns denied my request, citing confidentiality.

2. We learned eventually that Hunter was most likely abusing transdermal fentanyl patches. Fentanyl is a Schedule II drug (meaning it has a medical use but also a high potential for abuse) that requires a prescription. The patches are most commonly prescribed for hospice patients with cancer or for severe postsurgical pain. The patches are filled with medicated gel and are intended to be applied directly to the skin, where for approximately three days they provide a time-release dose. The drug can also be adminis-tered in the form of lozenges or lollipops, orally, nasally, or intravenously. Fentanyl patches are also sometimes prescribed for severely ailing pets.

Abusers often divert the unused patches—stealing from a relative to whom they've been legally prescribed, for example—and cut them into small squares, which are then burned, releasing vapor that is inhaled through a hollow tube. Because the patches are time-release, different parts of each patch hold different concentrations of the drug. This makes it difficult for abusers to know how powerful any particular dose will be. Sometimes the fentanyl patches are diverted after their intended use be-cause even used patches still contain significant amounts of the drug.

Some abusers chew the patches rather than igniting and inhaling them. Fentanyl users experience a euphoric high and often a deep sensation of relaxation. Higher doses can induce drowsiness, nausea, and sedation, slowing respiration to the point that breathing stops altogether.

How was Hunter getting fentanyl—or any drug for that matter? A family friend (call her Louise) who was several years older than Hunter, but whose years at Seattle High School overlapped his, later told me that at the time kids who wanted pot could buy it easily from fellow students. These teenage dealers often did not use the drug themselves but were paid to sell it by people higher up the drug distribution chain. Louise remembered that pot, Ecstasy, sometimes cocaine, and Adderall were usually on offer. Adderall was easy to get from fellow classmates for whom it had been prescribed to treat ADHD. Many of these kids hated the drug and were happy to sell their pills and use the money to buy pot. Most of these Adderall sellers were boys, Louise recalled, and girls—who used it as a study aid or to encourage weight loss—could usually get it free just by asking.

Louise never saw any opioid use at Seattle High, nor did she recall the presence of what in my high school years in Texas were called narcs—school district employees whose job it was to detect drug possession. There was a security guard who'd roll by the line of kids who smoked across the street from school, telling them to get to class. The kids would often walk instead to nearby wooded Cowen Park, ten minutes south of the school. And ten minutes farther south of Cowen Park, a quick walk or a few bus stops from Seattle High, was the University District, where, Louise recalled, you could buy anything. Within a few years, a friend of one of Louise's younger siblings reported, high school students openly acknowledged fentanyl's risk, using the catchphrase, "Don't fuck with fen."

When Hunter was smoking chopped-up fentanyl patches in spring 2010, black market use of illegally manufactured fentanyl was not widespread. According to the DEA, domestically produced illegal fentanyl was first detected in 1991 and traced to a lab in Wichita, Kansas. Over the next decade, DEA agents found and shut down a handful of other illegal fentanyl labs across the country. By 2007, fentanyl-related deaths were climbing in the Midwest and Northeast Agents traced the fentanyl-adulterated heroin to a lab in Mexico, and the lab was dismantled. By 2013, DEA agents and law enforcement officers across the country began to note a sharply increased number of fentanyl-related deaths. This statistic continues to rise. In King

County, where Seattle is located, for example, deaths in which fentanyl was involved rose from nine in 2008 to fifty-one deaths through the end of November 2018. Criminal organizations around the globe compete for the US market, with China and Mexico apparently the main suppliers. The drug is sold over the internet's so-called dark web and smuggled into the country through Mexico and Canada.

...

3. In the eight years since our frantic search, using the internet to locate drug rehab programs has become somewhat less confusing. The Substance Abuse and Mental Health Services Administration (SAMHSA) website, for example, has an excellent search engine that pinpoints rehab facilities by zip code and also a twenty-four-hour helpline. In late December 2018, Shatterproof, a national nonprofit organization whose stated mission is reducing the devastation addiction causes families, announced plans to build a ratings system of evidence-based addiction treatment programs. Shatterproof's effort is supported by the Laura and John Arnold Foundation and the Robert Wood Johnson Foundation and by a consortium of health insurers.

...

4. The language used to describe drug addiction is currently in flux. Many people in the recovery community now eschew the term "heroin addict" and similar descriptors in which the addiction fully defines the individual, considering these terms pejorative and derogatory. Preferred terms at present lean toward more neutral word choices: person with addiction (or with opioid addiction), person with opioid use disorder or substance use disorder, person battling addiction or struggling with addiction or addicted to heroin. Within the Narcotics Anonymous community, however, self-identifying as "an addict" during 12-Step meetings remains the norm, as was the case when Hunter was in treatment.

...

5. People who use needle exchange are also offered drug treatment services and medical treatment. Needle exchange falls under the category of harm reduction: an acknowledgment that drug use will exist whether society wants it to or not, whether legalized or illegal, and that given that fact, minimizing harm is in the best interest of the public health. Seattle's needle exchange program started in 1989 and operates throughout the city.

In 2018 the health department estimated that between 18,000 and 20,000 people who inject drugs live in King County. The county's rate of HIV infection among people who inject drugs has remained steady rather than increasing, a statistic other cities with needle exchange programs have in common. Needle exchange costs King County $1.2 million each year, as compared with a lifetime treatment cost of $385,000 for each person with HIV, which means, as the county's health department website points out, that by preventing infection in just three people a year, the program pays for itself. The state, county, city, and private donors fund King County's needle exchange program.

Although the needle exchange program was initially controversial, few Seattleites now object to a program that reduces disease transmission and keeps contaminated syringes off sidewalks and out of parks. Restroom stalls in libraries, on ferry boats, and in many other public and private facilities have sharp-disposal boxes, another example of harm reduction that provokes little controversy, and that serves as a constant silent reminder of the city's opioid epidemic. Other aspects of harm-reduction strategy remain highly controversial, particularly the Heroin and Prescription Opiate Addiction Task Force's 2016 recommendation that Seattle / King County establish test sites where people who use drugs intravenously can do so while being observed, so that if they overdose they can be revived with the overdose-reversal drug naloxone (brand named Narcan).

---

6. Each January, using about a thousand volunteers, King County participates in a one-night count of people within the county who are experiencing homelessness. In 2010, 8,559 county residents were counted. Of those, 5,800 were in emergency shelters and transitional housing, and 2,759 people lived unsheltered. By 2018, this already horrific number had greatly increased. In 2017, among the 11,643 county residents experiencing homelessness, 2,667 were in transitional housing, 3,491 in emergency shelters, and 5,485 living unsheltered. The 2010 count enumerated unsheltered individuals on benches, in parking garages and other structures, in cars and trucks, under roadways, in doorways, in city parks, in bushes and undergrowth, at bus stops, in alleys, and just walking around.

Seattle's most notorious homeless encampment was the Jungle, located south of downtown under the I-5 freeway. The Jungle coalesced in the

1990s. Living conditions there were dire, and the city periodically sent intervention teams to remove residents and, if possible, their possessions, before bulldozing parts of the camp. In the wake of ongoing crime, including several murders, Seattle closed the Jungle in 2017. Similar unsanctioned encampments immediately formed nearby.

In 2010, as now, people experiencing homelessness live in so-called tent cities. These are sanctioned by the city and operate mainly on church parking lots, moving from church to church every few months. In recent years, the city has opened "tiny house villages." Tiny house structures typically lack plumbing but provide shelter and relative privacy.

Like other cities with large homeless populations, Seattle struggles to balance the rights of all its citizens. City sanitation workers now regularly remove trash from all encampments, in 2017 removing 6,410,000 pounds of garbage from non-city-managed encampments. Neighbors debate the impact of city-managed encampments on neighborhoods, citing increased crime, more rodent problems, and a vast uptick of used syringes on nearby streets and sidewalks and in yards, bushes, and parks. Added shelter beds and spots in tiny houses fill instantly. Solving the issue of homelessness in Seattle feels out of reach.

As of 2018, Seattle was the fastest-growing city in the nation, with population up nearly 19 percent over the previous ten years. Housing prices have risen astronomically, and affordable housing lags far behind need. The Seattle Housing Authority operates the Housing for Choice Voucher lottery, a program that helps low-income families and individuals, senior citizens, and people with disabilities pay their rent in privately owned housing. In 2017 the program received 21,500 applications for the 3,500 places on the list. More than 35 percent of those came from people of color, who experience homelessness at disproportionate levels.

The tarps strung up near the freeway that commonly sheltered homeless people ten years ago have been replaced with rag-tag tents, some solo, some in clusters, erected on greenways and freeway berms throughout the city. Parks, especially those that are heavily wooded, provide places to pitch tents without immediate discovery. Many homeless individuals who have vehicles live in them. City ordinances require that vehicles on the street be moved every seventy-two hours, but many vehicles being used as housing are not operational. Owners risk returning to find that their vehicle has been towed and impounded.

Seattle struggles with all issues surrounding homelessness. The city is now trying to increase shelter capacity and rapidly rehouse people who become homeless, including people with substance abuse issues. Under the banner of Housing First, individuals with alcoholism and/or drug addiction are given access to "low barrier" housing, meaning that abstinence is not required. The hope is that, once housed, people will be more open to accessing addiction treatment programs. We have some day centers and hygiene centers and a navigation team that helps people through the process—but not enough of any of these forms of assistance, including housing.

In 2010, there were some resources specifically for homeless young people between 18 and 25: Teen Feed, offering free dinner every night in the U District, along with other services; Roots Shelter, also in the U District, providing overnight shelter, hygiene services, and on-site case management; University District YouthCare and other YouthCare drop-in centers, where homeless youth can find social support, a meal, and access to social services. As of 2018, these services all still exist and the need for them has only grown.

....

7. Chemically speaking, buprenorphine is a partial agonist. Every human cell contains myriad protein receptors on its surface—proteins with a highly specific shape. Each receptor is poised to receive certain chemical substances as a lock receives a key. When a substance binds to its companion receptor, a key turns in the cellular lock and a door opens, triggering instantaneous changes in cellular function.

A drug is called an agonist if it activates its companion receptor—in more simplistic terms, if its key opens a specific door. The brain's opioid receptors open the door, so to speak, to the heroin high. Another drug is an antagonist if it binds to its companion receptor and the door does not open: like a key that fits the lock but does not turn. Antagonist drugs do not exactly turn a receptor off, because a cell receptor with nothing bound to it is already turned off. But by binding to the receptor without activating its function, they block—antagonize—the receptor in question. Antagonists prevent the intended keys—the agonists—from opening the chosen door. As long as the antagonist occupies the receptor, an agonist cannot do the same.

Naloxone (also known as Narcan) is an opioid antagonist. It occupies opioid receptors and blocks them from agonists like fentanyl and heroin. As long as naloxone remains in a user's system, the would-be user can inject heroin but it will not work. Naloxone reverses overdoses by displacing heroin, fentanyl, or other opioids from their receptors. This reversal effect also puts the overdose victim into immediate withdrawal.

Buprenorphine's unique genius is its function as a partial agonist. It fits the lock and turns the key but lets the door open only a crack, enough to block withdrawal and enough to block the high of heroin but not enough for buprenorphine to itself produce a high.

Suboxone (buprenorphine and naloxone in combination) contains naloxone as a caution against abuse. Suboxone is intended to be taken sublingually and is prescribed in a solid form, as tablets or dissolving tape. Buprenorphine is absorbed by the digestive system, while naloxone is not. Only the buprenorphine works. Large doses of buprenorphine can produce a mild high if injected. If Suboxone is melted down and injected, however, the naloxone comes to the fore, blocking the effects of buprenorphine and heroin alike.

Suboxone received FDA approval to treat opioid dependence in October 2002. Suboxone is a private option, unlike methadone, which is dispensed as a liquid and must be taken at a clinic in a single daily dose. Methadone is a long-acting opioid agonist (full agonist, not partial) that blocks withdrawal without producing a high. Methadone is highly dangerous. Its metabolism in unpredictable and is affected by other drugs in a user's system. A small increase in daily dose can subject a user to fatal overdose risk.

The federal Drug Addiction and Treatment Act of 2000 (DATA 2000) requires physicians who want to be able to prescribe buprenorphine and other medications that contain it to pass an eight-hour course and meet other qualifications. During the first year after being credentialed, each doctor is allowed to treat no more than thirty patients, increasing to a hundred after the first year. In 2016, the 100-patient cap was increased to 275, and nurses and physician assistants became eligible to seek permission to prescribe. Prescribers must reapply every three years. Harm-reduction advocates criticize restrictions that limit buprenorphine prescribing, which severely curtail access to the drug. As of 2017, more than two million Americans suffered from opioid addiction, and by 2018, only about five percent of physicians in the country—some 43,000—could prescribe Suboxone for addiction treatment. In some parts of the country, finding doctors who can prescribe it and who also take insurance can be impossible. Medicaid coverage varies from state to state. Living in a major city, coupled with Barry's deep familiarity with Seattle's medical infrastructure, spared Hunter this inequity.

....

8. We understood eventually that Suboxone alone is not a magic bullet. The user's dysfunctional behaviors must also change. The rules for patients on Suboxone, which Hunter's doctor certainly would have explained to him, are: take your medicine every day; do not sell it; do not share it; see your prescribing physician on the appointed day. Respect boundaries. This is your medicine, and no one else's. If the patient is not firmly committed to following these rules, he will eventually break them and fail treatment— sell the Suboxone or share it with a friend who's in withdrawal. Either way, the patient runs out early, suffers withdrawal symptoms, and goes back to using.

I think now that if Hunter had been willing to augment the Suboxone prescription with some kind of outpatient treatment program, if Barry and I had made that a condition of his living with us, harm reduction with Suboxone might have stood a better chance of success. What had begun, with the inhaled fentanyl, as something that perhaps could still best be described as opioid abuse when Hunter entered rehab, had by this time spiraled into an entrenched opioid addiction. He needed multiple layers of support, not just Suboxone.

I now believe, although I did not see this at the time, that for Hunter (and, perhaps, many other young people with addiction) the social behaviors and social rituals associated with using drugs are, in themselves, addicting. This fact—coupled with recent discoveries about the ways in which opioid use alters those parts of the brain that govern the decision-making process—brings the efficacy of faith- and willpower-based abstinence programs as solutions to opioid use disorder into sharp question. Even medically assisted treatment for opioid use disorder is greatly enhanced by wrap-around social service care.

9. Vivitrol is the brand name for the depot (slow-release, slow-acting) injection version of the opiate-blocking and anticraving drug naltrexone that releases slowly over a month's time. Naltrexone is an opioid antagonist, meaning that it chemically binds with and fully blocks the effect of opioids. Naltrexone was approved for treating opioid addiction in 1984 and is also used to treat alcohol addiction. Any physician can prescribe naltrexone in oral or injectable form.

The fact that Hunter was on Barry's health insurance and that the policy had extensive benefits was critical. Each monthly shot of Vivitrol cost upward of $1,200. At the time Hunter was prescribed Vivitrol, many private insurers did not cover it.

10. Opioid-involved deaths in King County rose from 200 (10.6 deaths per 100,000) in 2008 to 258 (12.0 deaths per 100,000) in 2017, according to Seattle and King County Public Health. All local firefighters are paramedics, and they respond to overdoses everywhere: homes, dorm rooms, alleys, public libraries, department store bathrooms, grocery stores, the courthouse.

Heroin in this city, as a rule, is produced in Mexico and is distributed by Mexican drug cartels, moving from highly protected safe houses to street dealers down a chain. This is "black tar" heroin. Crude processing methods leave behind impurities that make black tar heroin sticky and tarlike or hard like coal. Black tar heroin is distributed primarily west of the Mississippi River. It is almost always injected.

Much of the heroin distributed east of the Mississippi comes from South America or Southeast Asia and is sold as white or brownish powder. It can be injected, snorted, or smoked. In the past, this purer form of heroin was referred to as China White. More recently, the term China White has been applied to heroin cut with fentanyl or to fentanyl by itself. China White is responsible for the current wave of overdoses in the eastern United States. Black tar is difficult to cut with fentanyl, although that will almost inevitably change. Heroin-adulterated fentanyl yields higher profits. Drug lords are working to find a way to add it to black tar.

The average cost of a single dose of heroin (0.1 g) in the US is between ten and twenty dollars. Heroin's effects peak at two hours but can be felt for up to six. Heroin users with high tolerance might spend $200 per day to maintain their addiction. Street users interviewed for a June 2017 documentary on Seattle's KOMO television stated that the price in Seattle is ten dollars. (The documentary can be viewed at https://www.youtube.com/watch?v=zi9gBT-47nI.)

---

11. The Oxford House website (oxfordhouse.org) does not currently mention transgender or gender-fluid residents.

---

12. Barry's brother, Colin, and his wife, Susan, have twin daughters. My sister, Susan, and her husband, Kevin, have twin sons.

---

13. Families of people with addiction live strung taut between the fear that their loved ones will be on the street and the terror of once again facing the peril of living with them. Sober houses can be a supportive environment for people in recovery. They can also function as parking places for the recently rehabilitated, offering respite for their families, who not infrequently foot all or part of the bill.

Oxford Houses operate under the umbrella of a well-respected nonprofit 501(c)(3) organization that has proven itself successful over time. Many other sober houses are independently operated and less forthright than those within the Oxford House system. Owning a sober house can be financially remunerative. Some houses take their residents' health to heart. But the entry criteria of many sober houses operating outside the Oxford House system may include insistence on several months of nonrefundable advance rent. Requiring nonreimbursable advance rent creates a built-in perverse incentive for the owners, who do better financially if their residents fail. The sooner a resident relapses and has to leave, the sooner the bed can be refilled and another chunk of advance rent collected. Few sober houses accept residents using medically assisted treatment options, such as Suboxone or naltrexone. Residents rely instead on their will power, coupled with the support of 12-Step programs.